WOMEN AND A NEW ACADEMY

Women and a New Academy

Gender and Cultural Contexts

Edited by

JEAN F. O'BARR

The University of Wisconsin Press

The University of Wisconsin Press
114 North Murray Street
Madison, Wisconsin 53715

The University of Wisconsin Press, Ltd.
1 Gower Street
London WC1E 6HA, England

Library of Congress Cataloging-in-Publication Data
Women and a new academy.
   Includes bibliographies and index.
   1. Feminism.   2. Sex role.   3. Intellectual
life—History.   4. Civilization, Occidental.
5. Feminist criticism.   I. O'Barr, Jean F.
HQ1154.W876   1989   305.4'2   88-40441
ISBN 0-299-11930-0
ISBN 0-299-11934-3 (pbk.)

Contents

WOMEN AND A NEW ACADEMY

Introduction

JEAN F. O'BARR

This is an essay collection born of that mother of invention, necessity. Each of the contributors researched, wrote, and presented her work within a particular institutional context—the development of a women's studies program at Duke University—that grew out of needs both intellectual and practical. Like many other colleges and universities in the United States in the 1970s, Duke University offered a variety of courses on women. These courses, developed within the traditions of the humanities and social sciences, reflected the interests of faculty members whose own research responded to the absence of women from the curriculum, and they were received enthusiastically by graduate and undergraduate students. Over time, it became clear that taking a course here and there, wherever it happened to be offered, was an inadequate institutional arrangement for the teaching of the new scholarship on women. Students needed a more thoughtful approach to this burgeoning field; they needed introductory multidisciplinary courses, advice on course selection, and assistance in identifying graduate and professional options. In short, they needed to see that an intellectual field of inquiry was being formed and to understand how the part they had experienced related to the whole. Thus, by 1980, the rudiments of a formal women's studies program were in the making.

The year 1983 marked the launching of the full program with the appointment of a director, the offering of an introductory course for undergraduates, the identification of affiliated faculty, and the organization of a concentration in women's studies within the curriculum. Campus response to the program was positive—enrollments soared, faculty research grew, activities proliferated. To those who were familiar with the growth of women's studies across the United States, the creation of the Duke program was both long overdue and parallel with developments elsewhere. But to those in the immediate campus community who were unaware of the women's studies movement, the activity raised questions that had complicated answers. What is the purpose of a

3

women's studies program? How would women's studies research relate to existing structures of knowledge? What can the new scholarship on women contribute to the way in which knowledge is organized into courses, departments, disciplines?

In response to our colleagues' interest, the women's studies faculty made the decision to devote a portion of our collective energies to the public presentation of our research. We organized a series of lectures on feminist reinterpretations of research based in Western intellectual history, in order to share our work with the community of educators at Duke.

The academic diet is rich in lectures—distinguished visitors come to share their latest findings with campus audiences, departments and specialized programs hold research seminars among themselves (or sponsor distinguished visitors), job candidates and graduate students have structured opportunities to present their work. It is relatively rare for a group of scholars, each from a different discipline but all belonging to the same institution, to participate in a public forum in which they address epistemological questions that stem from their own work, that touch the work of their colleagues, and that transcend disciplinary boundaries. Aware that both topic and format were innovative, the women's studies faculty developed the colloquium as a forum in which the emphasis would be on a scholarly discourse that was accessible to those from many perspectives and at many levels of familiarity with the new scholarship on women.

The colloquium put forward three goals: to describe, for a multidisciplinary audience of faculty, graduate students, and undergraduates, some of the new research on women; to link that work to the development of feminist theory; and to analyze the impact of the new information and ideas on the traditional disciplines. Colloquium attendance was high, it was diverse, it was engaged. As feminist scholars, we realized in an immediate and personal way that the work we were doing was provocative and far-reaching. Above all, we realized that the ideas that had been developed in the feminist community of academics—ideas included in the following essays—were unfamiliar to our closest and most sympathetic colleagues. Schooled in specific disciplines and not participant in the debates of feminist theory, they had not been exposed to the alternative assumptions and paradigms we had created to generate the new scholarship. The implications of the feminist undertaking were profound, and the gap between our understanding and theirs was striking.

Our story at Duke University is a common one to those who have developed women's studies programs at other institutions, each with its own particular plot twists. What is important about these stories, what makes them useful, is that they describe the pronounced connection we all explicitly sustain between feminist thought and feminist action in the academy. This surely is what distinguishes women's studies from the educational innovations of the past, this commitment to shaping education from the assumption that knowledge is culturally constructed. This surely is what fuels the challenging task of institutionalizing, bureaucratizing, formalizing women's studies in institutions that have been fundamentally shaped by the exclusion of women.

Before this benchmark symposium at Duke, research in women's studies was understood by most of the university community as an attempt to bring data and questions on women's lives into courses and research agendas. It was seen as a task of adding the missing—reading women's writing, analyzing selected women leaders, examining particular events or policies or problems specific to women—as the missing information complemented and supplemented what was already being taught. The discipline of women's studies was, in other words, the study of the anomalous, the correcting information, that which would not fit easily (or otherwise) into the traditions of the curriculum. And this, of course, is something of where feminist inquiry began some two decades ago. Recognizing the errors in statements about women that run through received knowledge and correcting those errors by adding new material was (and still is) basic to feminist scholarship.

But as feminist scholars began to do this, both at Duke and elsewhere, we noticed other kinds of problems with an academy that takes its authority from unquestionable knowledge (knowledge that has always been). Our efforts to include women had raised a second order of academic business for us: in view of how little was now known about women, how accurate were the conventional ways of generating, organizing, conceptualizing, and communicating knowledge?

At Duke, for purposes of the colloquium, we chose to emphasize one area of feminist scholarship, the reconsideration of ideas that are based in Western intellectual history. We recognized that much of the new work on women has a contemporary cast, addressing the late nineteenth and twentieth centuries and concentrating on postmodernism, the process of industrialization, and the study of class, race, and ethnic differences. We felt that we might make a contribution of our own to the evolution of feminist scholarship by taking up questions that challenge the epistemological assumptions of the Western curriculum. We wanted to demonstrate to our colleagues that feminist inquiry promised new thinking for the study of Western philosophy, culture, religion, and science. The essays that resulted from the colloquium are collected here, both to provide overviews of whole fields of endeavor (history and literature) and to explore selected topics that cross disciplines (political philosophy, medieval studies, biblical interpretation, church history, and the history and sociology of science).

Most readers will recognize as familiar to the feminist enterprise a number of theoretical positions that run through these essays: challenges to the idea of progressive historical change, to the separation of the private and public, to the concept of the individual as an autonomous being, to the confusion of nature with historically specific cultural constructs. Taken together, however, the essays form an outline of the complex relationship between ideology, knowledge, and power as it has influenced our consciousness of gender as a socially and historically specific cultural construct. Tracing the development of literary criticism and the study of English literature, Deborah Pope makes the point that the process by which a set of texts were selected for emphasis and honor tells us more about the masculinist values of those who have the power to select than about the inherent qualities of the texts themselves. Such a cult of expertise and elitism is built on rationales for exclusion that deny women the power to create symbolic representations of life while enhancing the privilege of men to do so. This idea also plays a role in Kristen Neuschel's essay, as she discusses the ideological power of notions about the differences between men and women. Ideological power—defined as the ability to contribute positive notions about one's self/life (shared reality) to community discourse and to have some of those notions prevail—requires access to verbal resources that allow for the development of conceptual categories with which to create and reinforce cultural meaning. The study of women's history and literature, then, becomes not simply exercises in redressing the historical absence of women from the curriculum, but rather transformative experiences in restoring to women the power and ability to influence/control the representation of knowledge and ideology.

The general task of restoring women's access to the processes by which cultural symbols are shaped is taken up in specific ways by other contributors. Sarah Westphal-Wihl, building on the work of Julia Kristeva and Hélène Cixous, challenges assumptions about the extent to which patriarchal values are embedded in courtly love traditions, arguing that some texts reveal a complicated politics of fantasy between women and men that are mediated through these traditions. Elizabeth Clark's and Carol Meyers' articles on women in the early Christian world and ancient Israel highlight the influence cultural systems have on the preservation and interpretation of knowledge over time. "I permit no woman to teach or to have authority over men," says 1 Timothy 2:11–15, a stricture that postbiblical traditions seized and promoted as a "natural" consequence of Eve's blunder in the Garden of Eden. Yet, as Meyers details, even this basic representation of Eve as Everywoman is questionable in historical context.

In fact, collusion between knowledge about "nature" and knowledge about "man" has had important ramifications for Western scientific knowledge as well as political philosophy. Angela O'Rand argues that contemporary efforts to measure individual capacity and sex difference can, by design or default, turn the tools of empiricism to the task of creating/maintaining cultural symbols of male privilege. And as Kathryn Jackson explains, the liberal political traditions that premise the values of Western education have both emphasized this collusion (in an emphasis on the "rational man") and embedded it in notions of equality fundamental to a feminist politics of knowledge.

Sandra Morgen suggests in the introduction to her article that paying greater attention to the history of ideas within a discipline might well foster the impact of feminist scholarship on the discipline. I would take this one step further to say that a new academy, one in which women were fully present at all levels of inquiry, may need to make central a reconsideration of those traditions of ideas in order to take the necessary next step toward an introspective, self-conscious knowledge base. Women's studies research, then, is in large part a critique of pedagogy as a system by which ideologies perpetuate themselves. As these essays show, the knowledge base of higher education evolved with implicit assumptions about the exclusion of women, predicated upon and perpetuated by the absence of challenge from women. Thus the new scholarship on women, by necessity, is a critique that at once redefines and replaces the underpinnings of contemporary epistemological discourse. A recognition of gender as the conceptual category that enmeshes knowledge, power, and ideology requires that we, as scholars and educators, self-consciously articulate and debate the assumptions from which we work.

In this volume, I hope we have accomplished two aims. First we present a feminist politics of knowledge to help us sort through the rubble of the old ideas dismantled. Second, and more important, we demonstrate a research agenda to help other educators to help create distinct and diverse understandings of knowledge making as fundamental to the educational process. Those of us who participated in this colloquium had, for a moment, a fantasy vision of a new academy in which we were purveyors of newly found cultural meanings. However aptly our efforts met the necessities of that day, such a moment is a reminder of the challenge we have still to present, for we are just now beginning to know the satisfactions of our intellects.

CHAPTER 1

Creating a New Past: Women and European History

KRISTEN B. NEUSCHEL

> All art is a dialogue. So is all interest in the past. And one of the parties lives and compre-
> hends in a contemporary way, by his very existence. It seems also to be inherent in human
> nature to turn and return to the past (much as powerful voices may urge us to give it up).
> The more precisely we listen and the more we become aware of its pastness, even of its
> near-inaccessibility, the more meaningful the dialogue becomes. In the end, it can only be
> a dialogue in the present, about the present.
>
> Finley 1977:15

With these words, the historian Moses Finley measures his own distance from
historians for whom the craft of history is a straightforward task of retrieval—
of seizing and making visible an object called the past. The most important
component of that past for early generations of historians in the nineteenth
century was the civilizing force of the nation-state and the political activity of
the elite through which it was realized. As the "objective" importance of the
political elite, their ruling apparatus, and their cultural hegemony came under
attack in the course of the nineteenth century, so too did the notion of the
objective nature of the past in general, and the assumption of its accessibility
to historians' probings. A significant minority within the historical profession
became concerned with and systematically devoted themselves to developing
new methods of historical inquiry. Not only did they anticipate Finley's assumption that the nature of one's questions in large measure creates the object
of historical investigation, but they also pioneered new investigatory techniques which a commitment to social and economic history required. Explaining the behavior not merely of a few leaders but of whole groups of people
required historians to treat values, intention, and causation not merely as
functions of personalities, but as complex economic, social, and cultural
problems (Iggers 1984:3–42).

There has been a long tradition within the historical profession, then, of principled and methodological challenge to the notion that history is the self-explicating story of the elite—an elite seen in isolation from both the cause and the effects of its power. Not surprisingly, some works of women's history date from this early phase of challenge (and some, like certain works in other areas of the discipline, remain classics in their field). It was not until after World War II, however, that the profession of history within the academy began to accept and reflect, to a substantial degree, the concerns of social historians, first expressed at the end of the nineteenth century (Iggers 1984:30–31). In the 1960s, both in Europe and America, a (renewed) call for a history of the past which reflected the commitments of the present came from the civil rights and student movements; and from the student movement came direct pressure to make the academy responsive to this demand. As the women's movement grew out of the civil rights and antiwar protests of the decade, women's call for an appropriate history was added to the agenda. But, as was the case with the renewed commitment to social history, it was the entry of large numbers of new and dedicated practitioners—most of them women—into the profession in the 1970s which ensured that the challenge would be taken up.

We shall see that the practice of European women's history, over the last two decades, bears the stamp of its origins. It developed within a discipline already in flux, responding to demands from within and without that a history be constructed which reflected the experience of all peoples. Also in the process of continuous development were modes of questioning and methods of investigation. Although traditional political history is still practiced within the discipline, history is today more often a multidisciplinary scrutiny of past societies, making use of tools borrowed from archaeology and sociology, demography and anthropology. Historians of women, then, were not the first self-consciously to ask, What ought to be the subject of historical investigation, and what questions must we ask and what data must we examine to illuminate that subject? Hence, many of the methods and data used to study women's history were not new with them.

Historians of women have pioneered new methods, when necessary, to illuminate the lives of women (Lerner 1979:172–75). But of greater importance to their task of constructing a history of women has been the theoretical task, unique to them, of investigating gender as a category of historical analysis and as a component of human culture through time. In so doing, they have departed from the conventional limits of social history by distinguishing the experience of women from those of other disadvantaged groups. Attention to the construction of gender roles and ideologies about gender in past societies has revealed material and ideological processes by which women's experience in the past was shaped. It has also revealed one of the primary means by which women's history has for so long been assigned a marginal status within the disciplinary practice of history. The fact that discourse on gender itself has had a history undercuts the assumption that gender is a constant in human culture. The marginalization of gender as a variable (in part sustained by the marginalization of actual women in history generally) has worked in two ways to keep the past of women from view: it has made women's past invisible by assuming it to be one of unchanging victimization and thus fundamentally ahistorical; it has thus kept the history of women from being integrated into broader historical processes where it would forcibly transform historians' understandings of "mainstream" historical issues.

Social and economic historians have creatively tackled problems of limited documentation in recent years and have uncovered a great deal about women's lives. Historians scrutinizing the impact of industrialization on workers and their families have manipulated and correlated census data to learn about family size, migration patterns, and occupational changes. Comparable sources for premodern (preindustrial) centuries have been exploited as well, despite the very great technical problems they present. Studies of parish records of births and deaths, when combined with studies of wills and marriage contracts, have resulted in profiles of artisanal and peasant communities—how households were constituted, how property was passed down, how families adjusted these practices in times of famine or economic decline. Of course, social historians' assumption that the family, for example, is a subject worthy of investigation made such forays into the documentation possible.

Some historians of premodern Europe have, over the past decades, been particularly imaginative in reconceptualizing what ought to be construed as historical structures and events. It was, in part, the disparity between the focus of conventional political history and the actualities of—the drastic material limits on—the exercise of power in the Middle Ages which led a group of medieval historians, more than fifty years ago, to become early leaders in the creation of a more "total" human past. It is ridiculous to focus solely on the policies of a given king, they argued, even if trying to understand the significance of his reign, because so little of what actually happened during the reign was within his ability to control. Not only must communities of people in his kingdom be considered, but so must technologies such as communication and armaments, and extrahuman forces such as geography, climate, and disease. Indeed, these historians argued, many of the structures which most affect human life exist on a material and temporal scale difficult for humans even to perceive: the geographical conditions which help determine that generation after generation of young men in certain regions of southwestern

France would "choose" to be shepherds; the ecological facts that generations of premodern peasants would face the identical problem of balancing pasture and cultivation in order to maintain soil fertility—drastically limiting, until industrial times, the amount of food produced and the number of mouths that food could sustain. It is the redefining of historical "fact" in these and other ways which can allow evidence of women's achievements to emerge. If the human environment—climate, soil, topography—and human physiology—nutrition and disease—are historically significant forces, then so are all human reactions to and interactions with these forces. Human ingenuity and achievement are to be found in every task of confrontation and adjustment. One of the most common coping mechanisms available to premodern families was the choice to adjust fertility, and one of the most important social efforts at all times was keeping *alive* those born—both primarily the work of women, as childbearers and domestic managers.

With this kind of methodological ground on which to build, historians of women and social historians more generally have already constructed an impressive body of knowledge about women's lives in the European past. It is revealing that in a 1983 review of scholarship on premodern women, a historian states confidently, "We all *know* that women in preindustrial society worked," and then proceeds to more specific issues (Hufton 1983:131, emphasis in original). We have moved from the need to establish that women *are* workers—so central to an acceptance of women as historical actors—to an understanding of the context in which they worked, and something of its significance for themselves, their families, and the wider community. From preindustrial times, well into the industrial age, the family carefully matched its labor power to the work necessary for its survival. Tasks were allocated according to the work which needed to be done (the entire family participating in the harvest, for example). Children were commonly apprenticed into trades or sent to work as servants or hands in nearby households when there was no work at home through which they could earn their keep. In this process of carefully balancing work, labor power, mouths to feed, and available resources, a woman's work was one of the most flexible instruments for the maintenance of the family. She would take in extra spinning or sewing, raise and sell additional produce, juggle extra domestic work for neighbors with her responsibilities at home. This meant, in preindustrial as well as industrial times, that adult women might enter and leave the paid labor force intermittently, according to the family's needs. Research concerning women's work in early modern towns reveals that women working in skilled crafts, although not, strictly speaking, wage laborers, experienced disabilities as workers reminiscent of those faced by female wage earners in industrial times; certain craftswomen in the sixteenth century, it appears, were denied the protection of guild membership and, in hard times, they could be denied work in favor of male craftsmen (Davis 1982). A picture of women's working lives through the centuries may thus be emerging in which urban women, particularly, formed a marginal labor pool, able to expand the number of workers in a given trade or job as the demands of that trade, and hence the jobs available, increased. Women thus experienced disabilities in the workplace as individual workers which men did not.

Research on women's work under industrialization has, from the first, concentrated on the deleterious effects of industrialization on women's work and, it is assumed, on women's power. The predominance of wage labor, it has been posited, resulted in the devaluation of domestic work, and the removal of much of the family's work from the home further devaluated women's work by making it invisible. In addition, women found it increasingly difficult to compete as independent workers in the marketplace. Industrialization, so this theory suggests, made working women powerless in the home and in the community despite their crucial economic contribution. Yet historians now also have evidence of what they had long suspected must be the case—that preindustrial times were not, in contrast, a "golden age" of harmonious work and family life for European women (Hufton 1983:126). As we have seen, the demands of the family economy meant that female workers were at most times disadvantaged, in comparison with men, in their search for independent economic power. Moreover, other evidence bearing on women's social power has come to light in the last decade which forces us to dispense with easy conclusions about the direct reflection in women's power in the family and the community of the work they did. A woman's power within the family, and her ability to go it alone, were directly affected by (widely varying) laws and customs regarding dowries and inheritances. The structure of households was also a factor; a young bride come to live with her husband's extended family, to name one kind of arrangement, might have substantial authority in the home only years later when she acceded to the role of matriarch. The agricultural economy, the availability of work, patterns of migration, household structures and property laws, village organization and state government, and religious identification all would have been factors in determining the experience of women within their families and their communities in preindustrial times.

Above all, however, it is the fact of the consistent (if occasionally more intense) persecution of women as witches which casts grave doubts on the existence of a preindustrial golden age. This is true not simply because of the numbers of women who suffered persecution, but because of the nature and significance of that persecution. That female witches appear, from what historians have so far uncovered, to have been socially vulnerable women—often older women eking out a living alone on the margins of the community (Hufton 1983:138)—only partly accounts for the ease with which they could be made targets during periods of economic, political, or religious turmoil. To explain this victimization more fully, we must find ways of reconstructing the web of socially available meanings by which women could be construed to be harmful, and such drastic persecution of them could be justified and successfully carried out. What, in short, was the content of the discourse about gender which prevailed in European communities? In this discourse lies the key not only to the vulnerability of women who "became" witches, but of women in all sorts of more routine circumstances.

The importance of ideological power—the ability to contribute positive notions about themselves to community discourse and to have some of those notions prevail—is easier to trace for upper-class women who are more likely to have left some of their own words to us. A well-known case is that of the medieval French noblewomen who were able to shape the positive images of themselves and of their roles contained in courtly love literature. Their ability to contribute to these images rose in part from their economic and political power within the aristocratic household, and in part from their consequent "cultural" power—that they presided over performances, and were in some sense the arbiters of composition, as well as actual authors themselves. Also important to the images of women and gender roles expressed in the literature was that in the feudal notions of reciprocal obligation between vassal and lord, a language of equality in personal relations was available to authors. Thus, these aristocratic women had access *to means* of ideological expression and *to images* which empowered them *in the terms of* the dominant social group— aristocratic men. They also had access to the material conditions which made courtly love relationships possible, including, for example, adequate resources to support, without threat to the patrimony, any bastard children who might issue from their liaisons (Kelly 1977).

Even in the case of these relatively visible aristocratic women, we cannot be certain how they actually behaved (did they openly enter into extramarital love relationships?). Some women might have behaved that way; what we can be more certain of is, first, that it was possible for them to imagine behaving in that way, and, second, what perceptual and material factors combined to construct that possibility (Kelly 1977:144). Reconstructing the comparable possibilities for nonelite women in most times and places is more difficult, not because women contributed to discourse on gender only when exceptionally empowered, but because that discourse, whatever its content, is more hidden from historical view. We must search for notions about gender roles where some residue of popular (largely oral) culture remains: in popular literature and art (such as mass-produced woodblock prints); in written descriptions of festivals, charivari, and religious ritual; in legal proceedings for offenses from wife beating to witchcraft; in—most precious of all—discussions and confrontations among individuals, recorded by observers. Efforts to penetrate elite and nonelite culture alike in order to depict the cognitive world, and not merely the material world, of past Europeans now dominate many subfields of European history, from studies of the popular reception of Catholic and Protestant Reformations to analyses of the political culture of industrial workers. These efforts are being pursued with the aid of the most recent spate of historians' interdisciplinary borrowings from ethnography, semiology, and sociolinguistics. Historians are currently concerned not with uncovering a static "body" of thought for a given age or region, but rather with the ways in which thought was constructed, particularly through the operations of language in its various guises: how certain verbal resources made available certain conceptual categories, how speech events or instances of symbolic communication created meaning within each culture; in short, how a discourse about political power, religiosity, gender roles, or anything else, was carried on—in what terms, according to what rules, and with what results.

Unfortunately, the historical discourse concerning gender has, so far, received far less attention than that concerning political power, religious authority, or class consciousness. In fact, the state of investigation into the crucial issue of witchcraft has been cited by feminist historians as an example of the limitations of current scholarship (Stuard 1981:139). It has been assumed that the marked upsurge of witchcraft prosecutions in some regions of Europe during the sixteenth century was in some way a reflection and result of the political, social, and religious turmoil of the period. That women were the usual victims of witch hunts is inevitably and sympathetically noted, but this fact of gender has not yet stood as the central issue to be investigated in witchcraft studies. Typologies of witch hysteria have been sketched, particularly in an attempt to explain the significance of the trials for the officials involved; did the eventual cessation of persecutions represent inroads of rationalism into an older, superstitious world view (Faure 1981:77)? However, witchcraft has not yet been considered primarily as an event in women's history, either as an actual event in the experience of a community of women or as an event in a broader sense, to be correlated with other contemporary trends in women's experience—changes in their legal, political, or economic status, or in religious experience—or in relation to conditions and changes in the community at large; in short, witchcraft has not been considered as an event in the discourse on gender.

The example of the treatment of witchcraft is symptomatic of the shortcomings of current scholarship on European women in general; women have been consistently a subject of historical study in recent years, but gender has not been. This in part, argues historian Joan Scott, is a result of what she terms the "integrationist" approach to women's history which has come from its simultaneous development with social history. Scott has recently observed that in much of the work concerning women which has appeared to date, "women are a department of social history" (Scott 1983:152). Scott calls attention to the tenacity of critical approaches and criteria of significance which predate a concern for gender and have circumscribed a critical focus on gender. Social history, she remarks, has largely been concerned with processes and systems such as industrialization or modernization; the experience of a group of people, whether workers, capitalists, or women, has been a means to investigating these broader themes. We have seen above, for example, that much research has been devoted to analyzing the effects of industrialization on the valuation and sexual division of labor. However, Scott (1983:151) asserts,

in all these studies, the explanation ultimately has to do with economic variables, not gender. Sexual divisions, their definition and elaboration are explained as a result of economic forces when, in fact, it is equally plausible and probably more accurate to suggest that cultural definitions of gender differences permitted the implementation of economic practices such as sex-segregated labor markets or the use of women to undercut the wages of skilled craftsmen.

Scott includes her own pathbreaking book, which located the context of women's work within the family economy, in this portrait of "integrationist" women's history. Similarly, she and other observers point out, women's personal, "private" lives have typically been analyzed within the context of the family, in the course of recent investigations of the historical development of the family: When and why does the nuclear family develop? When and why do strong affective ties between family members develop? When, in short, does the family become "modern"? (Family history itself is thus, in turn, a means of investigating broader themes.)

The consequences of the perpetuation of these kinds of questions as a principal framework for the investigation of women's history range from the perpetuation of antifeminist notions about gender to a failure fully to reconceive the historical record to include gender. Certain studies of women in the context of the family, like some studies of witchcraft, come perilously close to denying that women's experience is historically constructed; by equating women's destiny with that of daughter, wife, or mother (Faure 1981:75), or by accepting that women were inevitably the primary targets of witch hunts, historians allow female destiny to appear natural, and not socially constructed. When the discourse on gender remains invisible, women can appear in the historical record as workers, wives, even as protesters, but not as women. Specifically, we can understand their work, evaluate their economic contribution, delineate household and community structures, but women's power within family and community—the converse of their vulnerability to witchcraft, to physical and sexual violence, and to economic discrimination—will continue to elude us.

Considering gender, that is, considering female experience in light of male experience and vice versa, is a requisite to a full treatment of women in his-

tory. Studying gender ". . . consists of examining women and men in relation
to one another, of asking what the definitions or laws that apply to one imply
about the other . . . and what representations of sexual difference suggest
about the structure of social, economic and political authority" (Scott 1983:
153). Mainstream history—men's history—will be analyzed and accounted
for as fully in terms of gender as women's history will be, and as fully as
either is now understood in terms of class, or any other variable. Some examples of historical investigation along these lines have already been carried
out. The regional and chronological focuses for these studies have varied
widely, from medieval French noblewomen to twentieth-century Spanish
peasants, from Victorian society to Nazi society (Scott 1983:153). The conclusions reached by these various studies permit a glimpse of how a fully re-
defined historical record, and discipline, might be shaped.

One of the earliest of these works explicitly to treat gender as a category
was Joan Kelly's comparative consideration of the status of elite women during the High Middle Ages and the Renaissance, of which the study of medieval aristocratic culture, cited above, formed a part. In this analysis, and in
other work, Kelly pioneered the insight that women's status in any period was
the simultaneous product of their economic, political, sexual, and cultural
power, and of the content of prevailing ideologies about women. She also argued that the only historically meaningful evaluation of the degree of women's
power must be a relative one, in which their power in any one arena is measured against that enjoyed by men (Kelly 1977:139, 1976:812). Her conclusion that the Renaissance was no Renaissance for women, but rather represented a restriction of roles previously enjoyed, represents a challenge to
historical periodization: a conventional historical watershed is reevaluated as a
positive turning point only for one group, and not for a whole society. Moreover, she pursued, it was an advance for men in part *because* it was a period of
decline for women. The male experience of "Renaissance individualism" was
constructed *by means of* women's new dependent status.

Kelly thus explicitly analyzes men's and women's history in light of each
other. Not only her methods, but also her specific conclusions, have proved
useful hypotheses for later work, particularly the conclusion that the nature of
the boundaries drawn between public and private domains in a society are crucial in determining women's status in that society. Medieval noblewomen enjoyed political power because private and public arenas of activity were
largely the same; both public and private activity took place within the household of the noble family. The mere suggestion, implied in Kelly, that the
growth of the public sector—the eventual consolidation of the nation-state—
was not a universal good is hardly revolutionary in European historiography.
What is revolutionary is, first of all, an awareness of ways in which arenas of
human activity have been overlaid with meaning and value; the home, for ex-

ample, has come to be defined as a private arena of personal relationships, rather than recognized as a location of production and an arena of power, existing in relation to other economic and political structures. Second, also revolutionary is the exploration of the ways in which representations of gender identity have been fashioned as a consequence of and used as a means of expression of the distinction between public and private activity. Thus, Kelly's conclusion that the growth of Renaissance states was detrimental to women's power, and other historians' similar conclusions that the subsequent growth of nation-states was detrimental to women's power, *because* they were excluded are less important than their analyses of the ways in which gender identity, political power, and family life were constructed simultaneously, and in mutually relative ways, to produce the resulting exclusion. Another example can be found in studies of the eighteenth century. The conceptions of liberty articulated by Enlightenment *philosophes* and by representatives to French revolutionary assemblies have been reinterpreted as built on notions of gender as well as on "fundamental" concepts of natural rights. The subsequent exclusion of women from the benefits of the eighteenth-century revolutions cannot be dismissed as a mere failure in thoroughness by embattled revolutionaries; rather, it was a logical result of the republican vision which many revolutionaries were deliberately trying to establish (Kleinbaum 1977).

Other historians have recently considered the experience of and construction of gender integrally with other well-known historical topics, and their work points in parallel directions. The secularization of European culture—the subordination of church to state, the development of a this-worldly social and religious ethos, the rise of scientific rationalism—has been a consistent theme in the work of European historians because, it is argued, it constitutes one of the principal defining characteristics of European civilization. As in the case of the rise of the nation-state, historians no longer regard the rise of modern science, for example, as an unqualified good; some of the structural and philosophical shortcomings inherent in modern science have become apparent (and not only to historians) as the dangers of unlimited confidence in "scientific" knowledge have become clear in the twentieth century. A number of historians, over the years, have worked to situate the rise of modern science firmly within the social context out of which it grew; others (most notably Thomas Kuhn) have reconceived "science" in relative terms as human systems of explanation which have been replaced, historically, as they outlived their usefulness in accounting for observed phenomena. Women's historians, however, have also begun to add gender to the list of tools with which notions about the world system were fashioned, and which these notions in turn helped to fashion. Before the rise of modern science, one study argues, the natural world was conceived to be an organism, sensitive to human incursions and demanding that humans respectfully coexist with it. The most typical image for describing nature itself was that of the nurturing mother. But modern science, ". . . by reconceptualizing reality as a machine rather than a living organism, sanctioned the domination of both nature and women" (Merchant 1980:xvii). The author of this study charts the parallel growth of the ecology and women's movements in recent decades as protests against the exploitative "view of both women and nature as psychological and recreational resources for the harried entrepreneur-husband" (Merchant 1980:xvii).

Closely related are new insights into the nature and significance of the Protestant Reformation. Protestantism has been thought of as a more progressive religious system than Catholicism; it fostered an ethic of this-worldly achievement which, in turn, spurred commercial and industrial enterprise. As Natalie Davis concludes, Protestantism is thought to be "a more evolved religion, [which facilitated] the desacralization of society," because of its "transcendent and activist Father and less hierarchical religious symbolism" (Davis 1975:93). But as Davis and others have recently pointed out, it was Protestantism's transcendent Father which ended any possibility of sanctity cast in a female image; further, the dismantling of the hierarchy of saints, priests, and believers enhanced the spiritual and social authority of men in part because it placed adult women under the spiritual and moral authority of their husbands. Again, it is not only the effect of these movements on women which is the subject of attention, but also how the movement in question draws its character in part from its effects on women.

Many of the most successful recent attempts to integrate consideration of gender into historical analysis have been within the bounds of political history, since it is in political life, broadly defined, that ideas about legitimate power and authority are constructed and enforced (Scott 1983:154). It is often in political debates, campaigns, or movements that we can see the clearest examples of the simultaneous definition of the extent of the public sphere, of public policy created within that sphere, and of women in relationship to both. In a 1984 article examining debates over policy in fin de siècle France, Karen Offen traces the interrelationship of the debates by politicians, political theorists, and activists on three issues: the crisis over declining population growth, the crisis over national strength, and the challenge of the growing French feminist movement (Offen 1984). Although the potentially disastrous effects of France's population decline were linked, in most contemporary minds, with a feeling of crisis concerning the nation's security, historians have considered the issues separately. The heightened concern over national security, Offen remarks, has been discussed in the context of France's loss of the Franco-Prussian war; the issue of population decline and the feared further loss of national strength that it would cause has not been treated concurrently. Similarly, Offen continues, analyses of France's population decline have failed adequately to consider female agency as a crucial factor in the falling birth-rate. The literature on the issue is extensive, she notes,

> yet few works by demographers, or by demographic historians, acknowledge the fact—startlingly obvious to historians of women and the family—that fertility is not an abstraction. Rather, children are borne by women: aggregate statistics on nuptiality and fertility . . . depend to a great extent on discrete acts of consent by individual women as well as on the desires of men. Both sexes act within a concrete legal, socio-economic and cultural context that affects their social relationship. (Offen 1984:649)

Offen then proceeds to analyze the interrelationship of these three issues: the concerns over population decline and national security, and the debate on women's roles in state and society occasioned by the French feminist move-ment. Even a cursory glance at the sources, she argues, reveals to the historian willing to acknowledge it that the "woman question" was at the forefront of political discourse in France (Offen 1984:649). Notions about the proper role for women and questions of potential legal reforms to improve their lot were debated within a context of national hysteria over France's apparent failure to produce enough children. This shaped the character of the largest faction within the French women's movement and limited its goals to a demand for reforms to enable women better to fulfill their duties as wives and mothers. They demanded equality—but equality in difference; their demands for better legal and economic rights for women were all consonant with restricting women to a family role. Like Kelly, then, Offen analyzes the formation of ideologies by women within male-dominated political discourse, and demon-strates that positive ideologies had to be fashioned within those constraints.

Male politicians' receptiveness to feminist proposals for reform developed in tandem with efforts to solve the population problem. Hence, public discus-sions of women's roles were shaped under pressures which made it unlikely that women would be granted the same citizen status that men enjoyed. More-over, the way in which the proper role for women was most often described—as one of duties to the state by means of their labor in the family—drew on but also reinforced a vision of the republic as an organic unit to which everyone, male and female, is tied through indissoluble obligation. Over the years, as the population crisis deepened and as feminist pressure for reform continued, even the more moderate among bourgeois politicians gave in to "increasingly shrill patriotic rhetoric" which emphasized the interests of the nation over that of the individual (Offen 1984:671).

The previously hidden centrality of the "woman question" to political dis-course in fin de siècle France, should now "compel a rethinking of French—and for that matter, European—history as it has traditionally been written and taught" (Offen 1984:649). Precisely what such rethinking of European history will entail remains precisely to be spelled out by means of such studies. Clearly, research such as Offen's challenges the canons of historical importance by removing the barrier between public affairs and private lives; the allegedly private world of the family was in fact a focal point for public debate. And, in that debate, we can see that the various versions of the proper public order were founded on assumptions about the proper private social order. A rewritten historical record may not altogether dispense with conventional periodization; the world of politics will, if anything, take on added significance, since the nature of its importance in men's and women's lives, separately and together, will be more clearly revealed. Also, more attention will be given to discerning the political significance of struggles over gender identity and gender roles, wherever those struggles occur—that is, to scrutinizing implications whenever gender serves as an arena of discourse. Still, a recast European history will also need to give full weight to the events and achievements which the insights of social history have enabled us to value—the achievements of mothers in keeping their families alive against all odds, for example. Human action on this level must be given the full weight of event which we do not, currently, attach to it. A recast history will use time periods that include major demographic fluctuations and the invention of reliable contraception on a par with voyages of exploration and the invention of gunpowder. The only means to this end, however, is the inclusion of the variable of gender in all kinds of historical investigation, and especially within mainstream historical narrative, where it has seemed most irrelevant, and by means of which it is still most effectively marginalized.

WORKS CITED

DAVIS, NATALIE ZEMON
    1975   City Women and Religious Change. In *Society and Culture in Early Modern France,* pp. 65–95. Palo Alto, Calif.: Stanford University Press.
    1982   Women in the Crafts in Sixteenth-Century Lyon. *Feminist Studies* 8: 46–80.
FAURE, CHRISTINE
    1981   Absent from History. Translated by Lillian S. Robinson. *Signs: Journal of Women in Culture and Society* 7:71–80.
FINLEY, M. I.
    1977   Desperately Foreign. In *Aspects of Antiquity,* pp. 11–15. New York: Pelican Books.
HUFTON, OLWEN
    1983   Women in History: Early Modern Europe. *Past and Present* 101:123–41.

IGGERS, GEORG G.
  1984   *New Directions in European Historiography.* Middletown, Conn.: Wesleyan University Press.

KELLY, JOAN
  1976   The Social Relations of the Sexes: Methodological Implications of Women's History. *Signs: Journal of Women in Culture and Society* 1:809–23.
  1977   Did Women Have a Renaissance? In *Becoming Visible: Women in European History,* edited by Renate Bridenthal and Claudia Koonz, pp. 137–64. Boston: Houghton Mifflin Co.

KLEINBAUM, ABBY R.
  1977   Women in the Age of Light. In *Becoming Visible: Women in European History,* edited by Renate Bridenthal and Claudia Koonz, pp. 217–35. Boston: Houghton Mifflin Co.

LERNER, GERDA
  1979   The Challenge of Women's History. In *The Majority Finds Its Past,* pp. 168–80. Oxford: Oxford University Press.

MERCHANT, CAROLYN
  1980   *The Death of Nature: Women, Ecology and the Scientific Revolution.* New York: Harper and Row.

OFFEN, KAREN
  1984   Depopulation, Nationalism and Feminism in Fin-de-Siècle France. *American Historical Review* 89:648–76.

SCOTT, JOAN W.
  1983   Women in History: The Modern Period. *Past and Present* 101:141–57.

STUARD, SUSAN MOSHER
  1981   The Annales School and Feminist History: Opening Dialogue with the American Stepchild. *Signs: Journal of Women in Culture and Society* 7:135–43.

CHAPTER 2

Notes toward a Supreme Fiction: The Work of Feminist Criticism

DEBORAH POPE

My title is taken from a poem by Wallace Stevens, "Notes toward a Supreme Fiction." [1] Stevens' incessant concern in poetry was with the myriad and inevitable changes wrought in one's perception of the world by the workings of the imagination and cognitive process. Because of the nature of how we know our world—refracted, filtered, received as it is through language, through self, through time, and desire, and place—we can never finally have any way of possessing, of knowing "the thing itself"; we can only have "ideas about the thing." All of Stevens' poems, on one level, are pieces in a serial meditation on variously grand and minute, fertile and wintery transformations that the mind enacts on the world, the world sometimes resisting, sometimes colluding in these transformations, sometimes beyond determining. For Stevens, each poem, each moment of perception, posits a way of seeing, an "idea of order," but no ultimate, timeless, universal order is there. Even if such an absolute, final order was there, it could only have relevance through its entry into human cognition, awareness, and articulation. Because it could only be enacted through words and images, it would begin and end in a human construct mitigating its divinity, its ultimateness, and leaving it finally a "fiction."

The "supreme fiction" is Stevens' term for what such an ultimate order might be, with human fallibility inflected in it. It expresses both the longing we feel for a final coherence elevated beyond ourselves ("blessed rage for order"), and yet the impossibility of ever locating such a thing outside a time-bound linguistic construct and mediating consciousness that always qualifies its claims to absoluteness. Stevens would argue that the supreme fiction must always be striven for, because out of such endless recastings of imagination and perception come the only insights into ourselves and our world we are capable of having. The quest gives us necessary fictions, though none is likely

22

ever to be a finally sufficient fiction. While for Stevens the attainment of a supreme fiction was impossible, he was not beyond a certain prophetic assertion of what its fundamental properties must be, to contain the world and the mind, to be the elusive meaning of meaning. The three qualities he proposed form the three sections of the poem "Notes toward a Supreme Fiction": "It must be abstract"; "it must give pleasure"; "it must change."

I have begun with Stevens because his poem suggests a useful and relevant analogy for initiating a discussion of an understanding of literary criticism. Literary criticism is perhaps best conceived of as an exercise in supreme fictions, as the search for an ultimate idea of literary order. A literary text, in this analogy, is like the world itself—an entity that comes before us to be apprehended, interpreted, understood; and we can enter into the text and its meanings only through our language, through our experiences, through our interpretative strategies refined from other texts, through other fictions.

Literary critics have always tended to be on familiar terms with such confident, commendatory designations as supreme, but have generally been less than congenial to the implications of any specter of fiction in their constructs, and often extremely resistant to other ideas of literary order, other fictions that arise to dislodge their own. In that light, I will consider the nature of literary criticism; some of the "fictional" frameworks that have shaped it in the past; and the way in which recent feminist criticism is both revising and recasting the basis for a viable criticism of legitimately supreme aspirations. Stevens' criteria, with their rich suggestiveness, can stand as a measure for appreciating the power feminist criticism brings to literary studies. After all, the descent of literary criticism has never seriously disputed the first two criteria, abstraction and pleasure. *Abstraction* is an appropriate signification of the need for intellectual integrity in method, the dependence of criticism on rational assent, and a certain requisite high seriousness. *Pleasure* subsumes in it the search for what is humanizing, affirming, satisfying through its testament to value and completeness. It is in the arena of *change* where troubles stir and where feminist critics have met their most concerted resistance. Though they argue for a reanchoring of abstractions and challenge the conditions of intellectual assent, though they petition for the extension of literary and critical pleasures to a newly visible and vocal constituency, it is in the redirecting of an entrenched critical practice resistant not simply to change, but to the particular kind of changes feminist criticism necessitates, that its most basic challenges lie.[2] Feminist critics ask, What in criticism has been allowed to stand for the supreme? Where are the fictions? And whose world has criticism been invented to order?

Every discipline's ultimate concern is with epistemology. This being the case, we are all concerned in these essays with posing the questions most fundamental to university enterprises and intellectual inquiry: What has the status of knowledge? What gets valorized as worth knowing? What are the criteria evoked? Who has the authority to establish meaning? Feminists acknowledge that feminist criticism is a challenge to the way these questions have been traditionally answered. Indeed, even raising the questions causes controversy to flourish, since the issues questioned have long been the givens, the covert categories of our culture. But they are under fundamental scrutiny by feminist scholars who demonstrate that the phrasing of such questions and the answers given have explicitly and implicitly, consciously and unconsciously, rendered inconsequential, invisible, or nonexistent the experience and significance of women. That women have not had a role, or a sufficiently recognized role, in either the framing of these questions or the discovering of the answers has been the starting point of our task, as we have critiqued our individual disciplines and the paradigms they offer for understanding the relations of power and ideology to status and knowledge.

I am aware that literature may bear the dubious reputation among academic disciplines of seeming the least connected with any real world, of having the most dependence on the rarefied air of the university, of having the least to gain from any movement outward to considerations of the marketplace. I am more than mournfully aware that some even relegate literary study to the level of pretentious competitions in personal taste and unseemly gossip about writers' lives, or think it an extravagantly useless indulgence in the pursuit of arcane meanings and allusions whose ultimate purpose is the self-flattering exercise of a certain type of anal mind and the erecting of further barriers between those who know and those who do not. In either case, literary critics, to outsiders and even many insiders, can appear all too wrapped in the emperor's cloak of elitism and self-referential terminology, while literature itself may unfortunately be defined by the public as whatever it is nobody else is reading; indeed, as whatever it is nobody *can* read, except the handful of elect.[3] After all, what is readily available subverts the role and the expertise of the professional critic. It is no mystery why critics, out of self-preservation if nothing else, should tend to elevate the complex, the dense, the formal in their valuation of texts. This sense of literature as both disembodied and enclosed has been its curse, isolating it from any wide audience, and its self-justification as the dwindling, but noble preserve of what Matthew Arnold called "the best that has been thought and said."

What seems to many, however, an exaggerated retreat into the hieratic is arguably a defensive posture arising out of literature's ironic proximity to popular "taint." That is, people as a matter of course do not just sit down and "do" economics, anthropology, and biblical archaeology, but they do sit down and read—even, horrors, write. There is an interesting historical and psychological context for examining why literature and literary study in their present form carry the connotations they do, and it is directly related to femi-

nist concerns. For in fact the distinctions between popular and trained readers, accessible and privileged material, emotive and intellectual stances, carry gender inflections. An explanation may be sought in two factors: the historical origins of English literature as an academic field; and the corollary development that the critic is implicitly, if not always actually, male, and the reader is implicitly female. Scholars have located the origins of literature as a special field of academic study in the Victorian need for a spiritually uplifting and socially unifying body of national myth that would replace a religion devastated by Darwin, the Higher Criticism, and the operations of utilitarian capitalism; and in the unprecedented entry of women into institutions of higher learning. Over the strenuous objections to their frivolity, lack of rigor, and analytical substantiveness, and the dominance in them of mere taste and affectiveness, English studies were allowed into the universities when it was pointed out that these qualities made them the very thing to teach to the young women gaining increasing access to the universities. Eagleton's trenchant analysis of literature's academic rise offers this rationale: "since English was an untaxing sort of affair, concerned with finer feelings rather than with the more virile topics of bone fide academic 'disciplines,' it seemed a convenient sort of non-subject to palm off on the ladies, who were in any case excluded from sciences and the professions."[4] But literary study came into its own with the nationalism of World War I and the rise of Anglo-American New Criticism with its reaction against "feminine" taste mongering and impressionism, and its emphasis on a proselytizing zeal for masculine analysis, the rigorous intellectual scrutiny of highly technical formal properties of texts and their mind-bending, multiple ambiguities.

Yet the essential gender markings remained intact. Armed with the principles of New Criticism and the moral mandates of F. R. Leavis, the image of the literary critic has come down to us as "implicitly male," "cool," "magisterial," judgmental, Olympian, the "museum-guide" to tradition's artefacts; while the reader is implicitly female, "hot," eager, emotional, immediate, the perennial student in need of perennial instruction from the male critic, who has "mastered" his subject.[5] That women are the primary consumers of literature—whether "popular" or great—is easily evidenced by the grocery store checkout or the gender profile of any undergraduate English department. Yet at the level of our culture's designations of value and significance in art, women writers remain the least enfranchised, the least included. For a woman to study literature seriously is to study texts that are written by male authors, that enshrine masculine experience, and that are delivered under the authority of male professors and critics. Little wonder, then, that Showalter was led to make her classic observation: "A woman studying English literature is also studying a different culture to which she must bring the adaptability of the anthropologist."[6]

Feminist criticism began in this awareness of the need to address the invisibility of women's experience and significance in the way the dominant culture imagined itself. Women as writers, women as characters, women as symbols, women as readers have been kept invisible, unexpressed, or crucially distorted in the literary enterprise. As Adrienne Rich so eloquently asserts, for women to undertake the process of visioning and revisioning the whole of our literary heritage is "more than a chapter in cultural history; it is an act of survival." [7]

I want to focus on three interrelated areas of traditional literary study to which the revisionism of feminist criticism has particularly been directed: the gender markings of the literary canon; the aspiration of theory to neutrality and universality; the isolation of literary study from social and historical contexts. As both detractors and supporters point out, no monolithic creed accounts for all the methodologies and ideologies that go by the term *feminist criticism*. This pluralism is in itself a source of continuing controversy among feminist literary theorists, some of whom feel it is a weakness of the movement, and others of whom embrace it as one of the movement's great strengths. Nevertheless, some attributes clearly distinguish feminist literary criticism from other traditional critical schools. Applying the criteria of Stanley Fish, Kolodny argues that feminist critics do the best of what any other critics do by "challeng[ing] the assumptions within which ordinary practices go on." This challenge is pursued as one "seek[s] to overturn the interpretation of a single work, or recharacterize the entire canon of an important author, or argue for an entirely new realignment of genres, or question the notion of genre itself, or even propose a new definition of literature and a new account of its function in the world." [8] The difference is that feminist literary critics do these things in the service of women writers and the patterns of female relations to the world and the text. Feminist critics are particularly attentive to the way concepts of gender generate and structure literary texts, and the critical conventions governing those texts. [9]

Feminist criticism has been steadfastly resisted because, like the feminist movement in other areas, it is essentially political; that is, it relates literature to the social, cultural, and moral environment and to questions of power. Power in texts and power in criticism, like power anywhere else, is control of information. To put it more acutely, power is control of representation; it is control of language, the control of words: the words that can be used and the values they are determined to carry; the meaning they can be said to have. Power belongs to those who regard the authority to determine meaning as rightfully theirs. Feminist critics examine how assumptions of gender operate through the images, social codes, language patterns, and so on, that are reified by and transmitted through literature and literary criticism. As such, feminist criticism is inevitably connected to the most fundamental considerations of culture and cultural institutions, and brings a new scrutiny and skepticism to bear on such professionally powerful concepts as tradition, the canon, and standards of excellence, and shows how under the rhetoric of *universal,* these concepts have meant *nonfemale.*

Chroniclers of the rise of feminist criticism have identified several general areas of feminist enterprise, and have implied that these are to a large extent evolutionary, successive stages. In the earliest phase, described as "looking for the sins and errors of the past," [10] feminists consider the images and stereotypes of women in literature, and endeavor to correct the omissions and misconceptions about women (as readers and writers) in criticism. Despite the increasing shift in feminist discussion to issues of language, difference, and the construction of gender, this early corrective, compensatory approach remains to many their ideas of the standard feminist critique, and in practice it has addressed itself largely to classic male texts. However, as a number of feminist critics have acknowledged—notably Heilbrun, Kolodny, Showalter, Kaplan, among them—women scholars have increasingly moved on from "the task of revealing the ways in which patriarchy oppressed and misused women." There was widespread feeling that this work "was too easily done, too repetitive," and that it had the disadvantage of keeping the focus too centrally on male writers. [11] The work of feminist criticism has centered more and more on fundamental questions and explorations of the tradition itself—how "the Great Literary Tradition," the conventional canon enshrining a lineage of precursors and greats, has come to be accepted and perpetuated. Feminist scholars have directly confronted the means and implications of canonization and valorization of texts, calling down upon themselves the wrath of the literary establishment, in their persistent question of "what model accounts for our canonical choices?" [12]

A third branch of feminist criticism focuses its study squarely on women writers. Elaine Showalter's candidate for what to call this type of criticism—"gynocriticism"—has not achieved easy and precise currency, although the territory it was coined to designate is without question the site of most of the compelling and controversial debates shaping present feminist theory. The subject matter here, too, is often literary history, but the hitherto submerged history of the styles, themes, archetypes, and structures of writing by women. It investigates such areas as "the psychodynamics of female creativity"; "the trajectory of the individual or collective female career"; above all, it centers on "the essential question of difference." [13] This is the most recent and risky terrain feminists are mapping. Initially, difference was understood to refer to differences between male and female writers, a line of inquiry exemplified by Woolf's claim to be able to distinguish a man's from a woman's sentence wholly on the basis of distinctive styles. Others, taking up the challenge on the other side, early on tried to rehabilitate the reputation of women writers by arguing for their very indistinguishability from male writers, their comparable achievements within male categories and paradigms. But feminist scholars have by and large decamped from this effort to assimilate and accommodate women to the dominant modes of expression, and are exploring the evidence instead for separate and distinctive modes of expression. Here, the scholarly energy has been expended in foregrounding differences among women themselves, especially differences of race, class, and sexual identity.

Difference is, indeed, now the multifaceted, variably resonating catchword of a good deal of current feminist writing. On the one hand, it suggests a critique of the concept of a mythic, generic woman that tends to appropriate and deny distinctions of race, class, and personal and public history, while paradoxically, on the other hand, it underscores a largely French psychoanalytically derived concept of *difference* that seeks an essential, linguistic, gendered feminine (not necessarily female) that both inhabits and disrupts the liminal contours of discourse.[14] The most fundamental debates at this critical juncture in feminist theory align around divergences within and across these loose camps—divergences over concepts of language; shape and validity of data; reliance on patriarchal forefathers; notions of history and authorship; the materiality of experience; in short, the entire basis of their disputed epistemologies. The debates, urgent and provocative as they are, however, have at times been obscured by a disconcertingly nationalistic tone and tendency to reductive caricature. Regrettably, the much-bruited confrontations of a supposedly American-identified empiricist feminist criticism and a French "essentialist" theory more often than not oversimplify and thus distort the variances, subtleties, and intellectual allegiances of the theorists involved and the evolutions in the positions they have pursued.

Clearly, in any case, our understanding and determination of differences in women's writing and the feminine in language are intimately tied to, and await the outcome of, work in other analogous models of gender difference, such as those investigations being carried out in biology, linguistics, psychology, history, and anthropology. Though the dangers of reductionism, simplification, and even prescription are real and must be guarded against in any such critical undertakings, the potential richness and complexity make the efforts worth the risks. The limitation at this point is not the reductionist position that differences can be either neatly enumerated or scotched, but the position that this undertaking is anything more than invigoratingly inaugurated.

I want to return to the relation of literature, particularly canonical literature, to the forms of power in a culture. Literature is a form of socialization; it tells how—in what languages and images—we should understand our experience. From liberal and conservative forces alike, its justification is typically couched in terms of its usefulness for cultivating larger sympathies, instilling national and cultural identity, and serving as the conduit of moral concerns. As such, literature is monitory, exemplary, cautionary, both mythic and local to our culture and dominant ideology. Therefore what literature is selected out to be privileged over other forms tells us less about the inherent qualities of the text than it does about who has the power to select, and to what ideological uses a culture's assignment of aesthetic value is put. Following my opening questions on academic epistemology in general, we can rephrase them for literary study in particular: Who writes? For whom is the writing being done? Who criticizes? For whom is the criticism being done? Why do we read what we read as literature? Why don't we read other books? How is meaning assigned? Who has the authority to assign meaning? We need also ask, What happens before a book gets into the classroom? What happens when it appears there? Criticism and critical approaches not only reveal meaning in the work, but carry meaning as well; they even go some distance toward determining the meaning we find. Ideological and ethical implications inevitably inhere in critical strategies.[15] The feminist critic's concern is with how those values, reflective of white, male power structures, operate through literary institutions to exclude, consciously or unconsciously, nonwhite, nonmale writing and experience, and to privilege a set of more or less predictable texts whose effect is to further inscribe the power of white, male experience and significance on the world.

We recall the insecure, inauspicious beginnings of the academic study of literature. With the solidification of its acceptance, however, and the consequent professionalization of teaching, there emerged the desire to ground the critic's work on scientific principles, to give it a progressive, systematic basis. This was in part an attempt to give scholarly respectability to a field anxious to disclaim the reputation for being soft and concerned only with effete matters of taste and appreciation. I suspect that at the heart of literary criticism there is a severe, perhaps insurmountably self-defeating identity crisis over the ultimately insubstantial, elusive, and "fictive" object it pursues, that has accounted for its defensive concern with objectivity, empirical evidence, universalities, and purity, and its concomitant horror of relativity and indeterminancy. Thinking of its frustrated scientism, I might almost call it "genus envy," the longing for such equally confident systems of classification, hierarchies, and fixed characteristics. Yet as Barbara Herrnstein Smith points out in her brilliant study "Contingencies of Value," critics confront an essential conflict in trying to make literary criticism achieve the "rigor, objectivity, cognitive substantiality and progress associated with science and the empirical disciplines," and yet "remain faithful to the essentially conservative and didactic mission of humanistic studies . . . to illuminate and transmit the traditional culture values presumably embodied in them," which are inevitably more impressionistic, subjective, and variable.[16] Nevertheless, the literary theories and practices that determined the shape of modern criticism, and still remain powerfully influential today, held that criticism was apolitical, objective, and outside history, and the patterns of human experience and values to which it spoke, universal.

The New Critics were the most prominent force in professionalizing the study of literature and determining for their whole midcentury generation what literature and literary criticism was and should be. "New Criticism claimed to view the verbal object as in itself it really was, free from the distractions of biography, social message, or even paraphrase." [17] In their familiar phrases, the work of art was a "well-wrought urn," a "verbal icon." "The ethos of American New Criticism was clubby, gentlemanly . . . the critic [was an] educated aristocrat," and the aspects of literary art emphasized by midcentury critics—and many yet today—are precisely those aspects that intervene most between "literature" and a wide audience: formal techniques, exhaustive scrutiny for allusions, ambiguities, puns, tricks of language, multiple levels of meaning, irony, emotional restraint. Their standard served and elevated the modernist poetry of Eliot and Pound, and the metaphysical poets they championed, but its near-absolute hegemony as a critical standard tended to disparage any writing that did not fit it. As one critic observes, while the great classroom exercise carried out by this standard—the explication of text—"was effective as a classroom tactic and for exploring a great many powerful texts, it provided no useful basis for approaching that great body of literature that placed a premium on simplicity, transparency, and emotional directness—from American Indian chants and spirituals to Langston Hughes and Gwendolyn Brooks, from *Uncle Tom's Cabin* to *Daughter of Earth*.[18] Furthermore, as another critic adds, in New Criticism's extreme attention "to 'the words on the page' rather than the contexts which produce and surround them . . . it held at bay a great deal; it encouraged the illusion that any piece of language could be adequately studied in isolation. It was the beginning of the 'reification' of the literary work." [19] These forces tended to select out, and hence promote, a literature suited to complex analysis by enlightened specialists, almost to the point where accessibility was a liability. The more and more professional the profession thus became, the more selection tended to favor those texts that require *teaching,* that necessitate a translator so to speak. One can see the effect such aesthetic standards would have on elevating the position of the critics, of increasingly interposing the superior intellect and judgment of the critic (not coincidentally white and male) between the masses and "literature." So a cult of expertise and elitism entrenches itself on a restricted vision and tends to produce in the practitioners of that style an inability "to acknowledge the most fundamental character of literary value, which is its mutability and diversity." [20]

Here we encounter one of the most essential divides of literary theorists, a debate in which feminist critics are deeply engaged and highly partisan. This is the debate between those who see literary criteria as universal, objective, ahistorical, as the impartial reflections of self-evident excellence and the all-powerful test of time, and those who regard such designations of value and the standards of literary criteria as historically situated, time-bound, part of a continually shifting, changing social and cultural context. The latter is clearly the feminist position, and though it is one inevitably shared by others, the canon has been slow to reflect significant shifts, and even slower to give assent to the rationale such variability provides for the greater inclusion of women and the disadvantages they suffer in the operations of the dynamics of value. Despite the insight with which Marxists and other critics expose the cultural and ideological bases of literary criteria, they do not challenge the canon—they merely provide another means of interpreting it. While proliferating critical schools seem in such intense debate of late, they "essentially share an identical landscape, well-marked and mapped. Where they disagree is on the site from which it shall next be admired. As a result, their claims to innovation notwithstanding, it can hardly be said that such critics have radically dislodged the assumptions or presuppositions through which we read." [21] Feminists like Kolodny aim to redraw the boundaries altogether.

Feminists begin their critique of the literary canon with the "white father's effect"; "the white father's effect" underlies the crucial point that what is considered great depends on the process of selection and the power to select.

What is commonly called literary history is actually a record of choices. Which writers have survived their time and which have not depends upon who noticed them and chose to record that notice. Such power, in England and America, has always belonged to white men. That class has written the record called literary history, which is clearly shaped by the attitudes, conscious or unconscious, of white men toward nonwhites and nonmales. [22]

Kolodny bluntly calls literary history simply another "fiction" and points to the self-defeating circularity it brings to the classroom. As she so persuasively argues, simply being part of the canon "puts a work beyond questions of establishing its merits and, instead, invites students to offer only increasingly more ingenious readings" whose purpose "is to validate the greatness" already ascribed. Further, an artificiality enters in with the regrettable but understandable tendency to teach what one has been taught since "we read well what we already know how to read," that is, those works "from which we've developed our critical expectations and learned our interpretive strategies." So what we tend to select and teach, and thereby further enshrine, "usually follows our previous reading." [23] But in fact as she reminds us, we are not taught texts so much as we are taught, and teach, paradigms. That is, modern critical practice has institutionalized the mastery of interpretive strategies. It has instilled, and by its selection of texts affirmed, the acceptance and mastery of certain suppositions and methods that precede a text and color our under-

standing of it. This is a crucial recognition, and one that has been reached by a
number of prominent (male) literary critics. As Fish admits, "[interpretive]
strategies exist prior to the act of reading and therefore determine the shape of
what is read rather than, as is usually assumed, the other way around." [24]

This perception has an important bearing on the debate over such concepts
as "aesthetic quality" and "criteria of excellence," and those fundamental
questions about how we recognize what we do as "true," "real," or "signifying." What such critics, and feminists, acknowledge is that meaning is not
received, it is made—made in the two-way interaction between reader and
text. The "discovery" of meaning depends on many things existing prior to
the encounter with the text, most immediately the strategies one employs on
the text, but also upon prior agreement about what is meaningful, and other
variable factors such as "social and economic forces, by the spirit of one's
time and place and condition, by the conventions of one's language, and by
the drives and needs of one's psyche" and so on. [25] Once one knows a text
well, on subsequent readings one is as much calling up a memory of the text
(along with the supporting framework of critics one has assented to) as actually *reading* the text itself. It is very difficult, and becomes ever more so, to
read a text freshly. Feminist critics thus rightly point out the extent to which
women writers get lost from "the tradition" because of the formidable power
of existing, male-determined interpretive strategies. Because it is frequently
the case that women's writings, and much minority writing as well, does not
fit standard concepts of periodization, archetypes, lines of influence, etc.,
they are effectively rendered invisible or distorted by passage through an inappropriate critical lens.

We return to the questions, What is knowledge? What is meaning? What is
to be valued? Who has the authority to decide? The great illusion is that answers to these questions arise in a free marketplace, presenting their claims
equally, while the ultimate arbiters are truth, disinterest, intellectual integrity,
or particularly for literature, that almost glinting, back-lit phrase "the test of
time." Therefore there are those who cannot or will not see the virtual absence
of women writers from the serious study of literature as anything but the im-
placable hand of fate pointing them to the periphery. Yet this idea of a timeless
process in which merits are neutrally and universally weighed is a myth; there
is always someone with his hand on the scale. Herrnstein Smith shrewdly re-
buts such beliefs:

What is commonly referred to as the "test of time" is not, as the figure implies, an
impersonal and impartial mechanism; for the cultural institutions through which it op-
erates (schools, libraries, theaters, museums, publishing and printing houses, editorial
boards, prize-awarding commissions, state censors, etc.) are, of course, all managed
by persons (who, by definition, are those with cultural power and commonly other
forms of power as well), and, since texts that are selected and preserved by "time"

will always tend to be those which "fit" (and, indeed, have often been *designed* to fit) their characteristic needs, interests, resources, and purposes, that testing mechanism has its own built-in partialities accumulated in and thus *intensified* by time. . . . Also, as is often remarked, since those with cultural power tend to be those members of socially, economically, and politically established classes (or to serve them and identify their interests with theirs), the texts that survive will tend to be those that appear to reflect and reinforce establishment ideologies [emphasis in original].[26]

We have indeed come some distance since Wordsworth defined literature as "a man talking to men," and Anatole France described criticism as "the adventure of the soul among masterpieces." We must once and for all shear the myth of disinterest that has had an unnatural longevity in the literary hothouse, and has been the particular bane of the inclusion of women. We must see that the critic, like the author, cannot come to the task as an ideal spectator devoid of culture, history, politics, and public and private dispositions of all kinds. To understand this is not to be left only with bias and prejudice as the remaining contenders for meaning.

As Barnes suggests, no critic is able "to escape some classificatory schema"; in fact without some framework, one has no access at all. The object, the work, is in a sense only brought into being in its interaction with those who have access to it.[27] A further consideration is that a work can have an "overlay of meaning," necessitate a dialectic of interpretation that varying strategies can release.[28] It is important, too, to keep in mind that the recognition of an operative bias is not the point at which to finish a discussion, but the point at which to begin it. There is far more to feminist criticism than the "skeptical unmasking of concealed ideology, of false claims to neutrality, purity or nonalignment." The challenge of feminist criticism is "a prelude to the clarification of [what is worth] serving in the production of meaning"; it can be a "liberation of suppressed or forgotten meanings . . . [or] the envisioning of new meanings."[29] Above all, it is important to read literature, as a venerable critic once cautioned, "not so much with the intent to assign certificates of greatness, but to read each work as a more or less rich expression of our full and varied humanity and as an effective work of art,"[30] and to encourage in those to whom we teach it critical perceptiveness and independent thought. In doing so, it is to be hoped that we lose some of our dogma, arrogance, and limited vision.

Despite the tremendous increase in the visibility of feminist scholars and the presence of feminist-identified work in academic conferences, journals, and presses, feminist critical theory and practice remains an embattled enterprise within the discipline.[31] Thus, I have spoken as much about the considerable obstacles to feminist criticism as I have about the impact this work has made. I have raised more questions than answers. No feminist can fail to acknowledge the extent of the work that lies ahead. Yet the questions are clearly

vital, indispensable, ongoing conditions of the work. We recognize that the
first and continual task of criticism, of investigation in any field, is to frame
relevant questions. We can affirm already that without clear insight into, and
full account taken of, the powerful implications of gender, sexuality, the lived
and imagined experiences of women, in their interaction with, and distinctions from, the language, myths, images, and codes of cultural power, any
critical theory is seriously defective. As the poet Carolyn Kizer reminds us,
"We are the custodians of the world's best kept secret/ Merely the private lives
of one-half of humanity." [32] Thus, I see feminist criticism as walking a fron-
tier, and not yet—nor soon to be—nor even, perhaps, desiring to be, at the
point of easy summing up, preferring the interrogative posture to the de-
clarative as the truest to the potential of a "supreme fiction": the vision of that
site where we encounter the generative abstractions of an expanded theory and
discourse, the pleasure of enriched and deepened connections, and the continual renewal of transformation and change; where we see "truth" and "tradition" not as a landscape, fixed and immutable, but as a shoreline shifting
and altering as our archives of women's work, our hindsight into women's
past, our awareness of gender, and our insights into a fully human world open-
endedly grow.

NOTES

1 "Notes toward a Supreme Fiction," in *The Collected Poems of Wallace Stevens*
   (New York: Vintage, 1977), pp. 380–408.
2 For studies focusing on the impact of feminist theory in the academy generally,
   see, for example, Ellen DuBois et al., *Feminist Scholarship: Kindling in the
   Groves of Academe* (Urbana: University of Illinois Press, 1985); Paula Treichler,
   Cheris Kramarae, and Beth Stafford, eds., *For Alma Mater: Theory and Practice
   in Feminist Scholarship* (Urbana: University of Illinois Press, 1985); Teresa de
   Lauretis, ed., *Feminist Studies/Critical Studies* (Bloomington: Indiana University
   Press, 1986); Marilyn Schuster and Susan Van Dyne, eds., *Woman's Place in the
   Academy: Transforming the Liberal Arts Curriculum* (Totowa, N.J.: Rowman and
   Allanheld, 1985); Margo Culley and Catherine Portuges, eds., *Gendered Sub-
   jects: The Dynamics of Feminist Teaching* (Boston: Routledge and Kegan Paul,
   1985); Ellen Langland and Walter Gove, *A Feminist Perspective in the Academy:
   The Difference It Makes* (Chicago: University of Chicago Press, 1981); Judith
   Stiehm, ed., *The Frontiers of Knowledge* (Los Angeles: University of Southern
   California Press, 1976); Toward a Feminist Transformation of the Academy I, II,
   and III, in *Proceedings of the GLCA Women's Studies Conference,* ed. Katherine
   Loring and Beth Reed, Ann Arbor, Mich., 1979–1981, and Seeing Our Way
   Clear: Feminist Revision of the Academy, in *Proceedings of the GLCA Women's
   Studies Conference,* 1982; Evelyn Torton Beck and Julia Sherman, eds., *The*

Prism of Sex: Essays in the Sociology of Knowledge (Madison: University of Wisconsin Press, 1979).

3 Jane Marcus makes the provocative point that there may be a relation in recent years between the inroads of feminist criticism in the academy and the increasing resort of male critics to the tenuously abstracted in theory and language. Marcus suggests that feminist critics recovered the tools male critics had moved away from, i.e., textual criticism, recovery of manuscripts, biography, history, bibliography. "The more material and particular the labor of feminist critics became, the more abstract and antimaterial became the work of men. . . . The more we spoke in moral indignation and anger, the more Parnassian were the whispers of male theorists." J. Marcus, Storming the Toolshed, in *Feminist Theory: A Critique of Ideology,* ed. Nannerl Keohane, Michelle Rosaldo, and Barbara Gelpi (Chicago: University of Chicago Press, 1982), p. 218.

4 Terry Eagleton, *Literary Theory: An Introduction.* (Minneapolis: University of Minnesota Press, 1983), p. 28.

5 Sandra M. Gilbert, Life Studies, or, Speech after Long Silence: Feminist Critics Today, *College English* 40 (1979):853–54.

6 Elaine Showalter, Women and the Literary Curriculum, *College English* 32 (1971):856–57.

7 Adrienne Rich, When We Dead Awaken: Writing as Revision, in *Adrienne Rich's Poetry,* ed. A. Gelpi and B. Gelpi (New York: W. W. Norton and Co., 1977), p. 92.

8 Annette Kolodny, Not So Gentle Persuasion: A Theoretical Imperative of Feminist Literary Criticism, *Proceedings of the Conference on Feminist Literary Criticism* (Research Triangle Park, N.C.: National Humanities Center, 1981), pp. 3–20.

9 See, for example, studies focusing on feminist theory and literature such as those of Shari Benstock, ed., *Feminist Issues in Literary Scholarship* (Bloomington: Indiana University Press, 1987); Mary Eagleton, ed., *Feminist Literary Theory: A Reader* (New York: Basil Blackwell, 1986); Greene and Kahn, eds., *Making a Difference: Feminist Literary Criticism* (New York: Methuen, 1985); Showalter, ed., *New Feminist Criticism;* Judith Lowder Newton and Deborah Rosenfelt, eds., *Feminist Criticism and Social Change: Sex, Class and Race in Literature and Culture* (New York: Methuen, 1985); Judith Kegan Gardiner, Elly Bulkin, Rena Grasso Patterson, and Annette Kolodny, An Interchange on "Dancing through the Minefields," *Feminist Studies* 8, no. 3 (fall 1982):629–75; Myra Jehlen, Archimedes and the Paradox of Feminist Criticism, *Signs* 6 (summer 1981):575–601; special issue of *Diacritics* (summer 1982) on feminist criticism; Mary Jacobus, ed., *Women Writing and Writing about Women* (New York: Columbia University Press, 1979); Josephine Donovan, ed., *Feminist Literary Criticism: Explorations in Theory* (Lexington: University of Kentucky Press, 1975). Useful bibliographies of feminist critical writings are contained in the work of Showalter, *New Feminist Criticism;* DuBois et al., *Kindling in the Groves of Academe;* and Schuster and Van Dyne, *Women's Place in the Academy.* Also, the University of Wisconsin publishes regular listings and updates of its extensive feminist materials and collections, including specific interest bibliographies, such as literature and black and third world women.

10   Carolyn G. Heilbrun and Catherine R. Stimpson, Theories of Feminist Criticism:
     A Dialogue, in *Feminist Literary Criticism,* ed. Donovan, p. 64. Different desig-
     nations but similar conceptualizations of the various stages of feminist literary
     criticism are described by Sandra Gilbert and Susan Gubar, who refer to them as
     "critique, recovery, reconceptualization and reassessment" in their teaching
     handbook intended to accompany *The Norton Anthology of Literature by Women,*
     ed. S. Gilbert and S. Gubar (New York: W. W. Norton and Co., 1985). Similar
     formulations have been given to the evolution of feminist work in history and
     other disciplines.
11   Carolyn Heilbrun, A Response to *Writing and Sexual Difference,* in *Writing and
     Sexual Difference,* ed. Emily Abel (Chicago: University of Chicago Press, 1982),
     p. 293.
12   See especially Annette Kolodny, Dancing through the Minefield: Some Observa-
     tions on the Theory, Practice and Politics of Feminist Criticism, *Feminist Studies*
     6 (1980): 292–304; also essays on the canon in the work of Showalter, ed., *New
     Feminist Criticism;* Robert von Hallberg, ed., *Canons* (Chicago: University of
     Chicago Press, 1983); Paul Lauter, ed., *Reconstructing American Literature* (Old
     Westbury, N.Y.: Feminist Press, 1983).
13   E. Showalter, Feminist Criticism in the Wilderness, in *New Feminist Criticism,*
     ed. Showalter, p. 248.
14   For a sampling of work done by feminist critics on the writings of black and third
     world women, see Gloria Hull, Patricia Bell Scott, and Barbara Smith, eds., *All
     the Women Are White, All the Men Are Black, But Some of Us Are Brave* (Old
     Westbury, N.Y.: Feminist Press, 1982); Barbara Smith, ed., *Home Girls: A Black
     Feminist Anthology* (New York: Kitchen Table Press, 1983); Roseann Bell, Bettye
     Parker, and Beverly Guy-Sheftall (Garden City, N.Y.: Anchor Books, 1979);
     Mari Evans, ed., *Black Women Writers (1950–1980): A Critical Evaluation*
     (Garden City, N.Y.: Anchor Books, 1984); Barbara Christian, *Black Women Nov-
     elists: The Development of a Tradition, 1892–1976* (Westport, Conn.: Green-
     wood Press, 1980) and *Black Feminist Criticism: Perspectives on Black Women
     Writers* (New York: Pergamon Press, 1985). For sources on lesbian-feminist criti-
     cism, see Jane Rule, *Lesbian Images* (Garden City, N.Y.: Doubleday, 1975);
     Bonnie Zimmerman, What Has Never Been: An Overview of Lesbian Feminist
     Criticism, *Feminist Studies* 7, no. 3 (fall 1981): 451–76, reprint, in *New Femi-
     nist Criticism,* ed. Showalter; J. R. Roberts, *Black Lesbians* (Tallahassee, Fla.:
     Naiad Press, 1981); Margaret Cruikshank, ed., *Lesbian Studies* (Old Westbury,
     N.Y.: Feminist Press, 1982); Jean Kennard, "Ourself behind Ourself: A Theory
     for Lesbian Readers," *Signs* 9 (summer 1984): 647–62. For a selection of work
     on French feminist theory and Lacanian-influenced feminist theory see, for ex-
     ample, Elaine Marks and Isabelle de Courtivon, eds., *New French Feminisms*
     (Amherst: University of Massachusetts Press, 1979); Alice Jardine and Hester
     Eisenstein, eds., *The Future of Difference* (New Brunswick, N.J.: Rutgers Uni-
     versity Press, 1980); Toril Moi, *Sexual/Textual Politics: Feminist Literary Theory*
     (London: Methuen, 1985); Emily Abel, ed., *Writing and Sexual Difference;* spe-
     cial issue of *Contemporary Literature, L'Ecriture féminine* (summer 1983); spe-
     cial issue of *Signs, French Feminist Theory* (fall 1981). See also *Feminist Read-*

ings: French Texts/American Contexts,* special issue, *Yale French Studies* 62 (1981); Alice Jardine, *Gynesis: Configurations of Woman and Modernity* (Ithaca, N.Y.: Cornell University Press, 1985); Mary Jacobus, *Reading Woman: Essays in Feminist Criticism* (New York: Columbia University Press, 1986); *Feminist Directions,* special issue, *New Literary History* 19, no. 1 (autumn 1987); Jane Flax, Postmodernism and Gender Relations in Feminist Theory, *Signs* 12 (summer 1987): 621–43; *On Feminine Writing,* special issue, *Boundary* 2 (winter 1985): 99–110; Chris Weedon, *Feminist Practice and Poststructuralist Theory* (London: Basil Blackwell, 1987).

15   See Stanley Fish, *Is There a Text in This Class? The Authority of Interpretive Communities* (Cambridge: Harvard University Press, 1980); Edward W. Said, Opponents, Audiences, Constituencies, and Community, in *The Politics of Interpretation,* ed. W. J. T. Mitchell (Chicago: University of Chicago Press, 1983); see also the classic study of the self-replicating properties of entrenched intellectual methodologies by Thomas Kuhn, *The Structure of Scientific Revolutions* (Chicago: University of Chicago Press, 1962).

16   Barbara Herrnstein Smith, Contingencies of Value, in *Canons,* ed. von Hallberg, p. 6.

17   Said, Opponents, Audiences, Constituencies, and Community, 10.

18   Paul Lauter, Introduction to *Reconstructing American Literature,* p. xviii.

19   Eagleton, *Literary Theory,* p. 44.

20   Herrnstein Smith, Contingencies of Value, p. 14.

21   Kolodny, Not So Gentle Persuasion, p. 11.

22   Louise Bernikow, Introduction to *The World Split Open: Four Centuries of Women Poets in England and America,* ed. Bernikow (New York: Vintage, 1974), p. 3.

23   Kolodny, Dancing through the Minefield, pp. 8, 12.

24   Fish, *Is There a Text in This Class?,* p. 14.

25   Gerald Graff, *Literature against Itself: Literary Ideas in Modern Society* (Chicago: University of Chicago Press, 1979), p. 194.

26   Herrnstein Smith, Contingencies of Value, pp. 33–34.

27   Annette Barnes, Female Criticism: A Prologue, in *The Authority of Experience: Essays in Feminist Criticism,* ed. Lee Edwards and Arlyn Diamond (Amherst, Mass.: University of Massachusetts Press, 1977), p. 2.

28   Barnes, Female Criticism, p. 3.

29   Mitchell, Introduction to *The Politics of Interpretation,* pp. 4, 5.

30   Joseph Beach, *Obsessive Images: Symbolism in Poetry of the 1930's and 1940's* (Minneapolis: University of Minnesota Press, 1960), p. ix.

31   For a fascinating study of a long-term, university-backed project designed to acquaint traditionally trained faculty with the work of feminist scholars and the extent of entrenched resistance, see Susan Hardy Aiken et al., Trying Transformations: Curriculum Integration and the Problem of Resistance, *Signs* 12:2 (winter 1987): 255–75.

32   Carolyn Kizer, "Pro Femina," in *Knock upon Silence* (New York: Doubleday, 1963), p. 32.

CHAPTER 3

Power and Fantasy in Courtly Love

SARAH WESTPHAL-WIHL

. . . with a few rare exceptions, there has not yet been any writing that inscribes femininity; exceptions so rare, in fact, that, after plowing through literature across languages, cultures, and ages, one can only be startled at this vain scouting mission. It is well known that the number of women writers (while having increased very slightly from the nineteenth century on) has always been ridiculously small. This is a useless and deceptive fact unless from their species of female writers we do not first deduct the immense majority whose workmanship is in no way different from male writing, and which either obscures women or reproduces the classic representations of women (as sensitive—intuitive—dreamy, etc.).

Cixous 1981:248

Men produced most of the great secular works of medieval French and German literature: the Arthurian romances of Chrétien de Troyes and Hartmann von Aue; *Tristan und Isolde* by Gottfried von Strassburg; *Parzival* by Wolfram von Eschenbach; the political and erotic poetry by Walther von der Vogelweide; the lyrics of the troubadours and trouvères. Although the works of a few women authors have entered the canon—Marie de France writing in the late twelfth century, and Christine de Pisan writing about 1400—the male hegemony during the "classical decades" around 1200 seems nearly complete. Although the body of anonymous texts from the period may well contain some compositions by women, their workmanship, as Hélène Cixous states in the opening quote, differs little from that of male writing. Until we refine our tools of historical reconstruction or discover new manuscripts, the scholar of the secular, vernacular literature of this period will almost certainly study men's texts, or texts composed according to the literary conventions they established.

Still, the secular French and German literature written between 1150 and 1250 would seem to be a promising area for feminist research, since it is the first European literature of the postclassical era in which women play important, even key roles. The previous centuries had produced a vernacular, secular literature that we now call heroic. Its roots reach back to the oral poetry of the Germanic peoples during the early Middle Ages. The Old English epic *Beowulf* and the Middle High German *Song of the Nibelungen* are best known today. There are women in these stories, to be sure. The *Nibelungen* princess Kriemhild, who arranges to have her own family slaughtered with their retinue after they deprive her of husband and inheritance, is one of the most ambiguous heroines of medieval tradition. There are women in *Beowulf* as well: the diplomatic queen Wealhtheow who settles disputes before they reach the battlefield, and the mysterious and uncanny woman who appears from nowhere to mourn the death of the hero by wailing at his funeral pyre. Heroic epic, though, if it may be reduced to a single sentence, is about the fierce loyalties of men on the battlefield, engaged in wars that are destined to pit father against son and kinsman against kinsman.

In France around 1100, and later in Germany, there emerged another kind of epic based on the legends surrounding Charlemagne, and particularly his crusades against the non-Christian peoples of Spain. But here, too, the focus is on men's prowess in battle, fought now in the cause of faith, with assurance of salvation for anyone who falls in the line of duty. Women are more peripheral in this world than they are in the world of Germanic epic. We meet Roland's bride, Aude, only after Charlemagne's mournful return to France. When Charlemagne tells her of Roland's fall, she too expires, a love-death that expresses both the sorrow of the kingdom as a whole and her own complete loyalty to her betrothed. This act, though symbolic, is the only one that she performs.[1]

The new emphasis on women in the vernacular, secular literature of the High Middle Ages corresponds to the contemporary emergence of a new concept of gender. Since the end of the nineteenth century, scholars have called this concept courtly love. In this chapter I will examine some aspects of the ideology of courtly love that reflect women's historical role as the patrons of poets and composers. I will suggest some of the reasons why important women characters appear so suddenly, and even come to dominate the fictional world of this literature. I will then turn to the question of the representation of women in courtly literature. Since this topic must be treated selectively, I will concentrate on one convention of gallant discourse: the top-to-toe description of the female body, the *laudes membrorum* that seems to be a medieval equivalent of what modern feminist film critics have called the male gaze (Kaplan 1983:311–12). These panegyric catalogues are nearly ubiquitous in medieval courtly literature. The particular example I discuss forms the core of a German poem by one of the best known authors of the early thirteenth century, Walther von der Vogelweide.

Does feminist theory offer methodologies and insights that can help us to understand medieval texts? The answer is yes, although in practice most feminist criticism has concentrated on nineteenth- and twentieth-century literature. Before turning to my subject proper, I would like to examine briefly one spectrum of recent feminist theory. Although I make no attempt to be exhaustive, I will indicate which approaches are most productive for the study of medieval literature.

Feminist speculation on the status of language and literature cannot be separated from political or social analysis. Thus recent trends in feminist criticism may be juxtaposed to an overview of feminist political theory such as Julia Kristeva (1981) provides in her article "Women's Time." There she describes two generations of feminists (pp. 18–29). Each generation is defined by a different sense of its own identity, as well as of its temporality. It must be emphasized that these generations are not locked in a struggle for domination as between father and son; rather, they share a symbiosis in what Kristeva calls one "signifying space" (p. 33). The first generation includes women whose main concern is to achieve equality and power within a rationally conceived legal and social system. Kristeva describes the first generation as follows:

In its beginnings, the women's movement, as the struggle of suffragists and of existential feminists, aspired to gain a place in linear time as the time of project and history. In this sense, the movement, while immediately universalist, is also deeply rooted in the sociopolitical life of nations. The political demands of women; the struggles for equal pay for equal work, for taking power in social institutions on an equal footing with men; the rejection, when necessary, of the attributes traditionally considered feminine or maternal insofar as they are deemed incompatible with insertion in that history—all are part of the *logic of identification* with certain values: not with the ideological (these are combated, and rightly so, as reactionary) but, rather, with the logical and ontological values of a rationality dominant in the nation-state. (Kristeva 1981 : 18–19; author's emphasis)

The success of this generation has been particularly apparent in North America, where the woman's movement has taken a pragmatic approach to improving the conditions of women's lives.

Kristeva notes that the first generation's quest for equality entailed a simultaneous rejection of the traditional attributes of the feminine or maternal, as ideologically opposed to equality with the male. Their rejection of the "traditionally feminine" corresponds to the major concern of the earliest feminist literary critics—the misrepresentation of women in men's literature and, by extension, literature's complicity in the alienation of women from themselves and society. Mary Ellmann's *Thinking about Women,* published in 1968, marks the modern beginning of a broadly based feminist literary criticism concerned with misrepresentation. She exposes and condemns the stereotypes of the feminine—women are seen as formless, passive, unstable, confined, pious, both material and spiritual, irrational, compliant, and shrewish—that amount to an entrapment of women by a social and descriptive code that reserves such positive values as hardness, rationality, form, and reliability for men (1968:74–145).

The publication in 1975 by Patricia Meyer Spacks of *The Female Imagination* marks a shift from the problems of misrepresentation to a new interest in the writing of women themselves. Spacks shows in her own critical practice how attention to texts by women brings to light "the special point of view, delicately divergent though it may sometimes be" that distinguishes female from male writing (Spacks 1975:3). In a very short time, though, her innovations were advanced by the discovery of separate and coherent female literary traditions. Some of the most substantial successes of feminist criticism lay in restoring little-known texts by women, and revising literary history to account for women's themes and genres. This new field, named "gynocritics" by Elaine Showalter (1985:247–50), now comprises a mainstay of North American feminist criticism.

Although the methodological development of feminist criticism sketched so far includes a switch from male identification (how do women appear in men's texts? how do women's texts diverge from men's?) to female identification (what submerged female traditions have enabled women to write over the centuries? what other forms of expression has female creativity taken?), it still remains within the basic assumptions of the first generation. Its goals, which can be summarized as revisionist and historical, are compatible with the first generation's aspiration to gain a place in linear time as the time of project and history. Kristeva's criticism of this generation centers on its complicity with nationalism, insofar as its demands for participation are realized through identification with the logical and ontological underpinnings of the nation-state. In other words, Kristeva links the first generation faith in history and progress with the violence (militarism, aggression) of the institution of the state, and of the institutions that coexist within the state.

The second generation of feminists questions precisely those underpinnings, mainly by putting pressure on the logic of identity, especially as it is expressed by humanistic ideals. They tend to focus on the complexities of language both as an important tool of exclusion and repression and as the space where the muted experiences of women can be exposed literally for the first time. Kristeva describes the project of the second generation as follows:

Essentially interested in the specificity of female psychology and its symbolic realizations, these women seek to give a language to the intrasubjective and corporeal experiences left mute by culture in the past. Either as artists or writers, they have undertaken a veritable exploration of the *dynamic of signs,* an exploration which relates this tendency, at least at the level of aspirations, to all major projects of aesthetic and religious upheaval. Ascribing this experience to a new generation does not only mean that other, more subtle problems have been added to the demands for sociopolitical identification made in the beginning. It also means that, by demanding recognition of an irreducible identity, without equal in the opposite sex and, as such, exploded, plural, fluid, in a certain way nonidentical, this feminism situates itself outside the linear time of identities which communicate through projection and revindication. (Kristeva 1981:19–20; author's emphasis)

The second generation insists on the specificity of women's experience and psychology. Their stance is antihumanist, since they refuse to allow women's experience to be reduced to a variety of the human which has always been articulated as male. It is also antihistorical, since history, conceptualized as a project with a goal or teleology carried out in linear time, has never accorded women a "place." Specifically female experience is located in the corporeal, in the nonhistorical (cyclical, recurrent) experiences of the female body. The second generation feminists focus, therefore, on the body to reconstruct and symbolize women's consciousness.

Perhaps the best representatives of the second generation are a group of highly experimental French women writers who achieved prominence during the 1970s, and whose work has been advanced subsequently in the North American context. Among them is Hélène Cixous, whose views on the writing of the past starkly illustrate one difference between the first and second generation. She states that nearly all writing, regardless of the gender of the author, has been run by a male (libidinal and political) economy, and has served to perpetuate the repression of women by exaggerating sexual opposition rather than sexual difference:

I maintain unequivocally that there is such a thing as *marked* writing; that, until now, far more extensively and repressively than is ever suspected or admitted, writing has been run by a libidinal and cultural—hence politically, typically masculine—economy; that this is a locus where the repression of women has been perpetuated, over and over, more or less consciously, and in a manner that's frightening since it's often hidden or adorned with the mystifying charms of fiction; that this locus has grossly exaggerated all the signs of sexual opposition (and not sexual difference), where woman has never *her* turn to speak—this being all the more serious and unpardonable in that writing is precisely *the very possibility of change,* the space that can serve as a springboard for subversive thought, the precursory movement of a transformation of social and cultural structures. (Cixous 1981:249; author's emphasis)

Cixous refers to the containment and control of women that becomes possible when they are defined, in a culturally constructed minimal pair, as the opposite sex rather than the different sex. The repercussions of her statement, which hinge on an important distinction between opposite and different, are truly sweeping. All writing becomes not only the record of patriarchy but also its primary tool of repression. But her description of writing as the locus of women's repression, hidden by the "charms of fiction," also suggests that release is possible through analysis, either literary analysis or psychoanalysis, designed to unearth the repressed woman. Thus the other side of Cixous' theory of language as the locus of woman's repression is a boundless optimism about the ability of writing to transform individuals and society. Indeed, much of her own writing has a therapeutic quality, since she tries to establish contact with the woman who has been left out of the hierarchical oppositions that structure logic. Elsewhere she tries to transform language, to make it express what has never before been expressed, namely, women's "intrasubjective and corporeal experiences left mute by culture in the past" (Kristeva 1981:19).

Kristeva shares this optimism. At the end of "Women's Time" she advocates a third generation whose emergence is imagined in women's creativity:

. . . it is in the aspiration toward artistic and, in particular, literary creation that woman's desire for affirmation now manifests itself. Why literature? It is because, faced with social norms, literature reveals a certain knowledge and sometimes the truth itself about an otherwise repressed, nocturnal, secret, and unconscious universe? Because it thus redoubles the social contract by exposing the unsaid, the uncanny? And because it makes a game, a space of fantasy and pleasure, out of the abstract and frustrating order of social signs, the words of everyday communication? Flaubert said, "Madame Bovary, c'est moi." Today many women imagine, "Flaubert, c'est moi." (Kristeva 1981:31)

The new women's writing transforms the "abstract and frustrating order of social signs, the words of everyday communication." But Kristeva also attributes this transformational potential to the literature of the past, including the canonical texts produced by male authors such as Flaubert. Her speculation thus opens an ideological vista for feminist critics who study periods of near-total male hegemony in textual production. This vista is not so readily available in first and second generation theory.

North American feminists have tended to avoid the "masterworks" in favor of the more affirmative, and politically more pressing, task of recovering and interpreting women's writing. But avoidance need not become rejection in a process of revindication designed to compensate women, at least symbolically, for their social and economic subordination. Thus third generation theory will once again take up the challenge of the predominately male canon. This challenge means rethinking the first generation problem of the misrepresentation of women, using the second generation theories that see language as a locus of transformation as well as one of sacrifice and repression.

Psychoanalysis offers one very promising model, since it shows how narrative has an overt and a repressed content. An analogy can be made between repression in the mind of the individual and repression in social discourse, so that the psychoanalytical model takes on a political dimension. This analogy has been explored by E. Ann Kaplan in her feminist film criticism. She theorizes that the film is to the political unconscious what the dream is to the individual unconscious (Kaplan 1983:314–15). Another model emerges from what I would call rhetorical analysis, focusing on the mechanics of metaphor. In a word, it states that every metaphor has two sides, a vehicle and a tenor, or a literal and a figurative side, and that one side can never fully control the other, although the imperative of logic and understanding may force the reader to choose one over the other. Without making a simplistic identification of the two sides of the metaphor as male and female, this model at least suggests how fissures may appear in the ideology of masculine writing.

Feminist criticism of masculine discourse also necessitates some form of social and economic history as the context for literary studies. Although they conceptualize the mediation between language, society, and production in very different ways, most feminist critics insist that literature both portrays and affects the lives of real women. The student of medieval literature is particularly well served, since feminist historical research has produced substantial information on women in the Middle Ages. This research ranges from nonelite women to the highest nobility, one common perspective being the ways in which familial and marital status affected women's possibilities at all social levels. Studies of cloistered and other religious women fit into this pattern well, since throughout the Middle Ages the religious life presented the main, if not the only alternative to women who chose not to reproduce familial structures and the social institutions that were based on them.

The new courtly literature of the High Middle Ages consisted of erotic lyrics, which in their own time were actually sung before an audience but which now are read as poetry since the musical notation has, in most cases, been lost, and long narratives, written usually in couplets, whose modern generic term is the romance. The subject matter of the romance was the court of King Arthur and the deeds of his knights of the Round Table. Both poetry and romance celebrated courtly love. A century of interdisciplinary scholarship on courtly love has shown that it is not a unified poetical or conceptual system, but a very multiplicitous phenomenon that took different forms over time and changed from place to place.[2] Still, for the sake of orientation, I begin with C. S. Lewis' now classic definition that focuses on the male lover:

Every one has heard of courtly love, and every one knows that it appears quite suddenly at the end of the eleventh century in Languedoc. The characteristics of the Troubadour poetry have been repeatedly described. . . . The sentiment, of course, is love, but love of a highly specialized sort. . . . The lover is always abject. Obedience to his lady's lightest wish, however whimsical, and silent acquiescence in her rebukes, however unjust, are the only virtues he dares to claim. There is a service of love closely modelled on the service which a feudal vassal owes to his lord. The lover is the lady's "man." He addresses her as *midons*, which etymologically represents not "my lady" but "my lord." The whole attitude has been rightly described as "a feudalization of love." (Lewis 1975:2)

Lewis' description of the courtly lady as "whimsical" and "unjust" is one-sided; but his emphasis on the phrase "feudalization of love" points to an important political analogue. The feminist historian Joan Kelly (1984:22–23) has reiterated the importance of the relationship between feudalism, especially the set of political and social relationships known as vassalage, and the forms of courtly love. Kelly explains that vassalage is the military relationship between knight and lord. It distinguishes itself, at least in its earlier phase, by being voluntary. "At a time when everyone was somebody's 'man,' the right to freely enter a relation of service characterized aristocratic bonds, whereas hereditability marked the servile work relation of serf to lord" (Kelly 1984: 22). A model of love based on vassalage had an important implication for elite women, one which Lewis passed over. It introduced into heterosexual relationships the possibility of choice and mutuality. Partners entered into a relationship freely, and having done so, upheld numerous obligations. For men, these obligations entailed service or homage. Contrast Lewis' picture of the servile lover with Kelly's description of the knight, in which she stresses the voluntary aspects of courtly love:

As symbolized on shields and other illustrations that place the knight in the ritual attitude of commendation, kneeling before his lady with his hands folded between hers, homage signified male service, not domination or subordination of the lady, and it signified fidelity, constancy in that service. (Kelly 1984:23)

In the fictive world of romance, male service usually took the form of military action on the battlefield or in tournament. Often knights defended women's legal or social status. For poets, composition was an act of homage to the lady. The lady was also obliged to the man, although the nature of her obligation is more ambiguous, and determined, in part, by her marital status. To some extent her obligation is also tied to genre. In the erotic poetry her marital status is often unknown, but occasionally she is portrayed as another man's wife. The lover, who is also the poet or singer, may wish for anything from a smile or glance of recognition to a gift, a kiss, or even sexual intercourse.[3] In the romance the heroines are usually single or widowed, although Arthur's Queen Guinevere and Tristan's Isolde are important exceptions. All of these forms of obligation—the glance, the kiss, sexual intimacy—are recognized in the romance along with marriage. The widowed heroine is particularly interesting, since she often bestows her hand, as well as her lands and vassals, on her servitor.

Kelly's (1984:26) conclusion, that the structure of relations of courtly love is "nonpatriarchal," necessitates a radical reappraisal of these texts. Her methodology as a social historian establishes the context in which it could be performed. For in the same passage she asks what kind of a society could posit, as a social ideal, a love relationship that "despite its reciprocity, made women the gift givers [not the gift given] while men did the service?" What social conditions fostered these conventions, rather than the older ones of female chastity and dependence? Her brief answers deserve reiteration since their methodological implications are important.

First, she states that the literature of courtly love existed only because it "supported the male-dominated social order rather than subverted it." For example, it not only celebrated sexuality, it also enriched it with concepts of passion and sacrifice that also belonged to mainstream Christian speculation. And while the fiction of passionate love could assume antisocial dimensions, its forms still upheld the political ideal of vassalage. Finally, the prospect of choice in the selection of a sexual partner drew its power from the reality of feudal marriage, in which elite women were married for political or dynastic reasons, often at a very young age (Kelly 1984:26–27).

Kelly's approach to contradiction is useful for feminist scholarship, which must often deal with the question of how ideologies possibly favorable to women can exist within patriarchy. She denies neither the advancement for women implied by the sexual ethos of mutuality and choice, nor the opposed historical conditions of feudalism and feudal marriage. Other literary or social historians, faced with this paradox, have tended either to deny the progressive dimensions of courtly love or to situate it within a much more limited explanatory framework. Benton (1968:35) illustrates the former approach when he argues that "courtesy was created by men for their own [sexual] satisfaction, and it emphasized a woman's role as an object, sexual or otherwise." Even the feminist scholar Penny Schine Gold (1985:27) interprets the romance heroine as one who "serves as the inspiration for the passion of the man." Liebertz-Grün (1977:118–19) opts for the latter solution when she describes courtly literature as a form of protest fostered by elite women when faced with the ethical norms of feudalism, especially with respect to marriage, as well as the repressive sexual morality of the Church.

Second, Kelly (1984:27) stresses women's right to own and inherit fiefs and vast collections of counties, and to exercise the seignorial powers that went with them, as the legal and political basis that favored the literature of courtly love. This idea is not new. The link between women's legal and political status and the emergence of a literature in which women play an important role was already made eighty years ago. In her review of research on the sociology of courtly love, Liebertz-Grün (1977:76) discusses Eduard Wechssler's 1909 book, *Das Kulturproblem des Minnesangs*. Wechssler observed that in addition to ruling and owning land and passing it on to their heirs, women represented their absent husbands in all their functions as feudal and territorial lords. Since the wars and crusades that took men from their estates lasted months or even years, women achieved a great deal of independence and social prestige. Women who ruled in their own right, or who became vassals through the award of fiefs, often continued to rule their possessions independently even after marriage. Wechssler confined his observations to the conditions of southern France in the eleventh and twelfth centuries, but recent research has suggested that favorable political and legal status obtained for elite women in northern France, Hainaut, Flanders, west Lorraine, England, and parts of present-day Spain and Italy (Shahar 1983:127–31, esp. 128). Other evidence of women's favorable legal position in France in the eleventh and twelfth centuries includes their right to give and receive fealty, to enter into alliance with other rulers and to give military assistance in person, to appear as witnesses or parties in court and even to act as judges (Liebertz-Grün 1977:79).[4] Although a great deal of research and reevaluation needs to be done on these topics, particularly on the local level, Kelly concludes with confidence that courtly love "owed its possibility as well as its model to the dominant political institution of feudal Europe that permitted actual vassal homage to be paid to women" (Kelly 1984:30).

This part of Kelly's analysis shows how feminist theory rethinks older scholarship. Views similar to Wechssler's have been expressed for decades, but few scholars before Kelly gave priority to the still disputed link between women's legal and political status and the generally positive view of female sexual love found in courtly literature. For her, courtly love represents an "ideological liberation of [women's] sexual and affective powers" with a real social referent (Kelly 1984:26). Wechssler's understanding of the link was, by contrast, more restrictive. In his view, courtly poetry was a form of compensation for the sexual restrictions of feudal marriage (Liebertz-Grün 1977:77).

Feudal women also helped shape courtly love through the power of patronage (Bumke 1979:235–36). The decisive influence of two historical personages, Eleanor of Aquitaine and her daughter Marie de Champagne, is well known, yet it deserves reexamination in feminist contexts. Eleanor of Aquitaine was married to Louis VII of France at the age of about 15, divorced from him on the grounds of consanguinity, and married again to Henry II of England. According to tradition, Eleanor inspired the courtly love poetry of Bernart de Ventadorn, one of the most admired troubadours. Marie de France, who helped make the Arthurian stories the topic of literary discourse, may have been connected with Eleanor's court in England. We know for certain that Eleanor's daughter, Marie de Champagne, commissioned the composition of *Le Conte de la charrette,* a romance of Lancelot, from the French poet Chrétien de Troyes.

The patronage of a less well known daughter of Eleanor of Aquitaine was decisive for the development of German literature in the twelfth century

(Bumke 1979:236–38). Duchess Mathilde of Saxony, married at the age of twelve to the ambitious Bavarian duke Henry the Lion in 1168, may have commissioned the first known German version of the story of Tristan and Isolde from a poet named Eilhart of Oberge. It seems quite likely that she also motivated the German translation of the *Song of Roland,* for the translator, a cleric, dedicated his text to "the noble duchess, child of a mighty king." When Henry the Lion had to leave Germany in 1182 for political reasons, he and Mathilde found refuge with her father at the royal court in England before moving on to Normandy. There Mathilde received literary tribute from the troubadour Bertran de Born.[5]

The role of Eleanor and her daughters in shaping the literature of courtly love has long been recognized. Building on this recognition Joachim Bumke (1979) has gathered other references to female patrons, primarily in the German language realm. The number of names, and their geographical dispersion, suggest that patronage was quite widespread among women of elite standing. It might be argued that although far fewer women than men actually composed literature, their involvement as patrons placed them on an equivalent footing. Bumke makes some additional points that refine this hypothesis. For example, evidence of women's support for secular literature in Germany is strong for the late twelfth century—Mathilde's generation (p. 241). But for the early thirteenth century, the blossoming of German courtly song and romance, the evidence disappears. Women are named as patrons during this period, to be sure. But they tend to be associated with the composition of other types of texts, especially saints' lives (p. 239–41). No one yet fully understands the significance of this observation. An analysis would have to consider the possible prescriptive character of the saints' lives for noble women against the background of contemporary women's religious movements.

Yet Bumke's evidence for women's patronage shortly before the early thirteenth century is sufficiently strong that he cannot discount their continued involvement during the blossoming. He finds a great deal of indirect and circumstantial evidence in the literary texts themselves. For example, some romances such as Wolfram's *Parzival* are dedicated to an unnamed lady whose favor the poet hopes to receive. The lady is often given the right to judge the quality of the text. Although these *Minnewendungen,* or amorous turns of phrase, cannot be linked to specific patrons, they could indicate the first reception of the literature in a cabaret situation, where the ladies did perhaps actually pass judgment on the text, as well as on the quality of homage between lovers in the immediate social circle. Women would have played a leading role in such pastimes (Bumke 1979:241–42).[6]

Finally, Bumke states that in the romances, women are occasionally portrayed reading books. The ability to read and write was perhaps more widespread among women than among men. Contemporary pictures of noble women regularly show them with psalter in hand. Although their knowledge of Latin may not have reached beyond what was necessary for daily prayers, Bumke (1979:242–43) argues that their knowledge of French was probably substantial. The education of noble girls included instruction in languages, music, and various applied arts. He concludes: "On the basis of these educational presuppositions one can assume that women played an important role in the importation of French customs, forms of French social life, and French literature" (p. 243). Since the German literature of the High Middle Ages was regularly modeled on French texts, the mediating role of women may have extraordinary historical importance.

I have quoted Kelly's view that the courtly literature of the late twelfth and early thirteenth centuries is the first vernacular, secular literature in which women's "sexual and affective powers" are ideologically liberated. Before turning to one example of this literature, I would like to compare, very briefly, the Latin literary tradition. Throughout the Middle Ages, most texts were Latin. Latin was the lingua franca of the educated, who often felt more at home in this acquired second tongue than they did in their native vernacular. The richness and flexibility of medieval Latin made possible the development of science, theology, and philosophy, in short, the university. Above all, Latin was the language of the church and the monastery. Its significance as the universal language of worship and church administration cannot be emphasized too much.

There are important women authors who wrote in Latin, and it is nearly certain that feminist research on medieval women's monastic communities will discover many more of them. The milieu that supported the work of Hildegard of Bingen, born in 1098 as the youngest of ten children in a noble family, or of Hrotsvit of Gandersheim, the first known German dramatist, born about 940, must have produced other Latin texts by women.[7] And although they were officially excluded from the university, some women still managed to distinguish themselves there. One successful woman was Trotula, who very likely taught medicine at the University of Salerno, and who wrote, or dictated, two treatises on obstetrics, hygiene, and other topics around the year 1059. She has descended to modern times in the vernacular folk tradition as Mother Trot (Packard 1970:14–17).

Modern scholars have brought two complaints against the medieval women who wrote in Latin: that their Latin style is unusual or unlearned, or that they did not really write the texts credited to them.[8] The question of women's Latin style has a curious resemblance to the criticism of women's writing in the nineteenth and twentieth centuries. There, feminist scholars have successfully shown that women writers were working within separate but coherent traditions, and that comparison with the dominant male model of style will inevitably make their work seem aesthetically different, that is, inferior. Whether the

same will be found true of medieval women authors is one of the open questions of feminist scholarship. The second charge, that women authors did not
really write all or some of the texts attributed to them, reveals the worst sort of
bias and circular thinking. There are, to be sure, often great difficulties in fix-
ing the authorship of any medieval text. Most writers, like the medieval artists, did not sign their work, and we are left with often contradictory scribal or
traditional attributions or with purely circumstantial evidence. Yet doubtful
cases, when they concern women, seem to result in negative decisions, when
the same amount of evidence would pass as near proof of a man's authorship.
The modern debate about Trotula's authorship of the texts ascribed to her by
an extensive medieval tradition is instructive. Susan Mosher Stuard (1975:
537–42) examines this debate from a feminist point of view, and weighs the
evidence in Trotula's favor. The root of the modern skepticism is, perhaps, an
overly monolithic assumption about women's ignorance of Latin and their exclusion from the intellectual life of the time.

It would be impossible to generalize about the portrayal of women in the
mass of Latin literature written by men up to about the end of the twelfth century. But insofar as these texts were written in the service of the Church or
university, women's roles are fairly limited. Joan M. Ferrante's (1975) book
on *Women as Image in Medieval Literature from the Twelfth Century to Dante*
has a chapter on "Biblical Exegesis" (pp. 17–35) which strengthens this impression. In her discussion of female allegorical figures, she finds "a sympathetic portrayal of women only in personified abstractions" (p. 64).[9]

Ferrante has also written on the representation of women in courtly texts. In
her important article on "Male Fantasy and Female Reality in Courtly Literature," she stresses the significance of romance and lyrics as the first literature
in which women "play an important role, not as personifications of abstract
qualities but as human actors." But she finds the actual depiction of women
unsatisfying. Women function, she writes, "primarily as the inspiration of the
male poet, lover, or hero, and they are usually presented as projections of the
male ideal or the male fantasy, rarely as independent personalities" (Ferrante
1984:67). Later in the same article she states:

In the lyric, the fantasy consists of a "romantic" idealization of women as the love
object, and a complicated game of yearning, of temporary satisfaction and frequent
rejection, of alternating joy and frustration. By and large, the game, including the
woman who is at the center of it, is a figment of the man's imagination. (Ferrante
1984:70)

I would like to examine the depiction of women, and at the same time question Ferrante's theory that the woman-as-object is simply a male ideal or projection, by considering one example of the courtly love lyric. The text was
written in Middle High German, not in Provençal, but it contains all the ele-

ments that Ferrante describes. The poet speaks in the first person, in the role of the dolorous lover. The woman is presented as the mute but "romantic" idealization, the object of desire in the complicated love game of yearning and frustration. I have chosen this poem because it also comments openly on the depiction of women and the status of the female ideal. The poet, Walther von der Vogelweide, lived around 1200, and the poem was surely originally set to music. Here is my own, literal translation of the text:

> Those well-wrought women! If only they would
> express their gratitude! I will describe her
> lovable body worthily in my courtly song. I
> would like to serve them all, but I have chosen
> this one for myself. Another poet knows his own
> lady: he can praise her for all I care. Even
> if we had words and music in common, I would
> praise here, and he there.

> Her head is so wondrous, it could be my heaven.
> To what else should I compare it? It has
> heavenly luminosity. Two stars shine out from
> there. If only she were so near to me that I
> could see myself reflected! Then a wonder
> would occur: I would become younger, if she did
> that; I, desiring sick man that I am, would be
> cured of my sickness of desire.

> God took special care with her complexion. He
> painted priceless colors there, pure red and
> pure white, here rose-red, there lily-white. If
> I dared admit it even though it would be a sin,
> I would rather look at her than at the sky or
> the big dipper. Alas, what am I praising, man
> of little experience that I am? If I make her
> too great for me, the praise of my mouth will
> become the sorrow of my heart.

> She has a little red kiss (pillow): if I were to
> obtain that for my lips I could rise up from
> this anguish and be healthy for ever more. I
> would like to be near the place
> where she puts the pillow to her cheek. It smells, whenever
> one shakes it, as if it were full of balsam.
> She should give it to me; I would give it back
> to her as often as she pleased.

> Her throat, her hands, both feet are made to
> perfection. If I were to praise what lies in between,

then I would imagine to have seen more. I would not
like to have called out "cover up!" when I saw her
naked. She did not see me, when she shot me, so that
it stabs me now as it did then, whenever I think of the
dear place where she emerged pure from a bath.
(Walther von der Vogelweide 1965)[10]

The status and meaning of the female body in Walther's poem is illuminated
by contemporary feminist film theory. With reference to an essay by Mary
Ann Doane, Kaplan (1983) writes that "the female body *is* sexuality, provid-
ing the erotic object for the male spectator" (p. 316). Kaplan goes on to define
the male gaze as the masculine subject position in language and the unconscious, and to theorize the power relations it implies (p. 319). Briefly, her insight is that "men do not simply look; their gaze carries with it the power of
action and of possession that is lacking in the female gaze" (p. 311). Or
again: "Men's desire naturally carries power with it" in a gaze apparatus that
sets up a pattern of dominance and submission (p. 319).

Walther's poem, with its reification of the female body as erotic object,
shows that the masculine subject position is already well developed in medieval
courtly discourse. How, then, can we read this text from a feminist perspective? The problem, as Kelly approaches it, is not to deny or condemn the presence of a gender ideology that empowers the male gaze, but to show how the
text exposes that ideology's contradictions. Working within the discipline of
literary criticism, Myra Jehlen offers those who would read the "masterworks" from a feminist perspective advice compatible with Kelly's. Shakespeare, she argues, did not reject misogynist (or racist or antisemitic) conventions of discourse, but his "critical penetration" of them recognizes the
"complexity of all identity." She continues by linking convention to ideology:
"The kingly ambition of the bastard, the 'white' conscience or the Moor, the
father love of the Jew, the woman's manly heart: these complexities are expressed in the terms of the contemporary ideology, and in fact Shakespeare
uses these terms the more tellingly for not challenging them at the root"
(Jehlen 1982:193). Similarly, Walther reproduces the convention of the *laudes
membrorum* or top-to-toe praise of the female body, but in a way that "denatu-
ralizes" the link between the male gaze and the power of appropriation.

The first strophe is an artisan's introduction that forms part of a complicated
debate between Walther and another poet, possibly a competitor. The issue is
the degree of authenticity that conventional poetic discourse can attain.[11] At
stake is the *laudes membrorum* and other modes of panegyric reserved for
women. Walther takes the position that although poets use the same words and
tunes (might this text have been set to music composed by someone else?),
each nevertheless has only one woman in mind. In other words, Walther com-

ments on the problem of idealization as entrapment, recognizing that his tradition offers only one descriptive scheme, but conscious that the tradition is finally inadequate. The first strophe also contains a plea to women, perhaps the powerful patrons in his audience in what could be the cabaretlike scene of the poem's earliest performances. That Walther begs them for a "word of thanks" for his efforts shows that they, not the artist, are the more important persons in the relationship of patronage. It is significant that Walther makes his plea in his professional voice as poet.

In the following strophes Walther assumes the voice of a lover, bestowing praise on his lady's physical beauty. He admires the beauty or perfection of each part by comparing it to some substance of great rarity or intense color. But there are (at least) three points where he "errs" in his use of the *laudes membrorum.* Each "error" involves taking the convention, or one of its component formulas, literally. By making the convention progressively more unworkable, Walther thwarts its ideology of sexual appropriation.

Although less critical lovers would begin with the lady's hair, Walther commences rather oddly with her head, which he endows with the perfection of heaven. This comparison is lofty but puzzling. Is the common term between head and heaven luminosity, or roundness, or the image of perfection and bliss that each could afford the poet himself? Almost as if to forestall this question from the audience, Walther issues a defensive challenge: "To what else should I compare it?" His next simile justifies the previous one: if her eyes are like stars (and there are many examples of the *laudes membrorum* that say they must be), then her head is like heaven. By taking the amorous convention "at its word," Walther becomes entrapped in its alienating logic.

The third strophe flows smoothly through the conduits of convention as Walther compares the red and white of his lady's complexion to the colors of roses and lilies. But now the audience expects some reference to the lady's lips, since they are next in the catalog. Walther obliges them in the fourth strophe, although his opening line, "she has a little kiss that is red" exceeds the convention by increasing its erotic investment. "Red" is the formulaic term of praise, but lips have been converted into kisses.

Here Walther engages the assumption of sexual appropriation that sustains the convention, but in a way that simultaneously negates and exposes it. The Middle High German word for kisses, *küssen,* also means pillow. The audience, expecting "lips," hears "kisses," but the strophe continues in a way that makes "pillow" the most likely meaning. Our familiarity with the *laudes membrorum* entraps the poet and his lady in an eroticism that Walther seems to deny if the pun is foreclosed with the harmless "pillow." Or is he making an obscene joke, redoubling the convention to assert hyperbolically the power of his subject position? For this strophe employs the technical method of obscenity as Freud (1978:100) defined it in his monograph on *Jokes and Their Relation to the Unconscious:* "replacement by something small, something remotely connected, which the hearer reconstructs in his imagination into a complete and straightforward obscenity." The "little red pillow" perhaps replaces the lady's sexual organ. Medieval discourse from such diverse fields as moral theology, medicine, and courtly love heightens the plausibility of this obscene reading. All make use of another convention, the *quinque lineae amoris* or five stages of love (seeing, speaking, touching, kissing, coitus) that posits kissing as the penultimate step on the path to genital contact (Schnell 1985:26). The *quinque lineae* seem to cross the poem at this point, and Walther does not fail to draw this convention into his horizon of allusions. For if seeing and speaking correspond to the male gaze and courtly discourse, then touching, kissing, and coitus map the possibilities of power and action that the convention entails.

In his final strophe Walther finishes his inventory, proceeding downward from throat to hands to feet, praising all at once with a summarizing assurance of their perfection. In the last six lines he again surprises his audience by revealing the implicit logic of the convention. Walther claims that if he were to continue describing what is circumscribed by hands, feet, and throat, he would have to admit to having seen more of his lady than is normally permitted. That is, he actually states the silent assumption of the *laudes membrorum,* that a woman so described is not wearing any clothing. The poet who uses this convention is constructed as a voyeur, and Walther is committed to "having seen" his lady in a future perfect that forecloses other outcomes. Walther does not reject the role of poet-voyeur. In fact, he cannot do so and still deploy courtly discourse. Rather, he exposes its imperative by making it literal in the bath scene with which the poem ends.

One purpose of the bath scene is to free the lady of any complicity or cooperation. But as the poet's role is fixed as voyeur, the lady escapes as love personified, a blind medieval Venus with bow and arrow. This powerful female role is reasonably consistent with what we know of the status of aristocratic women as the influential financiers of literary men. One might object that it is still the poet Walther who endows the lady with this near-divine power of love magic, and that she still remains entrapped in the discourse of convention. But the closure of that conclusion is loosened by the poet's consciousness that his role as artificer is also limited. Walther, as an "erring" poet, makes no claim to master "reality," invariably presented as an amorous entanglement. It is left to the now absent lady to allow everything to turn out all right in the end. The end might be imagined as a secular paradise, modeled on an ideal of perfectly reciprocated love between woman and man.

Walther's "errors" teach the audience or reader how the sexual aggression entailed by the *laudes membrorum* becomes an imperative. Walther's own complex position—and, I would argue, that of many poets during the first century of courtly love—is illuminated if we compare this text to other uses of the convention. During the later Middle Ages, for example, obscene catalogs are common—a development that Walther anticipates. But I would like to present an earlier example that had great importance for the courtly poets of the High Middle Ages. Except for the *laudes membrorum* in the "Song of Songs," the first known examples are in the six elegies of Maximianus, an obscure figure who claimed to be a friend of Boethius (Ashton-Gwatkin 1975:13–14). Writing around 500 A.D., Maximianus used the convention twice to refer to women, once in his first elegy to state his preference in mistresses, and once in his fifth elegy in bawdy praise of a Greek dancer. In his reminiscence of the dancer, Maximianus seems to anticipate Freud's theory that the male libido for looking substitutes for a "primary desire to touch the sexual parts." [12] The progression from looking to touching is "naturalized" here in a way that is alien to Walther's courtly text:

> . . . Noble task and sweet
> To count her locks plaited in tresses neat,
> Her dusky locks against her skin of snow.
> Her breasts, so firm and pointed, seemed to glow
> Upon my eyes; their beauty made me gasp;
> And yet one hand could hold them in its grasp.
> Ah, how I loved the fold of thighs and groin,
> The slender waist, the plump and rounded loin.
> (Ashton-Gwatkin 1975:38)

By the eleventh century at the latest, Maximianus' elegies had become part of the school curriculum along with more staid authorities such as the distiches of Cato and Avian's fables (Schetter 1970:1). This "grammar lesson" suggests something of the learned, Latin culture against which the courtly, vernacular genres are positioned.

A second example from the Latin tradition deserves mention. By 1200, slender handbooks on literary composition recommended the use of conventions of representation codified by Roman poets and rhetoricians such as Horace, Quintilian and the pseudo-Ciceronian *Rhetorica ad Herennium* (Faral 1971:99). Originally, Roman jurists and authors used these conventions to help establish the character of their clients and heros. The medieval authors of the handbooks took the conventions out of their erstwhile legal context and reshaped them, aided by their study of classical literature, as fragments of poetic discourse (Faral 1971:102–3). Naturally, a Roman jurist would praise the virtue, wisdom, and integrity of his client. An author might present his hero in similar terms. Thus medieval poets inherited a descriptive scheme for men that emphasized these qualities. [13] The poets' model woman, by contrast, is all flesh and surface. Here is how Matthew of Vendôme, author of *The Art of Versification,* represents Helen of Troy.[14] It is another version of the *laudes membrorum,* whose ultimate source is not classical rhetoric with its legal roots, but the love poetry of the Bible:

> Her golden hair, unfettered by any confining knot,
> Cascades quite freely about her face, letting
> The radiant beauty of her shoulders reveal
> Their charms; its disarray pleases all the more.
> Her brow shows its charms like words on a page;
> Her face has no spot, no blemish, no stain.
> Her dark eyebrows, neatly lined twin arches,
> Set off skin that is like the Milky Way.
> Her sparkling eyes rival the radiance of the stars,
> And with engaging frankness play ambassadors of Venus.
>   (Galyon 1980:43)[15]

Matthew is presenting this convention for emulation, not for display and criticism as Walther does. His masculine subject position has a "natural" power of appropriation that is actually projected into the woman's gaze in the last line of the above quote. Similarly, his praise of Helen's brow which "shows its charms like words on a page" seems to say that her thoughts are easy to read. (She has only one thing on her mind.) But Matthew gets trapped much as Walther does, since the literal side of this simile, black ink on white parchment, is an awkward comparison that casts doubt on his skill as an "artisan." Matthew corrects his "error" in the next line, virtually wiping clean the implied ink stains: "Her face has no spot, no blemish, no stain." But the cover-up is not wholly successful, and the contradiction between the two sides of the simile remain to curtail his ability to "read" the *laudes membrorum* in terms of simple appropriation.

Walther disrupts the "natural" link between the male gaze and the power of appropriation in still another line from the poem. The third strophe begins, "God took special care with her complexion." This line constitutes another segment of conventional discourse. The topos that Walther uses is called *Deus artifex* or God as maker. It is found in Plato's *Timeus* as well as in the Bible. In Genesis 3:21, for example, God makes clothes for Adam and Eve out of the skins of animals. From this passage sprang the concept of God as tailor, one of his many roles as maker of the world and all that is in it. In the myths of the ancient world there are also numerous accounts of a creator god who appears now as a needleworker, now as a weaver, now as a smith, in the toil of creation (Curtius 1973:544–46).

In German courtly texts, the *laudes membrorum* very frequently appears with the topos of *Deus artifex.* Walther's joining of the two conventions is "syntactically" proper. The implications of this highly conventional linkage are quite important for understanding women's status in the fantasy world of courtly literature. The religious register to which *Deus artifex* belongs was normative for medieval people. When it is combined with the top-to-toe description of female beauty, the topos defies the gender hierarchy that places woman under the rule of man which is also rooted in Genesis. The woman appears instead as the direct product of divine artifice, not as the derivative of Adam's rib whose origin "explains" her social subordination. The poet himself, when he describes the lady, imitates the divine handicraft. But the convention that "God took special care" establishes her alterity and limits his voyeuristic power of appropriation. Courtly literature, as it is represented by this poem, is not pure male desire, but a complex fantasy of entrapment and paradisiacal escape.

NOTES

1 A good English language introduction to medieval literature is that of W. T. H. Jackson (1966). Of the role of women, Jackson writes: "It is worthy of note that in none of the Germanic epics is love between the sexes of any significance. The hero's conduct is never affected by considerations of affection for women (other than his blood relations). If he is married, it is family loyalty which sways him, and the highest compliment to his wife is that she behaves like a fellow warrior" (p. 28). A third type of epic, based on classical themes rather than Germanic or Carolingian ones, slightly preceded the Arthurian romance in France and Germany. The role of women in these stories, whose themes included love and adventure, was more substantial, and may be compared to that of women in the Arthurian romance.

2 The term *courtly love* or *amour courtois* was coined by Gaston Paris in 1883. The scholarship in French, German, English, and other languages on courtly love during the last hundred years is so vast that it defies any brief presentation. Two authors who present an overview of the subject are U. Liebertz-Grün (1977) and F. X. Newman (1968). In the following discussion I will mention only a few scholars who emphasize the historical role of women in the emergence of courtly love. Even within this important area I make no attempt to be comprehensive.

3 The few women who wrote erotic poetry—there are about twenty woman troubadours or *trobairitz* from Provence—are as frank about sexual desire as the men. Kelly (1984:29) quotes the following lines from a poem by the Comtessa de Dia:

> Handsome friend, charming and kind,
> when shall I have you in my power?
> If only I could lie beside you for an hour
> and embrace you lovingly—
> know this, that I'd give almost anything
> to see you in my husband's place,

but only under the condition
that you swear to do my bidding.

4   In contrast to the territories mentioned in this paragraph, in Germany the evidence
    for women's enhanced legal and political status is more ambiguous (Liebertz-
    Grün 1977:79). This fact suggests that there were other factors favorable to the
    emergence and advance of courtly literature. Put another way, we cannot make a
    simple equation between territories where women enjoyed prestige and a degree
    of legal equality and the success of courtly literature.

5   Bumke (1979:236–38; see also pp. 88–89, 111) accords Mathilde's literary pat-
    ronage "central significance in the establishment of French literature in Ger-
    many." The range of text types that we may associate with Mathilde—a chanson
    de geste, an early secular epic, and the courtly love poem of a troubadour—warns
    that we should not limit our understanding of women's patronage to any single
    theme or genre. Such combinations of genres which, as modern literary-historical
    categories, are barely compatible, are characteristic for the reception and con-
    sumption of texts in the Middle Ages.

6   Marie de Champagne and her courts of love serve as the prototype, although there
    is doubt about whether her "trials" actually occurred.

7   In addition, Bumke (1979:232–33) emphasizes the importance of women's con-
    tribution to religious literature in the vernacular in the twelfth and thirteenth cen-
    turies. He refers to Herbert Grundmann (1936), whose signal research on women
    as readers and writers in the Middle Ages is now being carried forward. On
    Hrotsvit and Hildegard, see Dronke (1984) and Wilson (1984).

8   The question, Did Abélard write Héloïse's third letter? is one of the best-known
    debates on the authenticity of a woman's authorship of a text ascribed to her in the
    manuscripts. Dronke (1984:142), in his well-reasoned reply to the skeptic John
    Benton, writes: "What underlies Benton's argumentation, however (though it
    never becomes wholly explicit), is the notion that in all that Abelard and Heloise
    shared intellectually, Abelard was exclusively the giver, the active partner. And
    this is purest prejudice." Dronke's *Women Writers of the Middle Ages* is an excel-
    lent and suggestive study, although it does not take feminist theory and criticism
    into account. Dronke (1984:6, 27, 30, 33, 36, 91) finds weaknesses in the Latin
    style of many of the authors he discusses, which suggests that women's relation-
    ship to the dominant Latin literary tradition will be a topic for feminist medieval-
    ists in the future.

9   The flowering of the vernacular, secular literature around 1150 in France and
    around 1200 in Germany ran parallel to a similar flowering of Latin songs and
    stories. These secular Latin texts should also be fertile ground for feminist
    scholarship.

10 Walther von der Vogelweide (1965: pp. 74–77, number 53, 25). The translation
    is my own and, like any translation, limits the semantic range of the original by
    the choice of English equivalents.

11 Authenticity may be equivalent to acceptability as judged by a woman patron in
    the public arena of medieval poetry.

12 Freud 1978:98. The Latin text of Maximianus' fifth elegy which contains this

laudes membrorum is edited by Tullio Agozzino (1970). The translation, whose lilting rhyme highlights the poem's implications, is by Frank Ashton-Gwatkin (1975).

13 Virtue in these handbooks is not an abstract or gender-neutral ensemble of attitudes and behaviors. According to Matthew of Vendôme, a virtuous woman negates all the female weaknesses and vices authorized by classical and Christian misogynist traditions. She must overcome her own nature and "become male." Thus Marcia, the faithful wife, makes the weaker sex the stronger one in a transformation that is equated with a miracle, something that cannot occur according to the laws of nature: "The yew yield honey and the hemlock smell of honey, / Were a firm faith to flourish in a frail breast. / A marvel—winter blossoms with spring flowers, the crow / Turns white; vinegar smacks of nectar, the yew of honey, / The myrrh of roses. Marcia glorifies womanhood . . ." (Galyon 1980:42).

14 Matthew's *Art of Versification* was written about 1175, probably as a textbook for his students at Orléans (Galyon 1980:4). The Latin text was edited by Edmund Faral (1971). I am quoting the translation by Aubrey E. Galyon (1980), who lists other translations on p. 116, n. 8.

15 Similar formulas of impersonal perfection are still part of the visual metaphors of advertising.

WORKS CITED

AGOZZINO, T., ed.
1970 *Massimiano: Elegie*. Bologna: Biblioteca Silva di Filologia.

ASHTON-GWATKIN, F., trans.
1975 *Max: Poet of the Final Hour. Being the Elegies of Maximianus the Etruscan*. London: Paul Norbury.

BENTON, J. F.
1968 Clio and Venus: An Historical View of Medieval Love. In *The Meaning of Courtly Love*, edited by F. X. Newman, pp. 19–42. Albany: State University of New York Press.

BUMKE, J.
1979 *Mäzene im Mittelalter: Die Gönner und Auftraggeber der höfischen Literatur in Deutschland 1150–1300*. Munich: C. H. Beck'sche Verlagsbuchhandlung.

CIXOUS, H.
1981 The Laugh of the Medusa. Translated by K. Cohen and P. Cohen. In *New French Feminisms: An Anthology*, edited by E. Marks and I. de Courtivron, pp. 245–64. New York: Schocken.

CURTIUS, E. R.
1973 *European Literature and the Latin Middle Ages*. Translated by Willard R. Trask. Bollingen Series 36, paperback ed. Princeton, N.J.: Princeton University Press.

DRONKE, P.
1984   *Women Writers of the Middle Ages: A Critical Study of Texts from Per-*
        petua (†203) to Marguerite Porete (†1310). Cambridge: Cambridge Uni-
        versity Press.
ELLMANN, M.
1968   *Thinking about Women.* New York: Harcourt, Brace and World.
FARAL, E., ed.
1971   *Les Arts poétiques du XIIe et du XIIIe siècle.* Paris: Librairie Ancienne
        Honoré Champion, 1924. Reprint.
FERRANTE, J. M.
1975   *Woman as Image in Medieval Literature from the Twelfth Century to*
        Dante. New York: Columbia University Press.
1984   Male Fantasy and Female Reality in Courtly Literature. In *Women's Stud-*
        ies: An Interdisciplinary Journal 11:67–97.
FREUD, S.
1978   *Jokes and Their Relation to the Unconscious.* Translated by James Stra-
        chey. Standard Edition, vol. 8. London: Hogarth Press, 1960. Reprint.
GALYON, A. E., trans.
1980   *Matthew of Vendôme: The Art of Versification.* Ames: Iowa State Univer-
        sity Press.
GOLD, P. S.
1985   *The Lady and the Virgin: Image, Attitude, and Experience in Twelfth-*
        Century France. Chicago: University of Chicago Press.
GRUNDMANN, H.
1936   Die Frauen und die Literatur im Mittelalter: Ein Beitrag zur Frage nach
        der Entstehung des Schrifttums in der Volkssprache. *Archiv für Kultur-*
        geschichte 26:129–61.
JACKSON, W. T. H.
1966   *Medieval Literature: A History and a Guide.* New York: Collier Books.
JEHLEN, M.
1982   Archimedes and the Paradox of Feminist Criticism. In *Feminist Theory: A*
        Critique of Ideology, edited by N. O. Keohane, M. Z. Rosaldo, and B. C.
        Gelpi, pp. 189–215. Chicago: University of Chicago Press.
KAPLAN, E. A.
1983   Is the Gaze Male? In *Powers of Desire: The Politics of Sexuality,* edited
        by A. Snitow, C. Stansell, and S. Thompson, pp. 309–27. New York:
        Monthly Review Press.
KELLY, J.
1984   Did Women Have a Renaissance? In *Women, History, and Theory: The*
        Essays of Joan Kelly, pp. 19–50. Chicago: University of Chicago Press.
KRISTEVA, J.
1981   Women's Time. Translated by A. Jardine and H. Blake. *Signs: Journal of*
        Women in Culture and Society 7:13–35.
LEWIS, C. S.
1975   *The Allegory of Love: A Study in Medieval Tradition.* Oxford: Oxford
        University Press, 1936. Reprint.

LIEBERTZ-GRÜN, U.
1977   *Zur Soziologie des 'amour courtois': Umrisse der Forschung.* Beihefte zum Euphorion 10. Heidelberg: Carl Winter Universitätsverlag.

NEWMAN, F. X., ed.
1968   *The Meaning of Courtly Love.* Albany: State University of New York Press.

PACKARD, F.
1970   History of the School of Salernum. Introduction to *The School of Salernum: "Regimen Sanitatis Salernitanum,"* by Sir John Harington. 1920. Reprint. New York: Augustus M. Kelley.

PARIS, G.
1883   Études sur les romans de la table ronde. Lancelot du Lac. Le conte de la charrette. *Romania* 12:459–534.

SCHETTER, W.
1970   *Studien zur Überlieferung und Kritik des Elegikers Maximian.* Klassisch-Philologische Studien 36. Wiesbaden: Otto Harrassowitz.

SCHNELL, R.
1985   *Causa amoris: Liebeskonzeption und Liebesdarstellung in der mittelalterlichen Literatur.* Bibliotheca Germanica 27. Bern and Munich: Francke.

SHAHAR, S.
1983   *The Fourth Estate: A History of Women in the Middle Ages.* Translated by C. Galai. New York: Methuen.

SHOWALTER, E.
1985   Feminist Criticism in the Wilderness. In *The New Feminist Criticism: Essays on Women, Literature, and Theory,* edited by Elaine Showalter, pp. 243–70. New York: Pantheon Books.

SPACKS, P. M.
1975   *The Female Imagination.* New York: Knopf.

STUARD, S. M.
1975   Dame Trot. *Signs: Journal of Women in Culture and Society* 1:537–42.

WALTHER VON DER VOGELWEIDE
1965   Si wunderwol gemachet wîp. In *Die Gedichte Walthers von der Vogelweide.* 13th ed. Edited by Hugo Kuhn, pp. 74–77. Berlin: W. de Gruyter.

WILSON, K. M., ed.
1984   *Medieval Women Writers.* Athens: University of Georgia Press.

CHAPTER 4

Recovering Eve: Biblical Woman without Postbiblical Dogma

CAROL MEYERS

Two words in the title require explanation, and the explanations will preview the nature of the discussion to follow. First, *Eve* is used in two distinct though related ways. As a name, it represents the first female appearing in the pages of the Bible: Eve as the female counterpart and companion of the first male. While she receives the etymological designation "mother of all living" (Gen. 3:20), it is in her role as wife that she comes to life in the narratives in Genesis 2 and 3. In her relationship to Adam, she dominates the Eden tale. Therefore I employ Eve as Everywoman or Everywife, standing for ordinary ancient Israelite women. These women are nearly invisible in the biblical canon, which is a product of and a reflection on the nature of a patriarchal, or at least formally androcentric, society.

Second, *biblical* refers to the Hebrew Bible, the body of sacred literature known as the Old Testament in the Christian canon. Consequently, by *postbiblical* I mean the views and dogmas associated with early Judaism and nascent Christianity as they appear in the literature produced after the second century B.C.E., that is, after the close of the canon of Hebrew scripture. According to this use of *biblical*, postbiblical literature would include the New Testament and early Christian literature, most deuterocanonical materials,[1] and the bulk of rabbinic literature.

Feminist critics well understand the role that the Hebrew Bible (Old Testament) plays in the current state of sexual politics. Thus feminist analysis of social patterns and cultural values comes up short if it refrains from tackling general religious values as well as the origin of those values in the authoritative texts of western religion. Yet the persistent reluctance for feminists to take on religion is understandable, for when they do so, they face difficult methodological questions as well as the antecedent problem of technical quali-fications. The relevant religious texts cannot be fairly assessed without a de-gree of competence in the requisite scholarly tools that, to a certain extent, only specialists can acquire. One cannot properly approach biblical materials without a knowledge of biblical languages, a familiarity with ancient Near Eastern history, and at least an acquaintance with the archaeological recovery of Syro-Palestinian antiquity. In addition, feminists who confront religion often find themselves working in opposition to "deeply held motivations, be-liefs, and life orientations. Of all feminist encounters with culture and with individual thought, and feeling," questions of religion and of the sacred texts that shape religion meet the most radical resistance from both institutions and individuals (Doyle 1974:16).

Nonetheless, we cannot ignore the biblical roots of today's sexual politics (Fuchs forthcoming). The emergence of the women's movement in recent de-cades has had, and is having, a profound effect upon biblical scholarship, where a feminist critique of western scriptural-based religion must properly begin. The practitioners of the discipline of biblical studies—the "guild" as Sakenfeld (1982:13) calls them, in contrast to and sometimes at cross-purposes with the "church," or the institutional manifestations of biblical reli-gion—are the ones who possess the tools for assessing those texts that have been so powerful in promulgating beliefs and preserving the power structures built on those beliefs.

Within the discipline of biblical studies today, the influence of feminist in-quiry at first glance seems rather enormous, mainly because the investigation of gender-related texts from a feminist perspective was practically nonexistent until little more than a decade ago. This situation is related to the dearth of female scholars in a field traditionally dominated by men and traditionally pursued most often in seminaries, which were almost exclusively male do-mains until quite recently. Yet, although there has been a significant growth in attention to gender matters in biblical scholarship, the situation leaves much to be desired for two reasons. First, in its admirable haste to respond to the de-mand of feminist considerations, biblical scholarship on gender matters has tended to be impressionistic (if not sloppy) and vulnerable to apologetic ten-dencies and to methodological weaknesses. Second, even where sound inves-tigation has produced excellent results, some congenial to feminists and some less so, a serious gap persists between the academicians' formulations and the incorporation of those insights into the beliefs and practices of those com-mitted to or acculturated by institutionalized religion.

The potential importance of responsible biblical scholarship to present feminist concerns has prompted the sort of inquiry that constitutes the second section of this essay. Since the path to contemporary biblical analysis as it relates to women is longer and more interesting than one might first imagine, I preface this study with a brief consideration of the development of feminist biblical scholarship.

HISTORY OF SCHOLARSHIP

As important as the recent impact of feminist concerns on biblical studies has been, it would be erroneous to suppose that biblical scholarship dealing with gender issues is an entirely new development. Our present awareness of the role of the Bible in sexual politics was adumbrated in a striking though, in its own time, ultimately futile way by nineteenth-century feminists (cf. Bass 1982:10–12). The issues the nineteenth-century women's movement faced were essentially the same as those that contemporary feminists confront when dealing with the religious history of sexual politics. It is instructive, then, to realize that many of those involved in the suffragette movement were keenly aware of the pernicious effects of religious doctrine based on biblical authority upon their attempts to achieve certain social and political rights.

The sporadic concern of the nineteenth-century women's movement over the oppressive nature of misogynist religion reached its culmination in the publication in 1895–98 of *The Woman's Bible*. This fascinating book was a product of a complex set of circumstances: the extensive changes occurring in American religion during the nineteenth century as the result of the War between the States, increased urbanization, and industrialism; the way those changes affected women and the women's movement as represented by the National American Women's Suffrage Association; the emergence at the same time and as the result of similar forces of a critical biblical scholarship that had considerable intellectual freedom to challenge doctrinal positions. Last but not least, *The Woman's Bible* was the product of the personal experience of its embattled author, Elizabeth Cady Stanton (Welter 1974; Griffith 1984). By the time *The Woman's Bible* was published, Stanton was a veteran of a half century of struggle on behalf of women's rights.

Theology in general was undergoing a liberalization in the post–Civil War period. The dogma of the Bible as literally God's holy word was challenged, partly under the influence of Darwinism, in strange anticipation of contemporary tensions in appraisals of biblical authority. The nineteenth-century liberalization in biblical studies held a powerful attraction for the women's movement. It is easy to see why. From the very beginning of the movement for women's emancipation, the Bible had been used to hold women in their "divinely ordained sphere" as prescribed in Hebrew scripture and, for Christians, in the New Testament as well. Church law and civil law, clergy and legislators, theologians and politicians—all had taught that "woman was made after man, of man and for man, an inferior being, subject to man"

(Stanton 1974:7). If western culture has been shaped by the Bible, sexism in western culture was insidiously rooted in such ideas about a biblical doctrine of women. Stanton summarizes well, in the introduction to *The Woman's Bible*,[2] the then accepted biblical position on women that she chose to confront:

> The Bible teaches that woman brought sin and death into the world. Marriage for her was to be a condition of bondage, maternity a period of suffering and anguish, and in silence and subjection, she was to play the role of a dependent upon man's bounty for all her material wants; and for all the information she might desire on the vital questions of the hour, she was commanded to ask her husband at home. (Stanton 1974:7)

The pervasive influence of such putatively biblical ideas shaped the gender-related legal and cultural patterns that still to some degree affect all Americans.

What could a nineteenth-century feminist do in the face of such conceptualizations of women in the ancient biblical community, women who were treated as the paradigms of female behavior and roles for all time? What might Elizabeth Stanton do to counter the arguments then used against women seeking the vote and other changes in their status? Three possibilities were open to her, as they are to today's feminist. First, she could reject the Bible entirely, discounting any authenticity or validity it might have and writing it off as so much mythical nonsense. Obviously this was an unlikely course for a politically astute nineteenth-century feminist. Whether it is politic today is not so compelling a question as is that of the theological implication of such a stance (cf. Pagels 1985:3). Second, she could allegorize, as had countless exegetes for thousands of years, so that biblical passages relevant to a concern for women's status could be interpreted according to ideas congenial to her feminism. *The Woman's Bible* in fact does show signs of this approach, but this is so notably in positions contributed by feminists other than Stanton. Third, she could go back to the original Hebrew, using the latest insights of the nascent discipline of biblical criticism, to recover the best understanding of the text. She would then be prepared to criticize and to reject as doctrine those portions of the Bible which she saw as degrading to women.[3]

Stanton wisely chose the third course and in so doing prefigured the shape of the contemporary intersection of biblical scholarship and feminist concerns. She ventured forth on her Bible project by forming a "revising committee" of about two dozen women and then creating subcommittees of eight members each to work on the biblical material, which she divided into major blocks. Although it was a committee endeavor in conception, Stanton's role was formative and dominant. Comments on individual units of biblical text were initialed by the contributors, and Stanton's initials occur far more frequently than those of all other members of the committee combined.

The new scholarship of the 1970s and 1980s on women and the Bible is heir to suffragette scholarship, despite the long hiatus separating the two. Contemporary biblical studies, however, particularly in the university, offer important conceptual and methodological advances that were not available to the authors of *The Woman's Bible*. I recognize three major advances along with some other developments that have peripheral relevance.

1. The discipline of biblical studies has been at least partially liberated from the control of those with a vested interest in having Hebrew religion or scripture provide the paradigms for modern belief. It is no longer the case that all biblical scholarship is carried out by scholars whose credentials include a divinity degree. And biblical scholars working outside seminaries can more easily accept the implications of a biblical world that was radically different from our own, partly because it existed so long ago and partly because the environmental and historical forces shaping it were so different from those shaping our world. Discovering that some values and roles portrayed in the Bible are culture- and time-bound and are relevant only to the ancient Palestinian setting is possible and even exhilarating. Discovering how others viewed the world and formed social relationships within that world, in ways that diverge from our views and social arrangements, can provide an enlarged sense of what it means to be human (O'Brien and Major 1982:1–2). Granted, sorting out ephemeral patterns and their associated values from the perennially valid truths that are also found in traditional religious texts is a challenging task, especially in the case of gender roles. But it is a task made possible by the other methodological advantages available to biblical scholarship today.

2. Feminists and biblical scholars of the nineteenth century were unable to identify their own cultural biases, which influenced and constrained their attempts to understand a biblical text on its own terms, in quite the same way as we can today. This statement is not meant to be arrogant back-patting for modern scholarship, which surely has its own biases to identify and acknowledge; but rather it highlights the developments in the resources now available to biblical scholarship. Biblical studies as a discipline have been altered forever by the twentieth-century archaeological discoveries of texts (for example, Dead Sea Scrolls, Gnostic documents from Nag Hammadi, sectarian fragments from the Nahal Hever) that bear upon traditional interpretations of many biblical passages, including gender-related ones. This development has been paralleled by the rediscovery of many long-ignored, extracanonical or deuterocanonical texts of similar antiquity, that is, from the last several centuries B.C.E. and the first centuries of the Christian era. These documents have helped identify the postbiblical biases, operating for more than two thousand years since the close of the canon of the Hebrew Bible, that profoundly shaped the traditional understanding of nearly all biblical materials relating to gender.

A case in point, perhaps *the* case in point, is the etiological narrative of the archetypal couple (Eve and Adam) in Genesis 2–3. This story has undoubtedly been one of the most influential pieces in western literary and artistic tradition as well as the source of much doctrinal characterization of woman. Until recently, both the opposers of the androcentric order as well as its upholders shared a misogynous reading of this apparently simple tale, and the standard interpretive reading has acquired a persistent canonicity of its own (Trible 1973a:35; 1978:72–73). The consensus of feminists rejecting it as well as of traditionalists invoking it proclaimed that the creation account laid forth at least a dozen gender-related dogmas (Trible 1978:73), of which the following are among the most tenacious and also the most erroneous:

1. A male God creates a man first and a woman second. This makes the man superior and the woman inferior.
2. Woman is created as a helpmate, a lower-order companion to stave off male loneliness.
3. Woman tempted man and is thus responsible for all human sinfulness.
4. Woman is cursed by pain in childbirth.

These ideas about the story, we now know, are *not* intrinsic to the text; rather, they violate its rhetoric, its integrity, and its cultural setting (Trible 1973b; Higgins 1976; Meyers 1983a). As extraordinarily persistent distortions, they arose for reasons we still cannot satisfactorily identify in the late biblical and early postbiblical period (see Prusak 1974), in the turbulent era in which early Judaism and nascent Christianity struggled to make sense, in the Greco-Roman world, of their Semitic heritage as contained in the Hebrew Bible. The landmark work of Trible (beginning with her two 1973 articles), and the related contributions of other scholars, stand forth as pioneering achievements in the task of discovering the original, artfully shaped values of those texts. Eve, or Woman, emerges at least as an equal to Man if not even as his intellectual and social superior. Genesis 2 and 3, read without the prejudices of postbiblical interpretations, can be counted among ancient Israel's best, not worst, statements about women.

In addition to the special case of the seminal narratives of Genesis 2–3, other traditional androcentric misinterpretations have insidiously affected the translation process which makes the Bible available in English to a Western audience largely unable to read the text in its original Hebrew. For example, the generic word for *human*, which permeates the creation tales and appears elsewhere in the Bible, is frequently if not universally translated *man*. In most cases the gender-specific potential of the word *man* is thereby erroneously attached to a Hebrew word that is almost always a collective singular designating *human* life, as a category to be distinguished from God on the one hand and the creaturely beings on the other. Biblical scholarship aware of feminist concerns can seek to rectify such ancient biases as they now become visible. It can do so with the added advantage of the sensitivity, provided by recent studies of gender and language, to the subtle power of language to shape attitudes and beliefs. The committee charged with revising the widely used Revised Standard Version of the Bible is removing gender-preferential words where none exist in the original and is also translating generic terms that are grammatically masculine in Hebrew (in which nouns are either masculine or feminine, there being no neuter) into inclusive English terms (cf. Metzger 1982). However, this admirable process can perhaps be pushed too far, as critics of the *Inclusive Language Lectionary* have asserted (Bailey 1984).

Another translation problem arises not so much from gender versus generic language but rather from the biases of the earliest translators. Take, for example, the familiar translation of Genesis 3:16, the so-called curse of Eve, which is not really a curse at all but rather a description addressed to the woman, and parallel to that addressed to the man, of her post-Edenic lot in life. That is, it is a description of reality, of the characteristic burdens of both men and women trying to eke out a living in a high-risk environment. The Revised Standard Version and most of the English versions provide the all too familiar sentence: "I will greatly multiply your pain in childbearing; in pain shall you bring forth children." Such translation incorrectly imputes the sense of "pain" to a word that means "toil," or physically productive work (see Meyers 1987), and that is never lexically associated with the birth process. The usual translation also incorrectly renders a word for "pregnancy" as "childbearing," and in so doing it fails to recognize the parallelism and intensification of the poetic line of that verse. A more accurate translation (see Meyers 1983a and 1988:95–121), sensitive to the role of the text as a sanction for the unending toil that males and females alike must experience in order to survive, is this: "I will increase your toil and your pregnancies; along with travail shall you beget children."

3. Biblical scholarship well into the second half of this century worked under a dominant assumption that claimed a distinctive role for religion, that is, that "religion functions as an independent variable, perhaps the decisive one, for which social organization and political organization then become dependent ones" (Kovacs 1980:2). There has been a considerable reluctance to look at ancient Israel as a living social entity. Ancient Israel, as the forerunner of Judaism and Christianity, has been surrounded by a "canonical sanctity" (Gottwald 1979:5) that impels those who examine it to seek abstract religious dimensions of its existence or to search for theological explanations of its meaning and existence. Such an approach stands in opposition to that of social scientists who classify religion, under the rubric of ideology or even of propaganda, as a form of communication using powerful verbal and visual symbols (Geertz 1973:167–72). Yet, though the communicative aspect of religion in complex societies, of which ancient Israel was one, is highly significant, religious ideology is hardly an epiphenomenon devoid of causal significance

(Frick 1979). Religion in archaic societies also served to legitimate and stabilize forms of social organization and activity, especially adaptive forms that would be difficult to establish without the authoritative force of religion.

The social scientific notion of religion as an integral rather than a discrete cultural expression, as a component of cultural identity rather than its sole foundation, has had an enormous impact upon biblical studies as a whole in the past two decades. Approaching religion as part of a cultural system opens up unprecedented opportunities for the study of gender in the ancient world. By bringing together textual exegesis, archaeological data, and historical geography or ecology, we can establish with some accuracy the nature of the biblical world. We can identify the locus of group life (in villages or urban centers), the socioeconomic patterns (a peasant society based on rainfall agriculture), the ecological features (relatively poor soils and inhospitable terrains subject to periodic drought), and the political orientation (tribal and then monarchical structures) of ancient Israel. Some of these features remained stable throughout the period of Israel's national existence (ca. 1200–587 B.C.E.). But others changed, and it is crucial to set particular biblical texts against the changing sociopolitical configurations, which they both reflect and sanction.

The last of these three methodological advantages, the ability to identify the physical and social landscape of ancient Israel, makes it possible to distinguish time-bound texts from universally valid ones. From the perspective of women's studies, it also allows for the discovery of the place of women in the biblical world apart from the place of women in the biblical text. The Bible as a whole is notoriously silent about women. The female figures that have survived in the pages of this androcentric document are almost entirely exceptional figures that tell us little or nothing about Everywoman. Let us consider Eve now not as the name of the archetypal woman of Genesis 2 and 3, but instead as the representative of these unnamed, unknown females hidden behind the male authors and actors who dominate the biblical record. I suggest that we can recover Eve as Everywife by establishing her social context and, with all the caution necessary in such a difficult task, by using information available from better documented, analogous societies. I have attempted elsewhere to do so for Eve as Mother (Meyers 1978, 1983b, 1988) and will only briefly summarize my conclusions here.

The Bible exhibits an extraordinary emphasis on female procreation and on the maternal role. One familiar example of this emphasis is the repeated injunction to "be fruitful and multiply." Another is the repetitive literary type-scene (in the matriarchal narratives of Genesis as well as in the stories of Hannah and of Samson's mother) of the barren woman striving valiantly and against all odds to conceive. This focus on procreation can be seen as an ideological sanction shaped by the demographic needs of Israel in its formative period (Iron Age I, ca. 1200–1000 B.C.E.). Several factors point to an urgent need for family growth in that earliest era of Israel's existence. These include the high infant mortality rate characteristic of premodern societies: osteological analysis of skeletal remains recovered from Palestine tomb groups show a death rate for infants and young children approaching 50 percent (Smith et al. 1981). In addition, early Iron Age populations were recovering from an extended era of recurring epidemic disease, which apparently affected the whole East Mediterranean area at the end of the preceding Late Bronze Age. More specifically for early Israel, the formative period was marked by the demands of a pioneer society trying to establish an agrarian base in previously unsettled, uncleared territory, an effort that required extra labor for clearing forested land, digging cisterns, constructing terraces, and building residences. The convergence of these factors mandated population growth and led to the formation of religious ideologies supporting demographic adaptation to the period's particular conditions.

This biblical sanction of female fecundity is typologically analogous to, although contrastive in function with, mythographic presentations known from ancient Mesopotamian societies threatened by overpopulation. The most notable example is the "final solution" to the human problem portrayed in the Atrahasis Epic.[4] In Atrahasis, unmarried females, orders of celibate priestesses, and stillbirths or infant deaths are construed as being in the general good by being portrayed as the will of the gods (Kilmer 1972). Maternity was not simply a personal issue in Mesopotamia or in ancient Israel; rather it was a social issue. The biblical emphasis on maternity was a particular cultural and adaptive response to a problem of underpopulation in an agrarian society, just as the mythographic sanction of a low birthrate in Mesopotamia was a cultural expression sensitive to overpopulation in an urban society.

WOMAN AS WIFE: REFLECTIONS ON THE DOMESTIC ECONOMY

Although the maternal role may be the most visible female category in the Hebrew Bible, the most comprehensive category for women was that of wife (ignoring daughter, since that category can be subsumed under "child" for the most part). We can assume that virtually all females who survived past puberty were married, since marriage was nearly universal for both sexes, but that fewer than 100 percent of adult women in the biblical world (virtually the same population as married women) became mothers. Eve as Everywife, if we are to form our judgments from an examination of the legal, historiographical, and aphoristic materials available in the biblical canon, was legally, socially, and economically dependent upon males (Bird 1974). That is, we can entertain the existence of a "biblical sexual politics" in reference to ways in which the Bible reflects and thereby promotes by virtue of its authoritative character the idea of female subordination to men.

But is it fair to attribute to the Bible such a designation? The question is a difficult and complex one because it involves the problem of separating current value orientations from ancient ones, and also the task of distinguishing stylized literary presentations from social realities. I would suggest, however, that the answer is no—that it is not fair to equate biblical patriarchalism or patrilinealism in its own context with a set of generally held Israelite beliefs endorsing an androcentric expression of female inferiority (cf. Rogers 1978). Any attempt to perceive the ancient Israelite woman as wife by determining her legal relationships to her husband and children is not adequate; it is only by examining the role of a wife in terms of her household (explained below) and by looking at the function of the household in Israelite society that her position can be evaluated. The notion of dominance and subordination, which underlies the concept of sexual politics and which may be a projection of western cultural ideas, can thereby be viewed against a more appropriate set of circumstances.

First consider the bias of the ancient literary sources. The biblical texts that are used to support the idea of female dependence and restriction are, by and large, the products of a literate, urban, male elite. Consequently, the views expressed in the relevant legal and cultic texts tend to be those appropriate to a social environment which had divergent public and private spheres of behavior and relatively specialized, gender-segregated roles. The biblical laws and narratives depicting women as secondary to men were formed or finalized in a setting that had separate public and private domains, women being barred from most areas of the public realms. But "Eve," representing the collective, nameless women of ancient Israel, lived a different life. For most, ancient Israel was an agrarian society. Even with the urbanizing tendencies that emerged under the monarchy (beginning ca. 1000 B.C.E. and lasting for four centuries), most Israelites continued to live as farmers and herders in small villages dotting the countryside.

The social location of Everywoman Eve in peasant villages is a crucial datum in the attempt to discern a woman's role. In peasant societies—and ancient rural Israel demonstrably was one (Chaney 1983; Gottwald 1983)—the relative status of females and males must be measured in terms of the dynamics of gender relations in the domestic and not the public sphere (Rogers 1978:148–49; cf. Friedl 1967). Within the Israelite villages, particularly in the formative Iron Age I period but also continuing into the monarchic era, there was relatively little development of specialized public roles to which extradomestic prestige (for men) would have been attached. For both women and men, life was largely domestic centered. Within that context, even if higher public status for men did exist in certain legal or cultic ways, complementary roles for women and men in the dominant, daily economic aspects of life would have been the norm. In the face of many biblical laws suggesting male cultic or legal dominance, other legal texts can be found that suggest near parity in terms of everyday domestic-oriented matters and subsistence tasks (Meyers 1983b). [5]

An interesting extra-Israelite verification is available from the classical world, where analysis of the legal documents also predictably reveals an emphasis on the restrictions and limitations of ancient women's lives. But such an emphasis, which arises in part from a concern for the transmission of landholdings and other property, is at odds with the information contained in less official sources. Such sources suggest, on the domestic level, mutuality, respect of husbands for wives and vice versa, and a dearth of evidence of either subjugation or submission. Lefkowitz (1983), in presenting these observations, arrives informally at conclusions similar to those reached analytically by Rogers (1978) and others:

Is it really fair to imply, as some of us have done, that ancient women would have wanted to live differently had they had the opportunity? What if any evidence can be found to support such a claim? For many years I doubted whether intelligent women took pleasure in leading an anonymous life of service to husband and family, but now I wonder if I have not been judging ancient women as I judge myself, by male standards of accomplishment. (Lefkowitz 1983:31–32)

Another, similar consideration that must enter into judgments of early Israel and other ancient societies is the virtual lack in ancient Hebraic thought of a concept of the individual as an autonomous being. As in most agrarian societies, the overriding concern for maintaining an adequate food supply shaped the economic roles of females and males, young and old, and made survival the powerful motivating factor for maintaining an efficient allocation of tasks and roles in a family-centered economy. Adults thus viewed their existence in relational terms, and the idea of a distinct personal identity apart from familial and social arrangements could not readily emerge (LeVine and LeVine 1985:31).

The possibility of a balance in gender relations in formative Israel has been suggested on the basis of oblique textual (biblical) evidence for the importance of the domestic setting and its agrarian context and also from ethnographic analogies (for example, Nelson 1974; Rogers 1975). These indirect sources for reconstructing the central role of early Israel's domestic life can now be supplemented, in a way not possible until the last decade, by the results of archaeological work on Israelite villages. Until recently, "biblical archaeology" (a misleading but popular designation for Syro-Palestinian archaeological investigations potentially able to shed light on the Bible, that potential usually being grossly overestimated) concentrated disproportionately on the urban sites most likely to provide verification for the political history recorded in the Bible. Such sites also possessed the greatest likelihood for yielding the monumental architecture and distinctive artifacts that make good museum pieces and good press. But the new archaeology (Binford 1962), interested in processes of cultural change and not in the high points of culture from a material perspective, has made its impact on Syro-Palestinian archaeology. Archaeologists are at last interested in village life (Callaway and Cooley 1971; Kempinski and Fritz 1977). Therefore, an archaeology of the family in ancient, rural Israel is now possible insofar as we can accept the assumption that uncovering domestic structures can illuminate the lives of their inhabitants.

Within certain limits that assumption is valid. Features of the domestic economy and therefore of social structure can be recovered through the analysis of floral and faunal remains, study of architectural accommodations to the stabling of animals, and examination of technological artifacts such as loom weights, grinding stones, and potters' wheels. The mode of life of the family as a unit can be reconstructed. But can the archaeology of the family be considered gender noisy? Can the mute walls and artifacts reveal the roles and relationships of the women and men who lived within the walls and used the artifacts? Until recently, the answer to these questions was largely and regretfully negative. It seemed that the archaeology of villages and their domestic components could shed light on family units but could not clarify matters of gender. Now a tentative, but positive, response to the question of gender and archaeology may be in order for ancient Israel in light of the identification of a certain pattern of domestic architecture that appears to have dominated Israelite villages and in view of how that pattern can be interpreted in relation to textual evidence and comparative ethnography.

The recent excavation of several highland villages has produced important data about domestic building patterns. Although individual, spatially distinct farmhouses occasionally can be identified in Israelite settlements, the characteristic pattern is that of compounds, or multiple dwelling units. These villages consist of an agglomeration of room clusters rather than of individual rooms or houses. Furthermore, the villages in which these compounds appear are composed entirely of such domestic units; they lack the special purpose buildings (storehouses, markets, temples, workshops) that are indicative of public activities in some larger villages (regional centers) and especially in urban sites. The clusters can be identified in terms of residential groupings as family compounds, composed of several individual units architecturally linked and sharing a common courtyard.

These clusters of dwellings or family compounds can be related to family organization at the extended or multiple family household level (Stager 1985). In the villages, the family compound, inhabited by an extended or multiple family unit with its shared space (the courtyard) for processing, storing, and consuming food, was the focus of daily existence. Domestic life, comprising the complex of activities carried out in a family compound, meant the interaction of more family members, young and old, female and male, than would be represented by only a conjugal pair and their unmarried offspring. This contradicts to some extent the commonly held notion that the nuclear family functioned independently in all of ancient Israel, as it probably did in cities, where single family dwellings were the norm. Because the archaeology of urban sites has predominated, the domestic pattern found in such sites was thought to be representative. Likewise, the existence of public areas in cities rightfully suggested the existence of distinct public roles for some, those some being almost exclusively males according to the undoubtedly reliable witness of biblical sources.

Comparative ethnography supports the interpretation of the village compound as the domicile of a multiple or extended, rather than a nuclear, family; and the biblical vocabulary articulating spheres of social orientation bears this out (Gottwald 1979:228–92). The most inclusive social grouping of ancient Israel is expressed in the biblical terms for "people" ('am) or "children of Israel." The next sphere is represented by "tribe" (šēbeṭ or maṭṭeh), which in turn consisted of "clans" or "phratries" (or "families," mišpāḥôt). At the center of this structure were the "lineages" and/or their constituent subgroups, extended or multiple families. By correlating this sequence with the archaeological data, we can identify the family compounds of the Israelite villages as the spatial location of the bêt 'āb, "family household." The term bêt 'āb literally means "household of the father" and primarily designates a living group, though it also can represent a lineage.

"Family household" as a phrase in English is composed of two words that are congruent to some extent but are logically and empirically different and in combination have important implications. Strictly speaking, "family" is a kinship term whereas "household" connotes both residence and social function (Bender 1967:493; see also Yanagisako 1979). The latter is more inclusive; household can include a set of related people and also buildings and outbuildings, wells, granaries, tools and equipment, fields and orchards even if they are not contiguous to the buildings, gardens, and animals (Gelb 1967:5). The English word "house," usually used to render the Semitic word (in Hebrew and its cognates) bayit/bêt, does not do justice to the broad nature of a term that was used chiefly to designate a "household" as the basic socioeconomic unit of society (Hopkins 1983; cf. Bartlett 1980). Hebrew bayit as "household" can be compared to Greek oikos, from which the Greeks coined the word oikonomia (economy) in recognition of the economic role of the household. Hence "family household" is an appropriate designation in its socioeconomic sense for the multiple dwelling unit or compound housing of Israelite villagers (cf. the clues to this residential pattern in the story of Micah's household in Judges 17–18).

The archaeological data thus far do not permit identification of the exact family structure of the compound's inhabitants. Either a multiple family or a joint family household (cf. the studies of Laslett and Wall 1972) is a possible interpretation; but an extended family (nuclear family plus older, younger, or laterally related unmarried relatives) is more likely on the basis of biblical data. In the latter case, only one married couple would have lived in the household at a given time. In either case, the household would usually be in flux, changing from multiple to extended and back as the senior members died and as the younger members married (Shorter 1973:343).

Domestic compounds, therefore, represented the living and working space of an extended or multiple family unit in Israelite agriculture villages. This contrasts with the nuclear family pattern associated with Israelite urban centers. The nature of the productive tasks associated with such peasant households would have involved complementary roles for female and male adults. The senior married woman of an extended family would have occupied an important if not preeminent managerial position. With the procreative role perhaps restricting female mobility, and with the demands of planting and harvesting field crops mandating male absence from the compound more often than female absence, the responsibility for many essential household activities and technologies would have been within the female's sphere. A similar pattern could be posited for the senior female and/or second generation females of a multiple family household.

For as long as the household was the major unit of society, various important societal functions were carried out almost exclusively within this unit. The economic function, in which virtually all of the labor necessary for subsistence was performed by household members, was obviously the central one. The production, processing, and allotment of resources took place within the household; and everyone had her or his vital role, which involved technological expertise associated only with that role, to play in the complex and multifarious assortment of essential tasks. In addition, the household was the focus of the education and socialization of the young, a process in which female responsibility was probably dominant. It was also the setting for family religious or cultic activities that involved all family members. And certain juridical and legal aspects of village life were rooted in the household unit and in the authority of the senior women and men of the household.[6]

In short, the household structure in an agricultural village entailed the interdependence of gender and the complementarity of essential roles. Although social or formal interactions beyond the family unit were patriarchal in structure, it is possible to posit that within the household neither female nor male occupied significantly higher status nor greater prestige. During the formative stages of Israelite life, the centrality of the household meant a relative lack of emphasis on suprahousehold arrangements and thus of male prerogatives. By

equating Everywoman Eve with the senior wife or female in a family compound in an Israelite village, we can then hypothesize that her life was not one
of an oppressed subordinate. The public-oriented biblical texts may give that
impression, and postbiblical traditions seized upon that impression and perpetuated it as dogma. Yet modern analytical methods can reconstruct the life
setting of typical Israelite peasant women and reveal that such women lived in
a world in which the dominant arena of life was domestic and was characterized by female-male interdependence and the authority of senior females in
crucial aspects of household life and thus of social life in general. The association of Eve, or Israelite women, with notions of submission, inferiority, or
dependence belongs to a much later world, in which a monarchic state controlled resources, in which urban life was conceptually dominant, in which
family structures were significantly different, and in which many other factors
contributed to the postbiblical revaluation, and devaluation, of Eve.

NOTES

1   The term *deuterocanonical* refers to the fourteen ancient works (e.g., Tobit,
    Judith, Ecclesiasticus, 1 and 2 Maccabees) that constitute the Old Testament
    Apocrypha. These books, which were included in the earliest translations of the
    Hebrew Bible, notably the Greek Septuagint and the Latin Vulgate, are not con-
    tained in the standard text of the Hebrew Bible. The early church, which utilized
    translated scripture rather than the Hebrew original, considered these works ca-
    nonical, or rather *deuterocanonical,* belonging to a second (and later) canon. The
    Roman Catholic Bible today still contains these books, but Protestants recognize
    only the books of the Hebrew Bible as canonical and hence omit the deuterocanon.
2   *The Woman's Bible* was republished in 1974 by Arno Press in an edition percep-
    tively entitled *The Original Feminist Attack on the Bible.*
3   A fourth approach, the creation of a new, nonsexist canon, was not a possibility in
    the nineteenth century, but has become manifest in recent feminist publications
    such as that of Ruether 1985.
4   The Atrahasis Epic is a long, rather fragmentary, Babylonian poem. The most
    complete text is an Old Babylonian copy, dating from about 1650 B.C.E. The poem
    begins with a description of the creation of the world and then of humanity. The
    appearance of the latter caused problems. The gods make several attempts to deal
    with "the noise of mankind" (overpopulation; shortage of resources), but these
    efforts do not have lasting success. Finally, the gods bring about a flood to destroy
    all people. The hero, Atrahasis—like Noah in the Bible and like Utnapishtim in the
    Gilgamesh Epic—builds an ark and escapes the flood. The postflood edicts of the
    god Entu and the actions of the birth goddess Nintu have the effect of decreasing
    population growth and thus resolving the recurring demographic problem.
5   Although females and males had shared economic roles in the agrarian settings of

early Israel, men apparently legally controlled the transmission of property from earliest times. I have elsewhere (Meyers 1988) discussed the complex dynamics and functional role of this situation, and I have suggested that it resulted in restrictive gender hierarchy only when land shortages, a market economy, and a central government extracting tax revenues replaced the domestic-centered economy of tribal Israel.

6 I treat the female role in these various household functions in considerable detail in *Discovering Eve: Ancient Israelite Women in Context* (New York: Oxford University Press, 1988).

WORKS CITED

BAILEY, L. R.
  1984   Tough Questions for Us All. *Review of Books and Religion* 12:1, 9.

BARTLETT, P.
  1980   Adaptive Strategies in Peasant Agricultural Production. *Annual Review of Anthropology* 9:553–61.

BASS, D. C.
  1982   Women's Studies and Biblical Studies: An Historical Perspective. *Journal for the Study of the Old Testament* 22:6–12.

BENDER, D. R.
  1967   A Refinement of the Concept of Household: Families, Co-residence, and Domestic Functions. *American Anthropologist* 69:493–504.

BINFORD, L. R.
  1962   Archaeology as Anthropology. *American Antiquity* 28:217–25.

BIRD, P.
  1974   Images of Women in the Old Testament. In *Religion and Sexism,* edited by R. R. Ruether, pp. 41–88. New York: Simon and Schuster.

CALLAWAY, J. A., AND R. E. COOLEY
  1971   A Salvage Excavation at Raddana, in Bireh. *Bulletin of the American Schools of Oriental Research* 201:9–19.

CHANEY, M. L.
  1983   Ancient Palestinian Peasant Movements and the Formation of Premonarchic Israel. In *Palestine in Transition: The Emergence of Ancient Israel,* edited by D. N. Freedman and D. F. Graf, pp. 39–54. Social World of Biblical Antiquity Series, 2. Sheffield, England: Almond Press and American Schools of Oriental Research.

DOYLE, P. M.
  1974   Women and Religion: Psychological and Cultural Implications. In *Religion and Sexism,* edited by R. R. Ruether, pp. 15–40. New York: Simon and Schuster.

FRICK, F. S.
  1979   Religion and Sociopolitical Structure in Early Israel: An Ethno-Archaeological Approach. In *Society of Biblical Literature Seminar*

    Papers, edited by P. J. Achtemeier, pp. 233–53. Missoula, Mont.: Schol-
    ars Press.

FRIEDL, E.
  1967   The Position of Women: Appearance and Reality. *Anthropological Quar-*
        terly 40:98–105.

FUCHS, E.
  forth-   *Sexual Politics in the Biblical Narrative: Literary Strategies and Patriar-*
  coming *chal Ideology in the Hebrew Bible.* Bloomington: Indiana University
        Press.

GEERTZ, C.
  1973   Religion as a Cultural System. In *Readings in Comparative Religion,* 3d
        ed., edited by W. A. Lessa and E. Z. Vogt, pp. 157–78. New York:
        Harper and Row.

GELB, I. J.
  1967   Approaches to the Study of Ancient Society. *Journal of the American Ori-*
        ental Society 87:1–7.

GOTTWALD, N. K.
  1979   *Tribes of Yahweh.* Maryknoll, N.Y.: Orbis.
  1983   Early Israel and the Canaanite Socio-Economic System. In *Palestine in*
        Transition: The Emergence of Ancient Israel, edited by D. N. Freedman
        and D. F. Graf, pp. 25–38. Social World of Biblical Antiquity Series, 2.
        Sheffield, England: Almond Press and American Schools of Oriental
        Research.

GRIFFITH, L.
  1984   *In Her Own Right: The Life of Elizabeth Cady Stanton.* New York: Oxford
        University Press.

HIGGINS, J.
  1976   The Myth of Eve the Temptress. *Journal of the American Academy of Re-*
        ligion 44:639–47.

HOPKINS, D. C.
  1983   The Dynamics of Agriculture in Monarchical Israel. In *Society of Biblical*
        Literature Seminar Papers, edited by K. H. Richards, pp. 177–202.
        Chico, Calif.: Scholars Press.

KEMPINSKI, A., and V. FRITZ
  1977   Excavation at Tel Masos: Third Season, 1975. *Tel Aviv* 3–4:136–58.

KILMER, A.
  1972   The Mesopotamian Concept of Overpopulation and Its Solution as Repre-
        sented in the Mythology. *Orientalia* 41:160–77.

KOVACS, B. W.
  1980   Contributions from Contemporary Sociological Theory to an Understand-
        ing of the Rise of the Israelite Monarchy. Seminar paper of Group on So-
        cial World of Ancient Israel, presented at Society of Biblical Literature
        Annual Meeting, Dallas, Texas.

LASLETT, P., and R. WALL, eds.
  1972   *Household and Family in Past Time.* London: Cambridge University
        Press.

LEFKOWITZ, M.
1983   Wives and Husbands. *Greece and Rome* 30:31–47.
LEVINE, S., and R. A. LEVINE
1985   Age, Gender, and the Demographic Transition: The Life Course in Agrarian Societies. In *Gender in the Life Course,* edited by A. Rossi, pp. 29–42. Hawthorne, N.Y.: Aldine Publishing Co.
METZGER, B.
1982   The Revised Standard Version. In *The Word of God,* edited by L. R. Bailey, pp. 28–44. Atlanta: John Knox Press.
MEYERS, C. L.
1978   Roots of Restriction: Women in Early Israel. *Biblical Archeologist* 41: 91–103.
1983a   Gender Roles and Genesis 3:16 Revisited. In *The Word of the Lord Shall Go Forth,* edited by C. Meyers and M. O'Connor, pp. 337–54. Philadelphia: American Schools of Oriental Research.
1983b   Procreation, Production, and Protection: Male-Female Balance in Early Israel. *Journal of the American Academy of Religion* 41:569–93.
1987   'āṣab. *Theologisches Wörterbuch zum Alten Testament* 6:298–301. Stuttgart, W. Kohlhammer Verlag.
1988   *Discovering Eve: Ancient Israelite Women in Context.* New York: Oxford University Press.
NELSON, C.
1974   Public and Private Politics: Women in the Middle Eastern World. *American Ethnologist* 1:551–63.
O'BRIEN, J., and W. MAJOR
1982   *In the Beginning.* American Academy of Religion, Aids for the Study of Religion, no. 11. Chico, Calif.: Scholars Press.
PAGELS, E. H.
1985   Women, the Bible and Human Nature. In *New York Times Book Review,* April 7, p. 3.
PRUSAK, B.
1974   Woman: Seductive Siren and Source of Sin? In *Religion and Sexism,* edited by R. R. Ruether, pp. 89–116. New York: Simon and Schuster.
ROGERS, S. C.
1975   Female Forms of Power and the Myth of Male Dominance: A Model of Female/Male Interaction in Peasant Society. *American Ethnologist* 2:727–56.
1978   Woman's Place: A Critical Review of Anthropological Theory. *Comparative Studies in Society and History* 20:123–62.
RUETHER, R. R.
1985   *Womanguides.* Boston: Beacon Press.
SAKENFELD, K. D.
1982   Old Testament Perspectives: Methodological Issues. *Journal for the Study of the Old Testament* 22:13–20.

SHORTER, E.
  1973   Kinship and Family Size in History. *History of Childhood Quarterly*
           1:342–47.
SMITH, P., et al.
  1981   Human Skeletal Remains. In E. Meyers, J. Strange, C. Meyers, *Excava-
           tions at Ancient Meiron,* chap. 7.2. Cambridge, Mass.: American Schools
           of Oriental Research.
STAGER, L. E.
  1985   The Archaeology of the Family in Ancient Israel. *Bulletin of the American
           Schools of Oriental Research* 260:1–36.
STANTON, E. C.
  1974   *The Original Feminist Attack on the Bible.* Reprint of *The Woman's Bible.*
           1895–98. New York: Arno Press.
TRIBLE, P.
  1973a   Depatriarchalizing in Biblical Interpretation. *Journal of the American
           Academy of Religion* 41:30–48.
  1973b   Eve and Adam: Genesis 2–3 Reread. *Andover Newton Quarterly* 13:
           251–58.
  1978   *God and the Rhetoric of Sexuality.* Philadelphia: Fortress Press.
WELTER, R.
  1974   Something Remains to Dare. Introduction to *The Original Feminist Attack
           on the Bible,* by E. C. Stanton. Reprint of *The Woman's Bible.* 1895–98.
           New York: Arno Press.
YANAGISAKO, S. J.
  1979   Family and Household: The Analysis of Domestic Groups. *Annual Re-
           view of Anthropology* 8:161–205.

CHAPTER 5

Devil's Gateway and Bride of Christ: Women in the Early Christian World

ELIZABETH A. CLARK

The materials out of which this paper is constructed might well promote despair among many feminist scholars. In the first place, the sources are exclusively literary—and to make matters worse, the literature is written *by* men *about* women. The literature, moreover, is so propagandistic and rhetorical that the attempt to extract historical information from it might seem futile. Far from hearing women's voices directly, we might reasonably question whether the male voices we hear can sound an authentic note. Thus, these sources, penned by church leaders whose views on women are barriers enough to a sympathetic reading, were constrained within contemporary literary conventions that seem to hide rather than reveal the full humanity of their subjects.

In addition, the women who served as the subjects of the church fathers' literary endeavors were from an elite class. Indeed, we can confidently assert that their social status and wealth contributed significantly to their selection as literary subjects. Although archaeology, inscriptions, and (for Egypt) papyri lend limited assistance to uncovering "ordinary" women's lives in the early Christian era, extended portraits of women almost exclusively concern those whose real estate holdings were scattered throughout a half-dozen provinces of the Roman Empire and whose annual income could have supported hundreds, probably thousands, of people.[1]

Yet discouragement occasioned by the sources is not the dominant motif of this paper, for women in early Christianity have been the subject of much lively writing in recent years. Spurred by the feminist movement of the past two decades, scholars with a raised consciousness of women's issues turned to the old sources with new eyes. Following a pattern we now recognize as typical in feminist scholarship, they first raised up for inspection the misogyny so prevalent in the writings of the church fathers.[2] Although this project is by no means complete, given the enormous corpus of patristic literature, a second task soon took precedence: to uncover the lives of actual women in early Christianity. Here a monumental task of historical reconstruction awaited them, since the meager materials pertaining to women had to be fleshed out and interpreted in light of scholarship on late antiquity in its social, economic, legal, literary, medical, philosophical, and educational dimensions, a task for which traditional theological education had not prepared them. Although older generations of male scholars had sometimes claimed that women's status was elevated by Christian ideology, few attempts had been made to detail the limits of that ideology or to uncover its economic and social correlates. The paper that follows will encompass both stages of historical research: although the church fathers' misogyny will be amply illustrated, the detailing of women's lives in ancient Christianity will receive attention as well.

I turn now to the problem suggested by the title of my paper: the dual evaluation of women by the church fathers as the "devil's gateway" and the "bride of Christ." The fathers' alternate condemnation and exaltation of the female sex is both striking and baffling. Their extreme ambivalence on the topic of womanhood has led some modern commentators to assert that women made progress in the early Christian centuries, and others, looking at different evidence, to conclude that they regressed. In this instance, both sides are right—depending on which groups of women they consider. To illustrate how women both "won" and "lost" is my present task.

First, listen to the voices of the church fathers themselves. Listen to the early third-century North African church father Tertullian harangue a female audience in his treatise *On the Dress of Women*. He exhorts Christian women to dress simply and modestly, and justifies his exhortation in these words:

If such strong faith remained on earth, as strong as the reward of faith expected in heaven, not one of you, dearest sisters, from the time she acknowledged the living God and learned about herself, that is, about the condition of women, would have desired a more charming dress, not to speak of a more brilliant one. She would rather go about in cheap clothes and strive for an appearance characterized by neglect. She would carry herself around like Eve, mourning and penitent, that she might more fully expiate by each garment of penitence that which she acquired from Eve—I mean the degradation of the first sin and the hatefulness of human perdition. "In pains and anxieties you bring forth children, woman, and your inclination is for your husband, and he rules over you" [Gen. 3:16]—and you know not that you are also an Eve?

God's judgment lives on in our age: the guilt necessarily lives on as well. *You* are the devil's gateway: *you* are the unsealer of that forbidden tree: *you* are the first forsaker of the divine law; *you* are the one who persuaded him whom the devil was not brave enough to approach; *you* so lightly crushed the image of God, the man Adam; because of *your* punishment, that is, death, even the Son of God had to die. And you think to adorn yourself beyond your "tunic of skins?" [Gen. 3:21][3]

Or again, listen to the words of John Chrysostom, bishop of Constantinople at the close of the fourth century. In the following passage, he warns male ascetics who have renounced sexual activity of the dangers that await them, the effeminacy into which they will sink, if they share a residence with a woman similarly vowed to celibacy. In his description of the feminine characteristics that will rub off on the man who attempts to live in such a situation, he compares this disgrace to the taming of a courageous lion:

Just as someone captures a proud and fiercely-glaring lion, then shears his mane, breaks his teeth, clips his claws, and renders him a disgraceful and ridiculous specimen, so that this fearsome and unassailable creature, whose very roaring causes everyone to tremble, is easily conquered even by children, so these women make all the men they capture easy for the devil to overcome. They render them softer, more hotheaded, shameful, mindless, irascible, insolent, importunate, ignoble, crude, servile, niggardly, reckless, nonsensical, and to sum it all up, the women take all their corrupting feminine customs and stamp them into the souls of these men.[4]

And yet, the fathers who utter such vituperations also lavish praise on women. The fourth-century church father Jerome had numerous female friends whom he frequently lauded. Sensitive to the fact that his male contemporaries might ridicule his praises, he defended his practice by an appeal to the New Testament:

An unbelieving reader might perhaps laugh at me for laboring so long over the praises of the ladies. He will rather condemn himself for pride than us for foolishness if he will ponder how the holy women who were companions of our Lord and Savior ministered to him from their own substance [Luke 8:1–3], how the three Marys stood before the cross [John 19:25] and how especially Mary Magdalene, who received the name "tower" (Magdala) from the zeal and ardor of her faith, was first worthy to see Christ rising, even before the apostles [John 20:11–18]. For we judge moral excellences not by people's sex, but by their quality of spirit. . . .[5]

The very man who claimed that women turn men into cowardly lions, John Chrysostom, had a close female friend and confidante, Olympias, whose merits he constantly sang in his seventeen extant letters to her. In the anonymous *Life of Olympias,* her many virtues are described:

No place, no country, no desert, no island, no distant setting, remained without a share in the benevolence of this famous woman; rather, she furnished the churches with liturgical offerings and helped the monasteries and convents, the beggars, the prisoners, and those in exile; quite simply, she distributed her alms over the entire inhabited world. And the blessed Olympias herself burst the supreme limit in her almsgiving and her humility, so that nothing can be found greater than what she did. She had a life without vanity, an appearance without pretence, character without affectation, a face without adornment; she kept watch without sleeping, she had an immaterial body, a mind without vainglory, intelligence without conceit, an untroubled heart, an artless spirit, charity without limits, unbounded generosity, contemptible clothing, immeasurable self-control, rectitude of thought, undying hope in God, ineffable almsgiving; she was the ornament of all the humble and was in addition worthily honored by the most holy patriarch John.[6]

Most interesting of all is the elevation of female martyrs and ascetics to the rank of "brides of Christ." A notable text that exploits this image is Jerome's letter to the adolescent heiress Eustochium, who had recently taken a vow of virginity. In his lengthy epistle to Eustochium praising her decision for the celibate life and warning her of the pitfalls she must now avoid, Jerome over and again rings the theme that she is to be "the bride of Christ." He opens his letter with the words of Psalm 45, "Forget your own people and your father's house, and the King [here meaning Jesus] will desire your beauty."[7] Since Eustochium is now the Lord's bride, Jerome feels constrained to address her as "Lady."[8] He reminds the girl's mother, his friend Paula, that she is now the "mother-in-law of God."[9] Throughout the letter, Jerome depicts Eustochium and her fiancé Jesus as swooning lovers, and often borrows the erotic language of the Song of Songs to sing this epithalamium that, paradoxically, celebrates sexual renunciation.[10] At the letter's conclusion, Jerome imagines Eustochium flying to heaven, where she is greeted by Jesus her Spouse. Eustochium, now united with her betrothed, cries to him in the words of the Song of Songs, "Many waters cannot quench love, neither can the floods drown it."[11]

How are we to account for the evaluation of the female sex as both devil's gateway and bride of Christ? How are we to account for the chilling negativity of some descriptions, given the praise of women's piety and steadfastness in others? The answer is threefold.

First, the church fathers inherited the literary traditions of classical paganism, of ancient Israel, and of primitive Christianity, which did not always accord the female sex the rights and dignity we today deem appropriate. Although virtuous wives, learned mothers, and brave heroines all can be found in the pages of classical literature, we also have such works as Juvenal's *Sixth Satire*, which in 661 lines catalogs the depravities, infidelities, cruelties, avarice, lies, extravagance, superstition, and murderous designs of wives. There is also the famous poem of Semonides in which the poet compares women to dogs, weasels, asses, monkeys, and other animals, and concludes that women are the greatest evil Zeus made.[12] Such proverbs as these passed down in the Greek tradition: "There are only two days on which a woman can refresh you: on the day of marriage and when she is buried";[13] "the grasshopper is to be praised as happy, since their females have no voices";[14] "O Zeus, what need is there to abuse women? It would be enough if you only said the word 'woman.'"[15] The literature of pagan antiquity contributed its share to the misogyny of later Western culture.

Although the Hebrew tradition did not portray women in general so negatively, female villains nonetheless lurk in the pages of Scripture: the names of Jezebel and Delilah became virtual synonyms for the treachery and deceit some church fathers thought characteristic of women. The Wisdom tradition of Hebrew Scripture, as well, was replete with images of "dangerous women," such as the "Madam Folly" of Proverbs 5 and the "loose women" young Hebrew men were warned to shun if they wished to escape "the Pit" of destruction.[16] And surveying the prophetic literature, we might wonder why the standard metaphor of the Hebrew prophets for Israel's apostasy was that of an unfaithful woman.[17]

Yet—and most interestingly—the canonical Hebrew Scriptures never so much as repeated, much less developed, the one story exploited by later Christians to restrict women's activities: the tale of Eve and the serpent in the Garden of Eden. The church fathers would not have accepted Carol Meyers' interpretation of the text,[18] for as early as the New Testament itself, Genesis 3 was singled out as *the* Old Testament passage most useful in rationalizing women's secondary status. I Timothy 2:11–15 provides our most explicit testimony:

Let a woman learn in silence with all submissiveness. I permit no woman to teach or to have authority over men; she is to keep silent. For Adam was formed first, then Eve; and Adam was not deceived, but the woman was deceived and became a transgressor. Yet woman will be saved through bearing children, if she continues in faith and love and holiness, with modesty.

As is evident, the author of I Timothy rests his case not only on Genesis 3; he also appeals to the creation story in Genesis 2, in which Eve is created second, after Adam (unlike the Genesis 1 rendition of creation, in which man and woman are created simultaneously). Church fathers cited these verses over and over again to justify woman's subordinate role. The church fathers believed the apostle Paul himself to have written the book of I Timothy (a view rejected by biblical scholars today), giving added authority to these words.

The "subjection" of women to which I Timothy refers concerns the penalty God placed on Eve for her role in the first sin, as described in the traditional English translation of Genesis 3:16: "I will greatly multiply your pain in childbearing; in pain you shall bring forth children, yet your desire shall be for your husband, and he shall rule over you." John Chrysostom, writing in the late fourth century, comments on these verses. Eve must accept servitude, he asserts; she must allow herself to be governed by a man and acknowledge her husband as a lord, since she did not bear her liberty well when she had it.[19] He claims, "When she misused her power, and although created as a helper was found to be treacherous and to have ruined everything,"[20] then God's words of condemnation fell upon her.

For Chrysostom, the implications for the present are that no woman may teach. "Why not?" Chrysostom asks rhetorically, and answers his own question:

Because she taught Adam once and for all, and taught him badly. . . . She exerted her authority once, and exerted it badly. . . . Therefore let her descend from the professor's chair! Those who know not how to teach, let them learn. If they do not want to learn, but rather want to teach, they destroy both themselves and those who learn from them.[21]

Without doubt, the most important conclusion the church fathers drew from the prohibition of women as "teachers" was that they were to be denied access to the priesthood. The female sex must "step aside" from the weighty task of caring for souls, Chrysostom intones in his treatise *On the Priesthood,* for "the divine law has shut women out from the ministerial office," however much they may desire it.[22] That I Corinthians 14:34 prohibits women from even "speaking" in church was taken as another indication that God's Word did not countenance women as preachers.[23]

In a fourth-century church order called the *Apostolic Constitutions,* yet another reason is given why women cannot be priests: Jesus nowhere sent out women to preach, despite a large female following that included his mother and sisters.[24] The author writes thus:

And if in what came earlier we did not allow women to teach, how can we assent to their being priests, which is contrary to nature? For this is an error of Gentile atheism to ordain women as priests to the goddesses; it is not in the dispensation of Christ. And more, had it been necessary for women to baptize, certainly the Lord would have also been baptized by his own mother, not by John, or when he sent us as well to baptize, he would have sent women with them for this purpose. But now, nowhere, neither by command nor in writing did he transmit this, since he knew the order of nature and the fittingness of things, being the Creator of nature and the Legislator of the arrangement.[25]

The limitation of women's roles in patristic Christianity could thus be justified by an appeal to biblical texts that upheld woman's subordinate status at creation, her guilt for the original sin, and the dangers women posed for men. Such readings of the Bible were only reinforced by misogynous views derived from the classical pagan tradition. The weight of ancient traditions was thus one factor that prompted the church fathers to denigrate the worth of women in general and to counsel limits on their roles.

A second reason why early Christian attitudes toward women and their roles in the church often appear negative can be categorized as sociohistorical. In the era of Christianity's precarious establishment, a variety of schismatic and heretical sects abounded, Christian by their own proclamation, but beyond the pale in the opinion of the Catholic church fathers. Since the "mainstream" church was in competition with these sects for adherents, it distressed orthodox churchmen that women found these groups appealing.[26] Although the fathers blame female attraction to these sects on women's weakmindedness and propensity to be led astray, it is not without interest that women appear to have been more readily accepted as religious leaders in the schismatic and heretical sects than they were in Catholic orthodoxy. Two examples of religious groups that gave women more opportunity for leadership than did Catholic Christianity will here suffice: Montanism and Gnosticism (an umbrella term for a wide variety of sects flourishing in the patristic era that offered to their enlightened adherents an escape from the evils of the material world and the celestial tyrants who governed it).

Montanism was a charismatic movement that proclaimed the imminence of the Kingdom of God, an enthusiasm that most Christians had abandoned by the mid-second century, when Montanism arose. Believers should prepare for the Kingdom's arrival by a life of disciplined renunciation, taught Montanus, the sect's founder. The Montanists believed that the Holy Spirit directly inspired their views and they highly esteemed prophecy in the name of the Holy Spirit. Women sat in the highest ranks of the movement, a phenomenon characteristic of spiritualistic movements throughout Christian history. Montanus included in his immediate circle two female prophetesses, Priscilla and Maximilla, believed by the Montanists to be direct vehicles for the Holy Spirit's revelations.[27] (Priscilla, for example, had a vision in which Christ appeared to her as a *female* to announce the descent of the heavenly Jerusalem.[28]) A scandalized church writer asserts that the Montanists even "magnified these females above the Apostles and every gift of Grace, so that some of them go so far as to say that there is in them something more than in Christ." [29] Moreover, church authorities report that Montanist women taught and prophesied publicly, indeed, baptized and celebrated the Eucharist. The women apparently appealed to Galatians 3:28 (in Christ Jesus "there is no male and female") and to the biblical tradition of prophetesses for scriptural support.[30] Despite the fathers' many criticisms of Montanism, they nonetheless conceded that this schismatic group was perfectly orthodox in its doctrine of God and its confession of Christ.[31]

The same could not be affirmed, however, of the various Gnostic sects: the church fathers unanimously condemned the Gnostic depictions of God and Christ. One aspect of Gnostic theology particularly reprehensible to the fathers was the Gnostic propensity to picture the Godhead as including female elements and powers, such as Grace, Thought, and Wisdom. Those Gnostics whose understanding of God approximated orthodox Christianity's might call on "the Father, the *mother*, and the Son," [32] thus offering praise to a Trinity with an explicitly female element.

Likewise, Gnostic Scriptures included episodes in which the female disciples of Jesus, especially Mary Magdalene, receive higher status as Christian leaders than they do in the gospels of Matthew, Mark, Luke, and John. Thus a Gnostic gospel entitled the *Gospel of Mary* singles out Mary Magdalene as the recipient of special and private teaching by Jesus, a point that enrages the hot-tempered Peter, who doubts the validity of her revelation.[33]

Women found expanded roles for themselves in some Gnostic sects more readily than in orthodox Catholicism. The Gnostic leader Marcus encouraged his female followers to view themselves as prophets. When he initiated a woman into the sect, it is reputed that he said to her, "Behold, Grace has come upon you; open your mouth and prophesy."[34] Even worse in the eyes of the church fathers was Marcus' allowing women to serve as copriests with him.[35] The heretic Marcion was reputed to have allowed women to baptize.[36] And the Carpocratian sect of Gnostics boasted a famous woman teacher, Mar-cellina, who journeyed to Rome as a representative of her movement.[37]

Orthodox churchmen reserved strong curses and condemnations for such practices. Tertullian, with whose view of woman as the "devil's gateway" we began, described a woman who led a Gnostic congregation in North Africa as a "viper."[38] In his treatise *On the Prescription of Heretics* (meaning the Gnostics), Tertullian further excoriates women as leaders of Gnostic sects. He writes: "These heretical women—how bold they are! They have no modesty; they are audacious enough to teach, to engage in argument, to perform exor-cisms, to undertake cures, and maybe even to baptize."[39]

How are we to explain the greater access to religious leadership allowed Gnostic women? Elaine Pagels suggests that the prominence Gnostics gave to the feminine element within the Godhead was the decisive determinant;[40] she here sees theology as the legitimation of a more liberal social organization.[41] Other scholars question her interpretation. They note that the Gnostic evalua-tion of the female divinities is ambiguous at best,[42] and hence provides ques-tionable support for Gnostic women's expanded leadership roles. Some of Pagels' critics attempt to offer other explanations. The Egyptian provenance of Gnosticism has been mentioned as a possible determining factor, for in Egypt women enjoyed more legal rights than in other areas of the Mediter-ranean world.[43] Still another possible explanation for the prominence of women's leadership in Gnostic sects rests on the supposition that Gnostics came from a wealthy and educated section of the population;[44] if the supposi-tion is correct, Gnostic women leaders may have received offices on the basis of their social and economic status. Whatever the precise reasons for the Gnostics' allowance of women religious leaders, such women leaders are firmly attested.

Over against the Gnostic allowance of women as religious leaders, ortho-dox Christianity upheld an ethic called by the New Testament scholar Gerd Theissen (borrowing from Ernst Troeltsch) "love-patriarchalism." In place of geniune equal rights and equal roles for women, mainstream Christianity preached an ethic of equality for all people—but one that was to be evidenced only "in Christ," not in the real world. Theissen writes, "In the political and social realm, class-specific differences were essentially accepted, affirmed, even religiously legitimated."[45] That in Jesus Christ there was no "male and female," as Paul put it,[46] was *not* translated into the bettering of women's position in the social-historical arena, as it was by the Gnostic and Montanist sects.

In the second and third centuries, the Christian church was engaged in the quest of its own "self-definition."[47] Striving to define itself in contrast to non-Christians without and dissenters within, the church drew firm lines, precise boundaries, between itself and these heretical and schismatic movements. Its desire for differentiation was all the stronger since the sects so often claimed that *they* possessed the correct understanding of Christian truth. To demarcate the boundaries between "us" and "them," the church fathers singled out for attack various features of the sects' allegedly misguided teaching and practice, such as the leadership roles of Gnostic women. In contrast to women in the sects, who allegedly engaged in blasphemous activities, no orthodox Catholic woman should teach, preach, baptize, exorcise, offer the Eucharist, or prophesy. Thus the mainstream church's limitations of women's roles can be understood in part as an aspect of its quest for self-definition.

The third reason for the church's limitation of women's roles may well have been the most important: for men, women were inextricably linked with sexuality, marriage, and procreation. Although many women today reject an identity that focuses on their sexual and reproductive capacities, we can nonetheless argue that women would be esteemed for their childbearing role (if for nothing else) in societies that placed a high value on reproduction, such as ancient Israel. But it was inevitable that when increasingly ascetic currents came to dominate Christianity, women as the symbols of sexuality and procreation would be accordingly denigrated.

The New Testament itself provides fuel for the ascetic fire. The Gospels represent Jesus as unmarried and report that he taught that those who become eunuchs for the sake of the Kingdom of Heaven were blessed;[48] that feeling lust in one's heart is as wicked as actually committing adultery;[49] that in the resurrection, there will be no marrying or giving in marriage.[50] Sentiments such as these were taken by later generations of Christians to mean that celibate living was an ideal recommended by Jesus himself to which people should aspire.

I Corinthians 7 serves to strengthen the ascetic resolve. There the only reason Paul gives for marriage is that it tamps down "the temptation to immorality'; those who are "aflame with passion" are advised to marry. Given that "the form of the earth is passing away," Paul thinks that Christians might better abstain from marriage with all its attendant responsibilities and "worldly troubles." Paul acknowledges that not everyone had his gift for celibacy, but he nonetheless wishes that all might have it. Marriage, he implies, is for those too weak to control their sexual desires. It promotes an "anxiety about worldly affairs." In contrast, those who remain single are able to expend their energies upon "the affairs of the Lord, how to be holy in body and spirit." Whether Paul would have given the same advice if he had foreseen that "the form of the world" was not to pass away is a moot question. Once Paul's letters were enshrined as Holy Scripture, Christians believed that his opinions were meant to hold for all time.

Marriage and reproduction could not be completely denigrated by the church fathers, however, for the church wished to praise the goodness of God's creation and the human body in contrast to some Gnostics who claimed that both the world and our bodies were the products of an evil creator or unfortunate accidents.[51] For some of them, reproduction was simply the nasty trick by which an evil creator had lured humans into becoming the agents for the further dispersal of spiritual particles amidst the gross material body and its animal passion. Faced with such a stark condemnation of reproduction, the church fathers felt compelled to recall God's first command to Adam and Eve in Genesis 1:28: "Be fruitful, multiply, fill the earth and subdue it."

That the fathers' championing of Genesis 1:28 was less than enthusiastic we can infer from a cursory examination of that most laudatory of all early Christian treatises on marriage, Clement of Alexandria's, written around 200 A.D.[52] The work is intended to refute Gnostic views of marriage and reproduction, and to demonstrate how orthodox Christian teaching differed from them.

In his survey of Gnostic teaching on marriage, Clement makes clear that Gnostics who live celibate lives are wrongly motivated;[53] they live ascetically because they hate the created order.[54] Clement agrees with them only to the extent that "to attain the knowledge of God is impossible for those who are still under the control of their passions."[55] Wishing to praise marriage, Clement feels compelled to explain why Jesus didn't marry; among the reasons he presents are that Jesus had his own bride, the church, and in any case, did not need a "helpmeet," since he was God on earth.[56] Clement compiled a list of biblical characters who married, and in his enthusiasm to sanction marriage, even included Paul![57] Clement concludes that marriage is an acceptable form of Christian life if, and only if, it is undertaken for the purpose of begetting children with a "chaste and controlled will."[58] He generously grants that it is possible to serve the Lord in marriage, as well as in celibacy[59] (one such service the partners render is to "suffer with each other and 'bear one another's burdens'"[60]). And if any further proof is needed that reproduction is good, Christians are reminded that Jesus himself was truly born.[61] Clement's is surely a very modest encouragement of marriage.

Later church fathers repeat his arguments and add some of their own. To Augustine, the church owes the view that the blessings of marriage include not just offspring and a control for lust, but also the sacramental bonding of the partners.[62] Hence marriage is given a religious status: the partners are united in a relationship like Christ's to the church,[63] and neither childlessness nor infidelity can rupture it. Augustine's stress on the sanctity of marriage is partly occasioned (as is Clement's) by his desire to combat the alleged excesses of the ascetic movement, with its lightly veiled suspicion of first marriage and its outright condemnation of second marriage.

We can gauge this rising tide of asceticism in early Christianity by several measures. One is the increasing attention given to the Virgin Mary. From the second century on, her status as *perpetual* virgin was increasingly stressed: Mary was not involved in sexual relations *after* the birth of Jesus any more than she had been before. The "documentation" (if we may call it that) for this view is provided by an apocryphal Gospel, the *Protevangelium of James,* which graphically offers physiological "proof" that Mary remained a virgin despite Jesus' birth (a woman attendant who doubted that a virgin had brought forth "made the test" and was punished by God for her unbelief).[64] Of course, the lauding of Mary's perpetual virginity raised some problems for scriptural interpretation, for the New Testament in numerous places mentions the brothers and sisters of Jesus. That problem did not daunt the great exegete of the fourth century, Jerome; in his classic treatise *Against Helvidius,* he explains that the alleged siblings of Jesus were in truth not blood brothers and sisters, but relatives;[65] the word "brother," he argues, is often used metaphorically in Scripture, just as Joseph is called the "father" of Jesus.[66] The point of Jerome's exegesis, of course, is to praise Christian virginity in general and that of Mary in particular.

A second such measure of growing ascetic concern lies in the attacks on remarriage from the late second century on. To be sure, Paul had written in I Corinthians 7 that he thought widows would be happier if they did not remarry,[67] but no more than the later author of I Timothy, who actively counseled the remarriage of widows,[68] could he have imagined the wholesale onslaught against second marriage that arose after his time.

Thus Tertullian, writing around 200 A.D., affirms that second marriage "resembles sexual defilement."[69] He mocks those Christians who confess that because the end of the world is at hand, we should take no thought for the morrow, yet are anxious for their posterity and the fate of their inheritances.[70] From Tertullian's vantage point, their expressed concerns are simply "pretexts with which we color the insatiable desire of the flesh"[71]—that is, those who wish to remarry are trying to excuse sexual indulgence. According to John Chrysostom, widows have no plausible justification for remarrying: they cannot even claim inexperience, having once been through the horrors of matrimony and childbearing.[72] He concludes that they must be either suffering from amnesia about the conditions of marriage, be craving worldly glory, or be governed by sexual lust.[73]

Jerome advises a young widow named Furia not to return to what he calls the "vomit" of marriage. He mocks her desire for children: "Do you fear the extinction of the Furian line if you do not present your father with some little fellow to crawl upon his chest and drool down his neck?"[74] He concludes his letter with the sobering exhortation, "Think everyday that you must die, and you will never think of marrying again."[75] Such denunciations of second marriage, when coupled with the exaltation of Mary's perpetual virginity, reveal that the values of early Christianity were undergoing a sharp transformation from the praise of motherhood and wifely virtue we find both in the Old Testament and in many Latin documents.[76]

An irony of early Christian history is that the ascetic movement, which had so many features denigrating of women and marriage, became *the* movement that, more than any other, provided "liberation" of a sort for Christian women. *If* they could surmount their identification with sexual and reproductive functioning, women were allowed freedoms and roles they otherwise would not have been granted. I do *not* posit that most women consciously chose the ascetic life as an "escape" from marriage. Nonetheless, their renunciations, motivated by religious concerns, served to liberate them from the traditional bonds of marriage. The advantages they received in adopting asceticism were practical as well as theoretical.[77]

In the fourth century, asceticism flowered. Indeed, our sources indicate that by the end of the third century, women were taking to the Egyptian desert to live as hermits;[78] in the first half of the fourth century, communal monasteries were established there for women.[79] Asceticism for women became popular in the West a few decades later: the 350s and 360s saw the adoption of "house asceticism" by noble Roman women, and in the 370s and 380s, they left home and homeland to found monasteries in Palestine. In the decades thereafter, monasticism spread all over the Mediterranean world. What advantages did this new way of life offer?

First, in the eyes of our male authors, asceticism allowed women to overcome the negative qualities associated with femaleness: lightmindedness, vanity, frivolity, and lack of intelligence were suddenly and miraculously overcome by women who undertook an ascetic program. Once these women swept away the old world of property, husbands, and children, they were inducted into a new status that elevated them above the deficiencies of the female condition. Sometimes they are said to have become "men"; at other times they are said to have become "angels." As Jerome phrased it, once a woman prefers Jesus Christ to a husband and babies, "she will cease to be a woman and will be called a man."[80] She was now considered a man's equal, not his inferior.[81] To those women who undertook the ascetic life, Jerome quoted Paul's words, that in Christ Jesus "there is no male and female," as an emblem of their new-found equality.[82] Once we recover from the shock of the fathers' androcentric bias, we can see that they affirm in the most positive terms of their culture (namely, terms of "maleness") that female ascetics had shed those negative characteristics which, to their minds, marked out women.

To be sure, the overcoming of the alleged deficiencies of femaleness was also manifest in earlier Christianity, namely, in martyrdom. Female martyrs are consistently called "virile," possessors of "manly spirit."[83] According to the fourth-century Latin churchman Ambrose, for example, Agnes, reputed to be a victim of the emperor Diocletian's persecution earlier in the century, is said to have risen "above nature,"[84] by which he means the "nature" of her sex, as well as "human nature" more generally. In his rhetorical rendition of Agnes' martyrdom, he claims that she was "undaunted by the bloody hands of executioners, unmoved by the heavy dragging of the creaking chains." Although girls of her age (namely, twelve) customarily cannot tolerate even a glare from their parents, and shriek when pricked by a needle,[85] Ambrose asserts that Agnes surpassed her sex as well as her age in bravery. He celebrates her:

What terror the executioner struck to make her afraid, what flatteries to persuade her! How many longed that she might come to them in marriage! But she replied, "It would be a wrong to my Spouse [i.e., Jesus] to anticipate some man's pleasing me. The One who first chose me for Himself shall receive me. For what, o murderer, do you delay? Let this body be destroyed, a body that can be loved by eyes of men I do not want." She stood, she prayed, she bent her neck. You could perceive the executioner tremble, as if he himself had been sentenced; the hand of the murderer shook, his face paled as he feared another's peril, when the girl did not fear her own. Thus you have in one victim a twofold martyrdom, of modesty and of piety: she both remained a virgin and acquired martyrdom.[86]

Likewise, the decidedly unfemale characteristics displayed by the North African woman Vibia Perpetua, martyred probably in the year 203 A.D., are vividly portrayed in the account of her martyrdom. On the day before Perpetua was to fight the beasts, she had a vision in which she was led to the arena. In her own words, she tells how in the vision an Egyptian was brought out to fight her. She reports, "I was stripped and I was made a man." She triumphs over her opponent whom, upon waking, she realized had been the Devil.[87] That to fight in the arena as one condemned to martyrdom might make one "manly" is here most graphically asserted.

Once the era of the Roman persecutions was over, however, martyrdom no longer offered a way for Christian women to demonstrate their "manliness." Asceticism was now judged to be the new arena in which a woman could exhibit her "manly courage." (The phrase is almost a tautology in Greek, since the very word for courage, *andreia*, indicates its masculine association.) The church fathers frequently asserted that asceticism was a new form of martyr-dom, one in which we could be martyred daily. Jerome, in *Epistle* 130, ad-dressed to a teenage heiress, Demetrias, who had abandoned her plans for marriage at the eleventh hour and taken a vow of perpetual virginity, imagines the timid young woman summoning up courage to announce her change of plans to her family. He pictures her saying:

What is to become of you, Demetrias? Why do you tremble so to defend your chas-tity? This situation demands candor and courage! If in a time of peace you are so afraid, what would you do if you were suffering martyrdom? If you cannot endure a scowl from your family, how could you bear the persecutors' tribunals? If the ex-amples of men do not challenge you, be encouraged and take confidence from the blessed martyr Agnes who overcame both youth and tyranny, who by her martyrdom won the victor's crown for the name of chastity.[88]

Thus the courage of an earlier woman stood as a model for the new "martyrs" of the postpersecution era, the ascetics.

Removed from the category of "womanhood" and its attendant complica-tions by ascetic devotion, females would learn (according to the fathers) that asceticism offered them unprecedented freedom: freedom from the domestic problems occasioned by slaves, money, in-laws, sick children, marital suspi-cion and jealousy, not to speak of the verbal abuse and physical blows to which the church writers attest many wives were subjected.[89] Ascetic women were exempt from the curse of Genesis 3:16. As Jerome put it:

When Jesus was crowned with thorns, bore our sins and suffered for us, it was to make the roses of virginity and the lilies of chastity grow for us out of the brambles and briers that have formed the lot of women since the day when it was said to Eve, "in sorrow you shall bring forth children, and your desire shall be for your husband, and he shall rule over you."[90]

Jesus' overcoming of original sin is here interpreted strictly as the advent of asceticism. For women, Eve's curse was undone through the adoption of the virginal profession.

For some ascetic women, another practical advantage of this way of life was the freedom to pursue friendships with the opposite sex. It is of interest that both Jerome and John Chrysostom, whose denigrating comments regarding women and marriage we noted earlier, cultivated circles of female ascetics with whom they maintained lifetime bonds of devotion. In fact, some of their contemporaries thought their relations with women were a bit overly close, and used that charge to discredit them.[91] In these circles of friendship, schol-arly pursuits were undertaken. Indeed, Jerome's circle in Rome can best be described as a late ancient coed study group. He and his female friends investigated Scripture, and many of his treatises and letters respond to the detailed questions posed by these ascetic friends. Some of them even learned Hebrew so that they could better appreciate the Old Testament.[92] When we consider how rare was the knowledge of Hebrew among *male* churchmen of the fourth century, their accomplishment is truly astounding.

Although the fathers disapproved of women speaking in public, we hear that some of these female ascetics carried on public debates. Marcella, one of Jerome's circle, is called by him the foremost student of Scripture in Rome after he departed the city. Jerome testifies that members of the clergy sought her out, so highly did they regard her. (The fact that she credited her answers to male authorities so as not to appear to be in violation of New Testament injunctions against women teaching is a quaint touch Jerome adds to his encomium.) Marcella is also represented as engaging in public debate during the Origenist controversy in Rome.[93]

Opportunities for travel in the form of pilgrimages to Egypt, the home of the desert fathers, and to Palestine, the locale of the holy places of biblical fame, also enriched the lives of ascetic women. For matrons, trips about the Mediterranean unaccompanied by fathers or husbands would not have been sanctioned. Yet when the travel was called pilgrimage, not only was it acceptable for female ascetics, it was laudable. One of the rare pieces of ancient Christian literature written by a woman is the account of the nun Egeria who, in the later fourth century, took a pilgrimage to the Holy Land and Asia Minor.[94] That her journey was one long marvel to her is abundantly evident from her chronicle, a travel diary that she composed for her sister nuns back home. Her excitement shines through her less than elegant prose as we follow her ascending Mount Sinai; viewing the spot upon which Lot's wife turned into a pillar of salt (now submerged in the Dead Sea, Egeria regretfully reports); journeying to Edessa, where she heard read the correspondence between Jesus and King Abgar, and to the impressive shrine of Saint Thecla in Isauria; and last, reverencing the sacred places in the Holy Land associated with Jesus' life and death.

Another such account of a female's pilgrimage to the holy places is Jerome's memorial of his friend Paula that details her visit to the desert fathers in Egypt and the holy sites of biblical fame.[95] Such a tour involved a veritable course in biblical geography. Paula saw, among other things, Cornelius' house in Caesarea, the valley where Joshua told the sun to stand still, the Bethlehem grotto where Jesus was born, and the cave in which Lot slept with his daughters— the latter provided an occasion for Paula to exhort the maidens with her against the dangers of drinking wine. She also crossed the Egyptian desert with "manly courage," Jerome reports, in order to visit the desert fathers; in doing so, she discounted "her sex and the weakness of her frame."[96] Thus pilgrimage provided to ascetic women increased opportunities for travel and on-site instruction.

A last and important contribution of asceticism was that it allowed some women to hold positions of religious leadership, even though orthodox Christian women were not to be ordained to the priesthood. Although Romans 16 calls Phoebe a *diakonos*, a deacon, and I Timothy 5 refers to a group in the church called "the widows," it remains unclear whether these titles meant the same in the earliest decades of Christianity as they did later. We know from patristic literature that the widows were a class of women devoted to prayer, but their office seems to have died out in the course of the fourth century. To replace them arose the deaconesses, vowed to the celibate life, who assisted with various liturgical functions involving women.[97] According to the Council of Chalcedon in A.D. 451, deaconesses were to be forty years old before they received office.[98] In Eastern Christendom, if not in Western, they underwent a genuine ordination to their posts,[99] unlike virgins and widows. We are fortunate to possess the prayer that was used in the ordination service for deaconesses:

O eternal God, the Father of our lord Jesus Christ, the Creator of man and of woman, who did fill with the Spirit Miriam, Deborah, Anna and Huldah, who did not deem unworthy that your only-begotten Son should be born of a woman, who also in the tent of witness and in the Temple ordained women as keepers of your holy gates: now look upon this your servant who is being ordained as a deaconess, and give her the Holy Spirit, and purify her from any defilement of the flesh and spirit [II Cor. 7:1], so that she may worthily accomplish the work entrusted to her and to your glory and the praise of your Christ, with whom to you and to the Holy Spirit be glory and adoration forever. Amen![100]

The deaconesses did not teach publicly in the church or baptize, but apparently they engaged in some private teaching of women. The fourth-century *Apostolic Constitutions* explains the deaconesses' mission: since the bishop could not send deacons to women's households without giving rise to scandalous rumors amid the pagan community and hence discrediting the church, deaconesses were sent.[101] Probably they engaged in preparing women to become baptismal candidates. Deaconesses must have been essential participants in the baptism ceremony, for in baptism, the candidates were anointed with oil on various points of their bodies and since it was not considered appropriate for the male officiant to anoint any portion of a woman's body below the forehead, the deaconess carried out this task.[102] With time, the office of deaconess died out, subsumed in that of the nun. Yet in the ascetic heyday of the fourth and fifth centuries, we hear of many deaconesses.

A number of celibate women were also able to found and direct women's monasteries. In some cases, an ascetic blood brother appears to have inspired the establishment of the women's monastery. Thus Pachomius, founder of

Egyptian communal monasticism, is said to have created a monastery for his sister to head.[103] Likewise, both Augustine and Caesarius of Arles wrote monastic *Rules* for convents of which their sisters had assumed leadership.[104] In other cases, the women themselves undertook the founding of monasteries. These were women of wealth who achieved their status as monastic superiors because they financed a monastery's construction. Into this latter category falls Chrysostom's friend Olympias (also ordained a deaconess, although she was under age),[105] who founded one of the first, perhaps the first, monastery for women in Constantinople.[106] Her *Life* reports that about two hundred and fifty women enrolled in her monastery, located next to the Great Cathedral of the city.[107] In addition, we know that Jerome's friend Paula founded, funded, and became the superior of a monastery for women in Bethlehem.[108] Similarly, Melania the Elder, in the late 370s or early 380s, built monasteries for men and for women on the Mount of Olives,[109] as her granddaughter, Melania the Younger, was to do several decades later.[110] Although the sources pertaining to these monasteries tell us much more about the women's piety, humility, and other Christian virtues than they do about the leadership they exerted as heads of monastic establishments, we nonetheless have firm testimony to the fact of the women's governance of monasteries as well as to the sisterly support they gave each other in the communal life.

In these several ways, then, asceticism provided new opportunities for women in the patristic era. The "progress" achieved by Christian women in this period is firmly linked to the ascetic program. For matrons, on the other hand, the traditional injunctions to subservience, submissiveness, and silence prevailed; to them, early Christianity brought no significant amelioration of status. The fourth-century Latin bishop Ambrose compares the lot of married women with ascetic ones in the following manner:

> The marriage bond is not then to be shunned as though it were sinful, but rather declined as being a galling burden. For the law binds the wife to bear children in labor and in sorrow, and she is in subjection to her husband, for he is lord over her. So, then, the married woman, but not the widow, is subject to labor and pain in bringing forth children, and she only that is married, not she that is a virgin, is under the power of her husband. The virgin is free from all these things, who has vowed her affection to the Word of God, who awaits the Spouse of blessing with her lamp burning with the light of a good will. And so she is moved by counsels, not bound by chains.[111]

Although the literary sources tell us little about married or nonelite women, celibate women, especially celibate elites, receive more attention than is sometimes assumed. As religious and monastic leaders, students of literature, pilgrims, and patrons, they prefigure the women of later centuries whose lives are being uncovered by feminist scholarship of our era.

NOTES

1   For Olympias' holdings, see the *Life of Olympias*, 5; for Melania the Younger's, see the *Life of Melania the Younger*, 7, 11, 14, 18, 20; and Palladius, *Lausiac History*, 61. According to the Latin version of the *Life of Melania the Younger* (15), her annual income was about 1700 pounds of gold (120,000 gold *solidi*). Although it is risky to estimate what 1700 pounds of gold could buy in A.D. 400, we have Gregory the Great's calculation from about two hundred years later that 80 pounds of gold would have been sufficient to support 3000 nuns for a year (Paul the Deacon, *Life of St. Gregory the Great*, II, 27). Melania's annual income may "translate" to be as high as $123 million.

2   The foremost example is probably the essay by Rosemary Radford Ruether, Misogynism and Virginal Feminism in the Fathers of the Church, in *Religion and Sexism: Images of Woman in the Jewish and Christian Traditions*, ed. Rosemary R. Ruether (New York: Simon and Schuster, 1974), pp. 150–83.

3   Tertullian, *On the Dress of Women*, I, 1, 1–2.

4   John Chrysostom, *Instruction and Refutation Directed against Those Men Cohabiting with Virgins*, 11.

5   Jerome, *Epistle* (hereafter *Ep.*) 127, 5.

6   *Life of Olympias*, 13.

7   Jerome, *Ep.* 22, 1.

8   Ibid., 2.

9   Ibid., 20.

10 Ibid., 1; 25.

11 Ibid., 41.

12 Semonides, frag. 7, in *Anthologia Lyrica Graeca*, ed. E. Diehl (Leipzig: Teubner, 1925), I, 3, 52–59.

13 Hipponax of Ephesus, in Stobaeus, *Florilegium* 68, 8 (*Ioannis Stobaei Anthologium*, ed. O. Hense [Berlin: Weidmann, 1958], II, 515).

14 Xenarchus, frag. 14, in *Comicorum Atticorum Fragmenta*, ed. T. Lock (Leipzig: Teubner, 1880–88), II, 473.

15 Carcinus, frag. 3, in *Tragicorum Graecorum Fragmenta*, ed. B. Snell (Göttingen: Vandenhoeck and Ruprecht, 1971), I, 213.

16 Proverbs 9:13–18.

17 Ezekiel 16; Hosea 1–3.

18 See Carol Meyers, Recovering Eve: Biblical Woman without Postbiblical Dogma, chap. 4 in this volume.

19 John Chrysostom, *Discourse 4 on Genesis*, 1.

20 John Chrysostom, *Homily 26 on I Corinthians*, 2.

21 John Chrysostom, *Discourse 4 on Genesis*, 1.

22 John Chrysostom, *On the Priesthood*, II, 2.

23 Ibid., III, 9.

24 *Apostolic Constitutions*, III, 6.

25 Ibid., III, 9.

26 For a fascinating analysis of how the author of the Pastoral Epistles attempted to keep women from deserting to heretical groups, see Jouette Bassler, "The Wid-

ows' Tale: A Fresh Look at I Tim. 5:3–16, *Journal of Biblical Literature* 103 (1984):23–41.

27   Hippolytus, *Refutation*, VIII, 12; Eusebius, *Church History*, V, 16.

28   Epiphanius, *Heresies*, 49, 1.

29   Hippolytus, *Refutation*, VIII, 12.

30   Didymus the Blind, *On the Trinity*, III, 41, 3; Cyprian, *Ep.* 75, 10; Epiphanius, *Heresies*, 49, 2.

31   Hippolytus, *Refutation*, VIII, 19.

32   *Apocryphon of John*, 2, 9–14, in *The Nag Hammadi Library*, ed. J. M. Robinson (San Francisco: Harper and Row, 1981), p. 99.

33   *Gospel of Mary*, in *Gnosticism: A Sourcebook of Heretical Writings from the Early Christian Period*, trans. R. M. Grant (New York: Harper and Brothers, 1961), pp. 65–68.

34   Irenaeus, *Against Heresies*, I, 13, 3–4.

35   Hippolytus, *Refutation*, VI, 35; Irenaeus, *Against Heresies*, I, 13, 1–2.

36   Epiphanius, *Heresies*, 42, 4.

37   Irenaeus, *Against Heresies*, I, 25, 6.

38   Tertullian, *On Baptism*, 1.

39   Tertullian, *On the Prescription of Heretics*, 41.

40   Elaine Pagels, *The Gnostic Gospels* (New York: Random House, 1979), pp. 59, 66.

41   Pagels, *Gnostic Gospels*, p. 164, n. 1. Pagels herself concedes that theology was not always the prime determinant for the sects' social practices, for neither the Marcionites nor the Montanists had divine female principles, yet they allowed larger roles to women.

42   Elisabeth Schüssler Fiorenza, Word, Spirit and Power: Women in Early Christian Communities, in *Women of Spirit: Female Leadership in the Jewish and Christian Traditions*, ed. Rosemary Ruether and Eleanor McLaughlin (New York: Simon and Schuster, 1979), p. 50; Raoul Mortley, *Womanhood: The Feminine in Ancient Hellenism, Christianity and Islam* (Sydney: Delacroix, 1981), pp. 55, 59, 62.

43   Mortley, *Womanhood*, pp. 61–62.

44   Kurt Rudolph, Das Problem einer Soziologie und 'Sozialen Verortung' der Gnosis, *Kairos* 19 (1977):36–39; on the intellectual status of Gnostics, see Hans G. Kippenberg, Versuch einer Soziologischen Verortung des antiken Gnostizismus, *Numen* 19 (1970):225. Pagels suggest that the move to equality found support "primarily in rich or what we would call bohemian circles" (*Gnostic Gospels*, p. 63). For the prominence of rich women among the supporters of Pelagius, see Peter Brown, The Patrons of Pelagius: The Roman Aristocracy between East and West, *Journal of Theological Studies*, n.s., 21 (1970):56–72, reprinted in *Religion and Society in the Age of Saint Augustine* (New York: Harper and Row, 1972), pp. 208–26. For the centrality of wealthy women to the Priscillianists, see Henry Chadwick, *Priscillian of Avila: The Occult and the Charismatic in the Early Church* (Oxford: Clarendon Press, 1976), pp. 20, 37–40, 144.

45   Gerd Theissen, Social Stratification in the Corinthian Community, in *The Social*

Setting of Pauline Christianity, trans. John Schütz (Philadelphia: Fortress Press, 1982), p. 109; see E. Troeltsch, *The Social Teaching of the Christian Churches,* trans. D. Wyon (New York: Macmillan, 1931), I, 79.

46 Galatians 3:28.

47 See the essays in the collection of E. P. Sanders, ed., *Jewish and Christian Self-Definition,* vol. 1, *The Shaping of Christianity in the Second and Third Centuries* (Philadelphia: Fortress Press, 1980).

48 Matthew 19:12.

49 Matthew 5:27.

50 Mark 12:25 = Matthew 22:30 = Luke 20:35–36.

51 See references in chapters 8–10 of Hans Jonas, *The Gnostic Religion: The Message of the Alien God and the Beginnings of Christianity,* 2d ed. rev. (Boston: Beacon Press, 1963).

52 Clement's *On Marriage* (*Miscellanies,* III) is translated in *Alexandrian Christianity,* ed. J. E. L. Oulton and H. Chadwick (Philadelphia: Westminster, 1954), pp. 40–92.

53 Clement, *Miscellanies,* III, 1, 4.

54 Ibid., 3, 12.

55 Ibid., 5, 43.

56 Ibid., 6, 49.

57 Ibid., 6, 52–53.

58 Ibid., 7, 58; 11. 71.

59 Ibid., 12, 79.

60 Ibid., 1, 4.

61 Ibid., 17, 102.

62 Augustine, *City of God,* XIV, 23.

63 Augustine, *On Marriage and Concupiscence,* I, 17, 19; 10, 11.

64 *Protevangelium of James* 19–20, in *New Testament Apocrypha,* ed. W. Schneemelcher, trans. A. J. B. Higgins et al. (Philadelphia: Westminster Press, 1963–66), I, 384–85.

65 Jerome, *Against Helvidius,* 16–17; 19.

66 Ibid., 18.

67 I Corinthians 7:39–40.

68 I Timothy 5:11–14.

69 Tertullian, *Exhortation to Chastity,* 9, 1.

70 Ibid., 9, 5; 12, 1; 12, 3; 12, 4.

71 Ibid., 12, 1.

72 John Chrysostom, *On Not Marrying Again,* 1.

73 Ibid.

74 Jerome, *Ep.* 54, 4, 2.

75 Ibid., 18, 3.

76 An analysis of cultural models in transition helps us to spot the conflict that was destined to arise when the new ascetic model for female living confronted the older reproductive one. Naomi Quinn of Duke University's Anthropology Department claims that such shifts in ideology are not simply reflective of economic conditions. Her claim seems appropriate to the present case, for there is

nothing in the economic circumstances, narrowly construed, of many female ascetics to explain their rapid and enthusiastic desertion of traditional ideas.

77 The rationale given their cause sounds similar to that of contemporary separatist feminists, who claim that women's subordination stems from their association with sexuality and reproduction, and who thus create separate women's organizations to free themselves from male domination. For a summary of the separatist position, see Alison M. Jaggar, *Feminist Politics and Human Nature* (Totowa, N.J.: Rowman and Allenheld, 1983), pp. 103, 105, 267; Alice Echols, The Taming of the Id: Feminist Sexual Politics, 1968–83, in *Pleasure and Danger: Exploring Female Sexuality,* ed. Carole S. Vance (Boston: Routledge and Kegan Paul, 1984), pp. 55, 58.

78 Athanasius, *Life of Antony,* 3.

79 *Life of Pachomius,* 5 (Pachomius founds the women's monastery for his sister).

80 Jerome, *Commentary on the Epistle of the Ephesians,* III (Eph. 5:28) (PL 23, 533).

81 Jerome, *Ep.* 71, 3, 3.

82 Jerome, *Ep.* 75, 2, 2.

83 E.g., John Chrysostom, *On S. Pelagia,* 2; *On S. Drosis,* 3; *On the Maccabees,* 1, 3; *On Saints Bernice and Prosdoce,* 4.

84 Ambrose, *On Virgins,* I, 2, 5.

85 Ibid., 2, 7.

86 Ibid., 2, 8–9.

87 *Martyrdom of Perpetua and Felicitas,* 10.

88 Jerome, *Ep.* 130, 5.

89 Augustine, *Confessions,* IX, 9; John Chrysostom, *On Virginity,* 40.

90 Jerome, *Ep.* 130, 8.

91 Jerome, *Ep.* 45; on John Chrysostom, see Photius, *Bibliotheca,* LIX (PG 47, 198): among the charges leveled against Chrysostom was that he saw women alone.

92 Jerome, *Epp.* 39, 1, 2–3; 108, 26, 3.

93 Jerome, *Ep.* 127, 9–10.

94 Translation by John Wilkinson, *Egeria's Travels* (London: SPCK, 1971).

95 Jerome, *Ep.* 108, 7–14.

96 Ibid., 14.

97 For a traditional view of the question, see Roger Gryson, *The Ministry of Women in the Early Church,* trans. J. Laporte and M. L. Hall (Collegeville, Minn.: Liturgical Press, 1980). For a less traditional view, see the forthcoming book of Karen Jo Torjesen, *Women's Leadership in Early Christianity.*

98 Canon 15, Council of Chalcedon.

99 *Apostolic Constitutions,* III, 15; VIII, 19.

100 Ibid., VIII, 20.

101 Ibid., III, 15.

102 Ibid.

103 *Life of Pachomius,* 5.

104 Augustine, *Ep.* 211; Caesarius of Arles, *Rules for the Holy Virgins.*

105 *Life of Olympias,* 3–6; Palladius, *Dialogue,* 56; 60.

106 Raymond Janin, *La Géographie ecclésiastique de l'empire byzantine,* vol. I:3, *Les Eglises et les monastères* (Paris: Institut français d'études byzantines, 1953), pp. 395–96.

107 *Life of Olympias,* 6.

108 Jerome, *Ep.* 108, 20.

109 Palladius, *Lausiac History,* 46; 54; Paulinus of Nola, *Ep.* 29, 10.

110 *Life of Melania the Younger,* 41; 49.

111 Ambrose, *Concerning Widows,* 81.

CHAPTER 6

Scientific Thought Style and the Construction of Gender Inequality

ANGELA M. O'RAND

> I would rather label the enterprise of setting biological value upon groups for what it is: irrelevant, intellectually unsound, and highly injurious.
>
> Gould 1981:107

Today we face a renewed interest in the national testing of our children's aptitudes. A concern to replenish the ranks of our scientific elite has brought about a flourishing of summer programs for the gifted and talented and the proliferation of special, sometimes statewide, high schools of science and mathematics. In our time, familial and class inheritance has grown less important, though by no means disappearing, while measured individual capacities and their social valuation have assumed enhanced importance. Our concerns to identify those with the "talent," the "gift," or the "capacity" reflect a quest for new social capital that serves more and more to stratify our society. In turn these qualities explain or justify the resulting social inequalities.

In theory, the possession of these unobservable capacities is an individual phenomenon that results from the asymmetrical interaction between genetic traits and environmental resources. Scientific methods are applied to measure and catalog these capacities through individual testing and distributional statistics. The methods and outcomes are, then, related to this theory of individual capacity. And in the spirit of this scientific rationality, the possession of certain capacities is gauged in quantitative form with measures of degree and not of kind.

Yet the primary social application of these concepts is to construct socially valued or devalued and disjunctive categories—to determine and establish categorical differences. The categories that emerge from the scientific testing typically comprise mutually exclusive "demographic" groups—whites and nonwhites, men and women. The testing for capacity assumes the a priori existence of these demographic categories as underlying determinants of individual differences. In this way a theory of individual capacity is converted into a statement about group differences. The scientific and social debates that then swirl round the construction of categories are, in spite of the dependence on individual "measures of degree" as evidence, actually about "differences in kind." And the compromise that is struck between precise quantification and qualitative categorization is the ranking of categories, no matter how trivial the measured "differences" between them nor how wide the individual variations within them appear (Bleier 1984; Lewontin et al. 1984). The compromise reflects the intricate relationship between social differences in society (and the ability of certain classes to stress the importance of one capacity over another) and the "sciences" for explaining them. Scientific explanation can come, then, to justify social inequalities either by design or by default.

The construction of gender inequality in modern societies is guided by this process. The scientific construction of gender-related capacities serves both to explain observed social outcomes (e.g., test score differences) and to denote them. The reduction of widely ranging individual scores to group averages analytically restricts explanation to the level of the group or category. Although the group mean is a derived value, it assumes the status of scientific fact. As such, it encourages the overestimation of homogeneity and the underestimation of heterogeneity within categories. And, most importantly, the statistic simultaneously represents cause (gender) and effect (intellectual capacity). This conceptual parsimony lends to the facticity of the statistic and provides the foundation for a shared view of the existence of gender-related differences across the disciplines.

The shared view of gender differences is a collective thought style that links the disciplines. The social sciences' measurement of social outcomes, the behavioral sciences' construction of capacities, and the biological sciences' determination of underlying causes are three separate scientific endeavors that share a common thought style regarding sex differences. Though these three disciplinary divisions operate quite independently of each other at a heuristic level, they are nevertheless associated and bound together by a shared view of how their respective objects of study—social differences, measured capacities, brain structure—probably relate to each other ultimately. The elements of this thought style and their impact on the scientific construction of sex differences and gender inequality are the subjects of the following analysis.

LUDWIK FLECK, SCIENTIFIC THOUGHT STYLE, AND CULTURAL PRECEPT

In 1935, Ludwik Fleck published *Genesis and Development of a Scientific Fact,* his historical study of the development of the Wasserman reaction in the diagnosis and treatment of syphilis. A Polish Jew, Fleck was a medical doctor of wide-ranging knowledge and interests. He published his study in Switzerland (because of prohibitions on the publication by Jews in Germany) the same year he was dismissed from his work in a bacteriological laboratory as part of sweeping anti-Jewish measures (Fleck 1979: 149–50). Fleck's work not only predated that of Thomas Kuhn (1962), but also provided for a more holistic understanding of the ties between scientific enquiry and culture.[1]

In his study of the development of the Wasserman reaction to syphilis, Fleck was able to integrate into its history the role of various cultural concepts such as folk notions about bad blood. These inherited habits of thought both within and outside the scientific community, together with the methodological conventions of science, led to the collective creation of the concept of "syphilis" and its treatment. And long after the development of the "fact"—the Wasserman reaction—the distinction between the "fact" as a cultural product and the original intentions and values of its producers became blurred.[2]

The central feature of Fleck's analysis was the notion of scientific "thought style." The relationship between culture and scientific thought style, in Fleck's view, is one in which scientific rationality is not necessarily isomorphic with but is nevertheless embedded within the broader cultural world view. As such, the relationship can be a force for promoting scientific change as well as for holding it back. Changes in cultural perceptions can provide new questions and insights into scientific investigations, while some inherited cultural precepts can legitimate the persistence of scientific thought styles that should be questioned. Similarly, scientific change can influence cultural conceptions either by altering them or reinforcing them. The history of the "construct" of syphilis, according to Fleck, is one of the confluence and reciprocal influence of cultural precept and scientific convention.[3]

Fleck developed a concentric model to characterize the cultural embeddedness of the sciences and the dissemination of scientific "facts." As facts are disseminated from their scientific, experimental center, they are increasingly abstracted from the immediate context of their discovery and are subject to popular application and interpretation. As such, facts gain a status autonomous of their experimental origins that can lead to their cultural appropriation—often resulting in their scientifically inappropriate application or use. Figure 6.1 portrays the model of concentric transmission for a scientific fact from the esoteric "journal" science at the core of a scientific specialty to the popular or "magazine" science in the wider society. The arrow in the figure represents the direction of diffusion. The speed with which scientific facts move from esoteric core to popular culture varies according to their cultural salience. Wider societal patterns place varying "demands" on scientific facts analogous to centrifugal forces pulling elements of esoteric science apart as they pertain to dominant and variant cultural patterns.

At the center of the model is journal science, which is skeptical and cau-

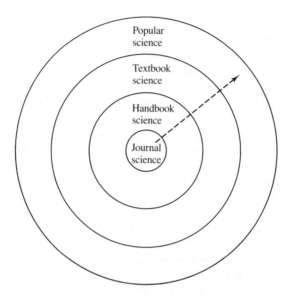

Figure 6.1. Fleck's concentric model of the development and diffusion of a scientific "fact"

tious in its generalization of the relevance of observations ("facts"). It is eso-teric science both in the sense that it protects a monopoly of expertise or "cul-tural capital" that certifies the facticity of special knowledge (Bourdieu 1975) and in the sense that it is usually identified by relatively specialized or idio-syncratic methodology and language. This is the social context of scientific discovery and knowledge production.

Immediately adjacent to journal science is handbook science. Handbook science applies abstracted facts to problem-solving situations closely tied to the esoteric purposes of the original research at the core. Accordingly, hand-book science applies facts, in recipe book fashion, to situations close to their experimental origins without reinterpretation or extensions.

Textbook science, however, in contrast to handbook science tends to con-nect the various disparate facts emanating from different esoteric cores into cognitively coherent systems using broader disciplinary and cultural precepts, biases, and—often—untestable concepts to tie everything together. In this medium, facts are meaningful as they relate to broader scientific thought styles, without much regard for the looseness of the fit. As such, textbook science is science in its most paradigmatic form (Kuhn 1962). Textbook science is also, however, "adjacent" to popular science and cultural precept. Thus, textbook science often comes to integrate scientific elements with the popular influ-ences of cultural biases and predisposing precepts.

Finally, popular science abstracts the fact even more from its core scientific origins and imbues it with cultural meanings, while deferring to the textbook construction of the fact for its legitimacy. In this way, facts can have a large impact on cultural precepts, though Fleck would probably and ultimately prefer to portray the general relationship as nonrecursive, that is, as an ongoing feedback process between the generative scientific center and the interpretive cultural periphery. This dynamic is manifest in the tie between textbook science and popular science, where popular science relies for its power on the legitimacy of textbook science. Yet, textbook science derives much of its holistic framework from cultural precepts in the general society.

Indeed, it is this nonrecursivity that, paradoxically, both promotes and, at times, inhibits scientific change. And it is the idea of nonrecursivity in the relationship between scientific fact construction and cultural consumption of these facts that seems particularly crucial to understanding the current climate in the disciplines and in the wider society regarding research on sex differences and gender inequality.[4]

THE GIFT, THE NORM, AND THE UNDERLYING CAUSE

Three cultural precepts, inherited from the past, undergird both the scientific investigation and the social acceptance of gender-related capacities. The gift (Bourdieu 1977; Bourdieu and Saint Martin 1974; and Bourdieu and Passeron 1977, 1979), the norm (Lewontin et al. 1984), and the underlying cause (Gould 1981) are cultural concerns that have influenced the development of scientific investigation and rationality since the eighteenth century. With clear mystical-ethical origins, the notion of the gift or talent gained greater currency with the rise of middle-class societies and the increasing individuation of inequality. The replacement of the family with elaborate educational institutions coincided with these developments, serving to rationalize or secularize the idea of the gift. The "ideology of the gift" transforms one's acquired capacities into intrinsic virtues (DiMaggio 1979:1464), and thus serves to define the expression of social capacities as inherent individual traits unevenly distributed in the population. The gift also retains something of its mystical quality in popular cultural precepts as something not to be wasted, hence something special to be fostered by others.

The history of the measure of intelligence illustrates the process of transforming gifts into norms, a process of the routinization of individual capacities into social categories. Gould's (1981) critical analysis of the rise of intelligence testing and its epistemological basis documents the relationship between the construction of the idea of innate intelligence and the influence of wide cultural biases, particularly regarding differences between racial and gender groups, on this construction. Following Broca's school of craniometry in the nineteenth century, which sought but failed to link intellectual capacity with head size, a research program developed to look for deeper biological bases for intelligence. By the early twentieth century, the idea of intelligence as an inherent trait was well on its way. The research tradition that Gould traces from Binet through Terman, Yerkes, and Spearman worked to confirm and characterize the "existence" of a global intelligence factor. This approach culminated in the identification of a single intelligence factor (Spearman's g) by which people could be ranked.

Beginning the second half of the twentieth century (about 1947), L. L. Thurstone, who questioned the validity of a global intelligence factor, initiated a line of research which replaced this idea with the notion of multiple forms (vectors) of intelligence. He argued that there were three "real" faculties of the mind—verbal, numerical, and spatial. The global score (g) was merely the average of these three. However, since each faculty was analytically distinctive and cognitively consequential, the separate scores were more meaningful than the global score. Verbal intelligence and mathematical-spatial intelligence, therefore, were deemed as both analytically and empirically separate forms of intelligence in the population (Gould 1981).

It is not accidental that Gould (1981:146–233) labels the construction of intelligence testing as an "American invention." The pragmatic concerns with individual testing and social categorization were not inconsistent within the context of a culturally pluralistic yet individualistic democratic society. The search for norms to achieve standards for homogeneity was an extension of this culture.

Today, mathematical-spatial intelligence is receiving considerable research attention since it is accorded a high cultural value (Caplan et al. 1985). The cultural belief is that an underlying mathematical-spatial capacity is crucial to the acquisition of the specialized knowledge and skills required for the more highly rewarded work of postindustrial society. As was true with Broca's craniometry and the global IQ, however, specialized intelligence is correlated with demographic groups and is used to "explain" social outcomes presumed to be related to specialized capacities. Outcomes such as the male domination of highly rewarded professions is seen as deriving from the male population's higher capacity, or gift, for mathematical-spatial intelligence. The gift is deemed to be the capacity that expresses, on the one hand, basic molecular and physiological makeup and, on the other hand, discernible social outcomes.

The norm and the underlying cause are inseparable from the construct of the gift or intellectual capacity. Distributional statistics generate average test scores that serve as indicators of underlying capacities. The capacities are, themselves, not directly observable. But the test scores—the norms—represent these capacities and become, especially through their introduction into textbook and popular sciences, something real in themselves. Norms are then used to validate the existence of the underlying construct in tautological fashion: the norm is first generated to gauge the outcomes of underlying capacities, then it becomes the measure of those capacities.

An illustration of this thought style is apparent in the construction of gender differences. The average scores on selected ability tests (for example, the Scholastic Aptitude Test) vary across gender "in favor of boys" repeatedly. And since the gender comparison implies that the groups are different, the scores are presumed to reflect the existence of real, underlying intellectual properties distributed differentially across sex. The test developers and administrators do not cite biological sources. But the thought style within which they operate leads to the attribution of these test scores to underlying biological causes. Biological differences between gender groups are presumed to be the underlying causes of the "measured" social regularities produced by their tests. However, the scientific thought style comes to treat the measures of outcome (the norms) *as if* they are the measures of underlying causes. In this way the outcome and the cause come to be related tautologically.

THE DISCIPLINES AND THE CONSTRUCTION OF
SEX DIFFERENCES

Despite shortcomings in clinical studies, it is now well recognized that sex differences are programmed from the beginning of ontogeny, are needed for reproduction, and have many consequences not directly related to fertility. We are fortunate that these times have afforded the support, technical developments, and intellectual climate necessary to produce the studies described in this series. (Naftolin and Butz 1981:1264)

Thus a special issue of *Science* devoted to the topic of sexual dimorphism was introduced by its editor. Reflected in this statement, and throughout the issue's papers, is a mixture of journal science—meticulous concern by authors with the limitations of their specific scientific studies producing tentative results about sex differences—and cultural precept—a faith in the existence of sex differences and the current intellectual climate that calls for them to be revealed. The papers, which review current knowledge among researchers in relevant specialty areas, range in topic from sex differences in genes and chromosomes and their effects on gonadal differentiation to gonadal hormone effects on organ systems, particularly the brain, gender identity, and behavior. Research on nonhuman species and selected clinical populations and case studies of humans dominates the subject populations in the literature reviewed.

The dynamic interplay between the skeptical knowledge (journal science) at the research level and the tacit and less skeptical acceptance of a particular thought style is reflected throughout these papers. Detailed critical reviews of current research in the authors' areas of expertise are coupled with the often uncritical acceptance of reported facts from outside areas that is based on the socially constructed thought style linking individual research efforts to the wider scientific quest.

An example of this differential criticism appears in a paper about the effects of prenatal sex hormones on gender-related behavior (Ehrhardt and Myer-Bahlburg 1981:1317) that very carefully reviews the current research in this area and criticizes the quality of the data in many instances. But in a section discussing the influences of prenatal hormones on cognition—a problem area outside the expertise of the authors—they nevertheless accept as fact that "sex differences in certain cognitive abilities are well known." The facts alluded to are that females tend to have higher verbal ability while males have higher spatial perception. As such, the authors accept, in textbook fashion, the facts of gender differences produced by other research specialties while following norms of skepticism about their own sphere of expertise.

Other papers in the issue exhibit the same thought style. What these papers on the state of the art in research on sexual dimorphism reveal is a tacit commitment to a thought style in this research area that begins with an implicit polarity, rooted in physiology, between male and female. As researchers, they disavow expertise outside their own research, but resort nonetheless to a thought style to locate their own work within the larger enterprise. The thought style is portrayed in Figure 6.2. Here the implicit causal chain in the construction of sex differences is captured. The disciplinary domains focused on different elements of the thought system are indicated. The five major problem areas are linked in a hierarchical system of cross-level determination.

The transdisciplinary thought style is deterministic, reductionistic, and hinged on a behavioral "black box," the unobservable construct of innate capacity. The linear model precludes the possible feedback relationship that can exist between points in the causal sequence. Genes influence the differentiation of the gonads, which in turn produce hormones. Testes secrete a higher androgen-to-estrogen ratio, which regulates the subsequent development of the individual male. The morphology, and ostensibly the functioning, of the brain is influenced by the biochemical properties and the developmental timing of the secretion of these hormones. And the specific androgen influence on brain organization is proposed to lead to greater lateralization (regional specialization) of the brain. This hormonal-morphological specialization is presumed to underlie the male's greater average mathematical-spatial capacity.

Extensive review and criticism of this scientific explanation of capacity and the construction of sex differences has been presented by Bleier (1984). Her work on the hypothalamus, an organ critical to hormone regulation in human development over time, leads her to reject the determinism of this thought style. Her detailed examination of the literature and its reasoning uncovers repeatedly that generalizations are based less on solid research findings than on social precepts. Contradictory experimental results, unrepresentative

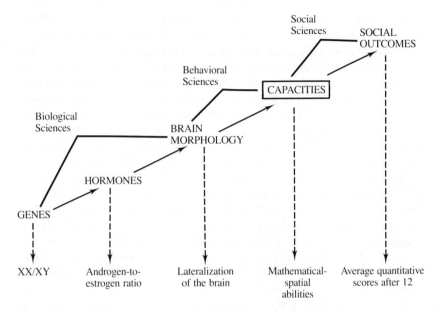

Figure 6.2 Thought style in the construction of sex differences

samples (accident victims, sexual anomalies, prisoners), partial data (single-item parameters), cross-species generalizations, and time-censored cross-sectional studies seeking to test developmental hypotheses are among the technical shortcomings widespread in this literature.

The primary theoretical issues that Bleier addresses concern nonplasticity and bias toward ascribing qualitative differences. In her research, Bleier specifically focuses on the question of nonplasticity in the relationship between hormones and brain and brain-related organ morphology. Nonplasticity refers to the theoretical assumption of fixed developmental states as opposed to more dynamic and fluid patterns of development. Her research on the hypothalamus points to a feedback process in the relationship between hypothalamus and hormone levels, both of which are continuously responsive to sensory input over time. The continuous responsivity negates the idea of fixed states. The reductionistic and deterministic bias of the dominant thought style, however, precludes this notion. Instead, it suggests that biologic sex grows out of a linear sequence of states beginning with genetic determination and continuing with genetically determined (and fixed) gonadal androgen-to-estrogen ratios that set an inevitable course for the timing and organization of brain development. Hormone mixes become fixed traits in the dominant paradigm, taking on a categorical, static character. The development consequence of fixed hormone ratios is an equally static concept of fixed brain structure.

However, even accepting that androgenic hormones play a conditioning role in brain organization, hormone ratios vary continuously—rather than discretely—between and within sex groups as well as within individuals across time and behavioral context. Accordingly, quantitative variations in hormone mix responsive to ongoing sensory inputs in the human body make the concept of a fixed state highly problematic. Bleier's recovery of this quantitative variation suggests a dynamic plasticity, not a categorical determinism.

The problematic relationship among genes, hormones, and brain morphology is recognized in the biological research community. For this reason alone, the research agenda has been set for many decades to come. Yet, the cautiousness and conservatism that leads to the recognition of this problematic relationship is abandoned when it comes to the collective belief regarding sex difference in cognition and its presumed inevitable relationship to brain organization. The (scientific) jury is still out in the case of biological proof; but the thought style prevails nevertheless.

The pivotal element in the thought style, however, is probably the most problematic concept of all. Capacities represent the real *black box* in the entire system. They are the unobservables, whose empirical referents are the scores on paper and pencil texts. Their existence is presumed by social outcomes. To construct capacities requires reference, on the one hand, to underlying causes and, on the other, to social outcomes. The idea of capacity has no meaning outside the thought style, but is derived completely from it.

An exemplary paper on capacities reveals this. Benbow and Stanley (1980) published findings on sex differences among nearly ten thousand "intellectually gifted" junior high school students between 1972 and 1979. Gauging mathematical reasoning ability by scores on the mathematics portion of the Scholastic Aptitude Test, they found that boys persisted over the period to score higher than girls, though the gap narrowed between them (from 190 points to 30 points) by the last observation year (1979). Among the concluding remarks in the two-page article was the attribution that differences in scores probably reflect the greater male spatial ability. Of course, their study was not one on ability but on outcome, so that this statement of ability derives not from their research but from the dominant thought style.

A four-year follow-up citation analysis of this paper in the social science literature (using the Social Science Citation Index for 1981 to 1984) traces the "impact" of the paper on other disciplines and interested groups. It also reveals the transmission of the "fact" produced by the Benbow-Stanley study beyond its context to a wider community. The article averaged over twelve citations annually, already more than the average annual mean of one citation for all articles referenced by the Citation Index.[5] Of the twenty-seven journals containing articles with citations to this Benbow-Stanley paper, over half were education journals, including the *American Journal of Education, Gifted Child Quarterly, Harvard Educational Review, Journal of Special Education, Journal of Educational Research,* and *Journal of Educational Psychology.*

The review of the citing articles in these journals generally repeats the pattern reflected in the *Science* issue summarized earlier. The pattern is defined by two contradictory norms of skepticism: one allows for less critical acceptance of "facts" produced outside of one's specialty and the other for greater criticism and skepticism of results obtained within one's specialty. Both norms operate comfortably (and sometimes simultaneously) within the thought style. As such, the citation patterns illustrate the centrifugal impact of the "fact" and its compatibility with prevailing expectations in other cultural and scientific spheres.

A content analysis of the citing references reveals the complex operation of the thought style of sex differences.[6] At least three patterns of relationship between "fact" and thought style emerge. One pattern reflects the skepticism of journal science, which disputes the specifics of knowledge claims made by authors (including Benbow and Stanley). Here, fully one-third of the citing references either criticize directly the Benbow-Stanley results and the thought style that gives them meaning (Brush 1982; Hirst 1982; Eckart 1982; Plake et al. 1982; Freed 1983a, b; Kimball 1981) or review the technical shortcomings of the research literature on gender and ability (or achievement), but do not always abandon explicitly the thought style (e.g., Betz and Hackett 1983; Denno 1982).

The second involves the occasional a priori strength of the thought style in the interpretation of contradictory results by researchers. One study of students' self-concepts, grades (in geometry), and gender found that gender did not significantly influence self-concept (Peterson et al. 1983). Yet the authors interpret their results by first turning to other authors, including Benbow and Stanley, to reestablish the fact that self-concept is positively associated with achievement in mathematics and that "there are more males among the highest achievers in mathematics" (Peterson et al. 1983:123). Their own results are then eclipsed by the received view of the thought style.

The third pattern—one less characteristic of the esoteric center and more characteristic of the popular periphery—is the simplistic synthesis of disparate correlations into a "fact" that draws its legitimacy wholly from the thought style rather than from any systematic research. Gowan (1984), formerly a high school mathematics teacher, argues that the associations among gender (maleness), height (tallness), and mathematics achievement (high grades in solid geometry) can be attributed to testosterone ("testicular volume"); he does not argue from evidence collected by his research but from cultural bias. He concludes his essay by drawing a parallel between teaching mathematics to women and teaching squirrels to swim or tortoises to fly (Gowan 1984:190).

CRITIQUE AND SYNTHESIS

Nearly simultaneous with the Benbow-Stanley report were other reports and reviews aligning sides in the controversy (Kolata 1980; McGlone, 1980; Jacklin 1981; Schafer and Gray 1981; Marshall 1984; Struik and Flexer 1984). And since 1980, several lines of critique of both the facticity of particular findings and the thought style that links facts to cultural precepts have developed. A feminist and a philosophical, antideterministic critique have emerged to question the facticity of sex differences and to challenge the thought style. Bleier (1984), Keller (1974, 1981, 1983a, b), and Hubbard (1982) framed the initial feminist critique. The antideterminist position, in addition, subsumes much of the feminist critique under a broader attack on reductionist science and its ideological implications for the social control of all individuals (Lowentin et al. 1984; Gould 1981). In addition, a specific line of attack within the behavioral sciences—one not tied to feminism or to the philosophy of biology—has developed to question the ontological and methodological bases of fact production regarding gender-related capacities.

One of the most influential "textbook" accounts of sex differences is the classic Maccoby and Jacklin (1974) review of the state of the sex differences literature, probably the most highly cited reference in this area. In this reference, the authors drew the conclusion that male superiority in visual-spatial tasks had been demonstrated in adolescence and adulthood, but not in childhood (p. 351). It is notable that the literature that received their most critical assessment was largely (almost entirely) composed of childhood studies. The analysis of literature on older samples is primarily secondary. Yet, this reference and its statement about male superiority has been treated repeatedly as the last word. Even the authors (see Jacklin 1981), are more tentative and critical of their own earlier statement than the wider citing community influenced by the thought style regarding sex differences that leads it to assimilate the Maccoby-Jacklin reviews to a particular position.

Critiques of this thought style are growing within the behavioral sciences. A recent review by Caplan et al. (1985) is exemplary of this critique. Generally, these reviewers demonstrate that there is indeed little consensus on the definition of capacities and, importantly, a paucity of evidence that "spatial abilities," specifically, is a legitimate construct. Like Bleier's (1984) critique (though they are not familiar with this critique), they challenge the pattern of converting small quantitative differences into categorical differences based on gender. In addition, they argue that studies not finding gender differences often go unpublished due to theoretical biases that cling to the belief in differences. Those studies that are published follow what the authors refer to as the "box score approach" to analysis on gender differences. This analytic style takes small statistical differences in gender behaviors across contexts and argues that categorical differences must exist because of the persistent pattern observed time and again. Thus, why there are no female chess masters, or few female mathematicians or physicists of great accomplishment, comes to be listed with the results of experimental studies of paper-and-pencil performances of children and young adults. Further, they systematically criticize the facticity of the results produced by several major studies claiming statistical differences. All in all, the journal science in the specialty cognitive sex differences is less tied to the belief in sex differences than are other fields such as developmental psychology or social psychology which choose to presume these differences.

Among the more important challenges to the thought style are two recent evaluations and criticisms of the gender-related "capacities" research tradition. Pleck (1981) challenged the construction of the masculinity idea in psychological research. According to Pleck, the measure of masculinity, comprising such capacities as aggression, is traceable in the modern period to the MMPI (Minnesota Multiphasic Personality Inventory) and its so-called *m-f* (male-female) scale. The scale of traits was developed, however, on a particular unrepresentative set of samples during the 1940s. The original test battery was administered to 54 male soldiers, 67 female airline attendants, and 13 homosexuals; the median years of education were eight years. Heterosexual rapists were used as a control group with whom the homosexuals were compared.

Pleck's critique, however, goes beyond a criticism of the representativeness of the samples. He argues that the *m-f* scale and later iterations of it grew out of a culturally conditioned paradigm that he believes persists to this day in the behavioral sciences. The paradigm is conditioned by cultural attitudes toward nonwhite male populations, homosexuality, and femininity. He argues that the strength of the paradigm derives less from the reliability coefficients that have accompanied many of the personality inventories than from its compatibility with prevailing cultural prejudices.

Selkow (1984) directly addresses the problem of assessing capacities by evaluating the sex bias intrinsic in items from seventy-four psychological and education tests. Her content analyses of these tests reveal sex biases in most instruments. These take several forms: (1) the relative frequency with which men and women are used in illustrations and context items; (2) the sex and age ratios of men and women to children of different genders; (3) the incidence of men and women in nonoccupation and occupation roles; (4) the incidence of men and women in stereotypical occupational roles; (5) the numbers of occupations depicted for men and women; (6) the relative numbers of references to famous men and women; (7) the assignment of stereotypical emotions, language, or dress to men and women; (8) the use of language that demeans or excludes women; and (9) the application of separate forms (and norms) for male and female test takers.

Selkow's description shows, for example, that the Wechsler Adult Intelligence Scale has more content relating to males than content relating to females and portrays females in stereotyped fashion. The Wechsler test for children is similar. The Metropolitan Achievement Tests in math tend to portray more males as adults and more females as children. Selkow has not conducted a quantitative analysis of these data, but her detailed inventory reveals the persistent cultural stereotypes in psychological and cognitive assessment inventories still in use in this country.

Both Pleck and Selkow, along with Jacklin (1981) and others (e.g., Caplan et al. 1985), are writing in response to the mushrooming literature on sex differences. But the value of their studies is more than technical. They challenge the dominant paradigm or question the thought style that promotes the construction of sex differences, despite repeated revelations of faulty measures, unrepresentative samples, and nonrobust statistics.

This line of critique is compatible with Fleck's original formulation of the power of thought styles in the construction and persistence of scientific facts. Facts do not speak for themselves, but derive their believability within larger conceptual-cultural contexts. Challenging the thought style is more difficult than demonstrating the unreliability of specific quantitative results. Yet, it is in the larger context that the scientific agenda is set.

SOCIAL BEHAVIOR AND HOLISTIC EXPLANATION

The antideterministic challenge to the construction of gender-related categories or other classification endeavors comes from the biological sciences, where the hegemonic status of molecular biology forces the issue of determinism to be viewed as problematic. Bleier's critique is antideterministic, but more explicitly feminist in focus. Gould (1981) and Lewontin et al. (1984) provide critiques with broader applicability. All three emphasize the need to conceptualize complex social behavior as a system, characterized by the interaction and mutual, though sometimes asymmetrical, influence of its elements. Biological potential and limits cannot be defined as "traits" represented by statistical—and static—norms, but rather as ongoing systems of relationships. Finally, potentials and limits cannot be reduced to more basic biological (molecular) levels, but can be understood only in relation to the elaborated social and biological contexts in which they occur.

This alternative to the dominant thought style is presented in Figure 6.3.

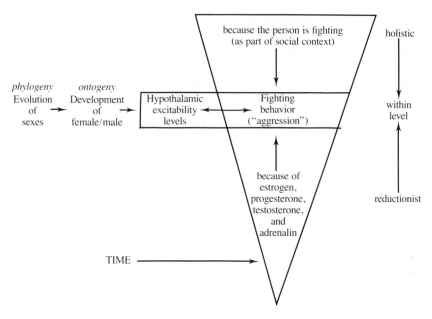

phylogeny *ontogeny*
Evolution   Development
of →   of →
sexes   female/male

Figure 6.3. O'Rand adaptation of Lewontin-Rose-Lamin model of causal explanation in biology

Here the Lewontin et al. (1984:281) illustration of causal explanation in biology is applied to the case of a complex social behavior—fighting—which is often explained in terms of an underlying capacity—aggression—said to be gender specific. The reductionist explanation for fighting behavior is aggressiveness, as this capacity is influenced episodically by hormonal levels. The alternative Bleier "explanation" can be found in the center of the scheme, where the double-headed arrow depicts the reciprocal effects over time of hypothalmic excitability levels and patterns of behavioral response to sensory inputs, such as fighting within a particular social context.

The holistic explanation requires all the elements in the system to be considered simultaneously in their relationship to each other. As such, it is a relational theory. Social behavior is not reduced to properties or to traits, but is understood as the dynamic configurations of interacting systems. Patterns and regularities can be accounted for in the scheme, but so can anomalies and irregularities.

Probably the most important feature of this alternative thought style, however, is that it is proposed as both a scientific and a cultural paradigm. As a cultural, and even political, paradigm, the feedback to the esoteric research center of science is inevitable. The debunking of the dominant thought style leads not so much to the abandonment of fruitful research in molecular biology, as to the self-conscious recognition of the relationship between cultural precept and the construction of scientific fact.

Fleck observed that the esoteric circle of the scientist and the broader cultural context interpenetrate. The scientific world view reproduces the cultural system. And in the case of the assessment of capacity it can tacitly participate in the "rank ordering of the world" (Lewontin et al. 1984) by applying the cognitive authority of science to the construction of inequality. The alternative vision that feminism brings to the biological sciences could widen significantly the questions for research—not narrow them. Unlike the dominant thought style, feminism is self-reflective, conscious of its partial vision. Such consciousness inevitably opens the search for more views, and more views are a stimulus to research.

NOTES

1 Kuhn encountered Fleck's work before publishing his provocative sociological construction of scientific change (Kuhn 1962). Yet, Fleck's account of the social embeddedness of facts and of human thought remains more radical than Kuhn's notion of paradigmatic incommensurability and conflict. Despite Kuhn's sociology of scientific community and change, his ontological position with respect to facts was steadfastly realist.

2 A recent interpretation of Fleck's analysis of the "thought collective" in the development of scientific fact is offered by Weissmann (1985). Weissmann compares some aspects of the history of the development of the Wasserman reaction, particularly how the ultimate outcome of the research (the Wasserman reaction) differed considerably from the original intentions and actions, to modern episodes in the history of science. He suggests that the discovery of the structure of DNA, for example, followed a similar developmental course with early mistaken assumptions, false experimental starts, and final hindsights embedded in collective thought styles.

3 The "relativism" of Fleck is not identical with the relativism of the "strong programme" (Bloor 1976) in the sociology of science and related philosophies. Instead, his version of relativism is one of embeddedness rather than of epiphenomenon. The latter is clearly an oversocialized view; the former is one that permits boundaries between science as practice and culture as content.

4 Nonrecursivity is a property of the objective relationship between culture and science. It should not be confused with the more subjective notion of reflectivity.

5 According to Eugene Garfield, Director of the Institute for Scientific Information, which produces the science citation indices, the average paper in the Science Citation Index is cited about ten times over ten years. This means that the majority of papers are cited far less frequently.

6 This analysis was aided by the independent review of these materials by Laurie de

Freeze (1986), whose participation in the Study of Mathematically Precocious Youth, on which Benbow and Stanley based their work, provided valuable insight into the study.

WORKS CITED

BENBOW, C., and J. STANLEY
  1980   Sex Differences in Mathematical Ability: Fact or Artifact? *Science* 210: 1262–64.

BETZ, N. E., and G. HACKETT
  1983   The Relationship of Mathematics Self-Efficiency Expectations to the Selection of Science-based College Majors. *Journal of Vocational Behavior* 23:329–45.

BLEIER, R.
  1984   *Science and Gender: A Critique of Biology and Its Theories on Women.* New York: Pergamon Press.

BLOOR, D.
  1976   *Knowledge and Social Imagery.* London: Routledge and Kegan Paul.

BOURDIEU, P.
  1975   The Specificity of the Scientific Field and the Social Conditions of the Progress of Reason. *Social Science Information* 14:19–47.

BOURDIEU, P., and J. C. PASSERON
  1977   *Reproduction in Education, Society, and Culture.* Beverly Hills, Calif.: Sage.
  1979   *The Inheritors: French Students and Their Relation to Culture.* Chicago: University of Chicago Press.

BOURDIEU, P., and M. DE SAINT MARTIN
  1974   Scholastic Excellence and the Values of the Educational System. In *Contemporary Research in the Sociology of Education,* edited by J. Eggleston, pp. 338–71. London: Methuen.

BRUSH, L.
  1982   Review of *Women and Mathematical Mystique,* edited by L. H. Fox, L. Brody, and D. Tobin. *Harvard Educational Review* 52:105–8.

CAPLAN, P. J., G. M. MACPHERSON, and P. TOBIN
  1985   Do Sex-Related Differences in Spatial Abilities Exist: A Multilevel Critique with New Data. *American Psychologist* 40:786–99.

DE FREEZE, L.
  1986   Reaction to the Benbow-Stanley Study. Research paper, Duke University.

DENNO, D.
  1982   Sex Differences in Cognition: A Review and Critique of the Longitudinal Evidence. *Adolescence* 68:779–88.

DIMAGGIO, P.
  1979   Review Essay: On Pierre Bourdieu. *American Journal of Sociology* 84: 1460–73.

ECKART, D. R.
    1982   Microprocessors, Women and Future Employment Opportunities. *International Journal of Women's Studies* 5:47–57.
EHRHARDT, A. A., and H. F. L. MEYER-BAHLBURG
    1981   Effects of Prenatal Sex Hormones on Gender-related Behavior. *Science* 211:1312–317.
FLECK, L.
    1979   *Genesis and Development of a Scientific Fact.* Chicago: University of Chicago Press.
FREED, N. H.
    1983a   Forseeably Equivalent Math Skills of Men and Women. *Psychological Reports* 52:334.
    1983b   Prospective Mathematical Equivalency by Gender. *Psychological Reports* 53:677–78.
GOULD, S. J.
    1981   *The Mismeasure of Man.* New York: W. W. Norton and Co.
GOWAN, J. C.
    1984   Spatial Ability and Testosterone. *Journal of Creative Behavior* 18: 187–90.
HIRST, G.
    1982   An Evaluation of Evidence for Innate Sex Differences in Linguistic Ability. *Journal of Psycholinguistic Ability* 11:95–112.
HUBBARD, R.
    1982   The Theory and Practice of Genetic Reductionism—From Mendel's Laws to Genetic Engineering. In *Towards a Liberatory Biology,* edited by S. Rose. London: Allison and Busby.
JACKLIN, D.
    1981   Methodological Issues in the Study of Sex-related Differences. *Developmental Review* 1:266–73.
KELLER, E. F.
    1974   Women in Science: An Analysis of a Social Problem. *Harvard Magazine* (October):14–19.
    1981   Women and Science: Two Cultures or One? *International Journal of Women's Studies* 4:414–19.
    1983a   *A Feeling for the Organism: The Life and Work of Barbara McClintock.* San Francisco: Freeman, Cooper and Co.
    1983b   Women, Science and Popular Mythology. In *Machina ex Dea,* edited by J. Rothschild, pp. 130–50. New York: Pergamon Press.
KIMBALL, M. M.
    1981   Women and Science: A Critique of Biological Theories. *International Journal of Women's Studies* 4:318–33.
KOLATA, G.
    1980   Math and Sex: Are Girls Born with Less Ability? *Science* 210:1234–235.
KUHN, T. S.
    1962   *The Structure of Scientific Revolutions.* Chicago: University of Chicago Press.

LEWONTIN, R. C., S. ROSE, and L. J. KAMIN
  1984   *Not in Our Genes: Biology, Ideology and Human Nature.* New York: Pantheon Books.
MACCOBY, E. E., and C. N. JACKLIN
  1974   *The Psychology of Sex Differences.* Stanford, Calif.: Stanford University Press.
MARSHALL, S. P.
  1984   Sex Differences in Children's Mathematics Achievement: Solving Computations and Story Problems. *Journal of Educational Psychology* 76: 194–204.
MCGLONE, J.
  1980   Sex Difference in Human Brain Asymmetry: A Critical Survey. *Behavior and Brain Sciences* 3: 215–63.
NAFTOLIN, F., and E. BUTZ, eds.
  1981   *Sexual Dimorphism.* Special issue of *Science* 211: 1263–321.
PETERSON, K., G. BURTON and D. BAKER
  1983   Geometry Students' Role-specific Self-Concept: Success, Teacher and Sex Differences. *Journal of Educational Research* 77: 122–26.
PLAKE, B. S., C. J. ANSORGE, C. S. PARKER, and S. R. LOWRY
  1982   Effects of Item Arrangement, Knowledge of Arrangement, Test Anxiety and Sex on Test Performance. *Journal of Educational Measurement* 19: 336–42.
PLECK, J.
  1981   *The Myth of Masculinity.* Cambridge, Mass.: MIT Press.
SCHAFER, A., and M. GRAY
  1981   Sex and Mathematics. *Science* 211: 229.
SELKOW, P.
  1984   *Assessing Sex Bias in Testing: A Review of the Issues and Evaluations of 74 Psychological and Educational Tests.* Westport, Conn.: Greenwood Press.
STRUIK, R. R., and R. J. FLEXER
  1984   Sex Differences in Mathematical Achievement: Adding Data to Debate. *International Journal for Women's Studies* 7: 336–42.
WEISSMANN, G.
  1985   *The Woods Hole Cantata: Essays on Science and Society.* Boston: Houghton Mifflin Co.

CHAPTER 7

And Justice for All? Human Nature and the Feminist Critique of Liberalism

KATHRYN JACKSON

Contemporary feminist theory poses a challenge to the tradition of liberal political thought. This tradition, with its assumed values of liberty, equality, and justice for all, is the dominant perspective (or, some might say, ideology) in Western political theory and practice. More than any other perspective, liberalism has structured the basic terms in which our political ideals, conflicts, and values are defined. This is so despite the fact that, historically, liberal theories presupposed the exclusion of women from the political or so-called public sphere. It was assumed that women were more appropriately situated within the domestic or private sphere, and this was largely beyond the scope of legal or political intervention. Justice for all was in fact justice for men only—for only they were deemed capable of holding equal rights and political liberties.

Feminist theory was born of this tradition when early feminists, such as Mary Wollstonecraft, Harriet Taylor, and John Stuart Mill, recognized that a genuine commitment to the central values of liberalism required that the rights of equal citizenship be extended to women just as much as to men.[1] They objected not so much to the theory of liberalism or its assumed values as to its inequitable application and unjustified exclusion of women from the world of politics. Similar assumptions have motivated the thought of more recent liberal feminists. For example, Betty Friedan and the philosopher Janet Radcliffe Richards assume, along with the early feminists, that justice for all is possible if only the central liberal values and principles are properly extended to women through the mechanism of legally protected rights.[2] According to this

*Research for this article was generously supported by a research leave provided by Duke University during the 1986–87 academic year.

view, the main problem with traditional liberalism is simply that it has excluded women. Liberal feminists argue, however, that this problem can be readily corrected by recognizing the fundamental equality between women and men, and by including women fully within the scope of politics.

Although liberal feminism is prevalent in the world of political action—it is assumed, for example, by the activities of groups like NOW (National Organization of Women), and NARAL (National Abortion Rights Action League)—it is no longer favored in the theoretical writings of contemporary feminists. While these writers adopt a wide range of theoretical perspectives, and though their writings can be distinguished into a variety of categories (such as Marxist, socialist, radical, psychoanalytic, and postmodern),[3] they nonetheless share a fundamental belief regarding the incompatibility of liberalism and feminism. They generally assume that the theoretical perspective defined by liberalism is incapable of accommodating the ideals and goals of feminism, regardless of how these are defined. While contemporary feminist scholars admit that liberal feminism was an important stage in the development of a feminist consciousness and in the achievement of political status for women,[4] they nonetheless argue that it is not now possible to be both a feminist and a liberal. Alison Jaggar's claim that "liberal feminism contains contradictions that threaten ultimately to shatter its own philosophical foundations,"[5] reflects this widely held view.

The particular reasons for rejecting liberal feminism are varied, and differ in general terms according to the theoretical assumptions of the writer. The Marxist feminist will, for example, have specific reasons for rejecting liberalism which are different from those offered by the psychoanalytically oriented feminist. Nonetheless, some strands of criticism cut across the various theoretical perspectives. One of the most fundamental of these focuses on liberal assumptions about human nature. It is argued that every liberal theory depends upon a conception of human nature which is at best a conception of the nature of men (or perhaps of some men) only. Women cannot therefore be included within the scope of politics defined by liberalism, because its most fundamental assumptions are irrelevant to their experience. The male bias of liberal theory is considered to be so fundamental that it cannot be corrected. And hence, liberal feminism is viewed as an untenable position.

The critique is not just historical but is conceptual as well. While it is true that liberal theories have traditionally assumed a biased conception of human nature, this does not in itself show theoretical incompatibility between liberalism and feminism. To show this, it is necessary to establish that no liberal theory could be developed without these unacceptable assumptions about human nature.

The purpose of this chapter is to examine some of the central elements of the feminist critique of the liberal conception of human nature, and to consider the extent to which the conceptual case against liberalism is thereby established. Is there really an inevitable contradiction between the liberal and the feminist perspectives, or are there ways in which liberal theory can respond to the feminist critique without losing its liberal character? This question motivates the discussion that follows.

Three liberal assumptions about human nature are most objectionable from the feminist perspective. These are rationality, psychological egoism, and abstract individualism. As conceived in the context of liberal theory, these are closely related and may even be mutually dependent. Each will be considered here in turn. Since the critique involves not just an examination of the human nature claims but also the way in which these structure liberal theory, the theoretical significance of each supposedly human characteristic is also considered.

RATIONALITY

In historical theories of liberalism the exclusion of women from the political world was often justified by reference to their assumed deficiencies regarding rationality. The capacity to reason was regarded as the primary criterion for citizenship status, and was assumed to be the basis on which men alone were fit for moral and political activity. By virtue of their reason, men could rise above and control nature. But by virtue of their reproductive capacities, women were assumed to be less rational than men—closer to nature, and hence, like the rest of nature, more liable to the control of rational men.[6] The inferiority of women was therefore considered to be a biological rather than a social fact, and the significance of this assumption in the specification of the human good is significant.

For men as rational beings the realization of the good requires moral and political interaction. Women, however, are deemed to lack precisely those qualities necessary for full participation in the public or political world. Therefore only men are suited for citizenship. In their private lives—in those aspects of life considered immune from state intervention or direction—each man is considered sovereign. Thus in the ideal world, every man is quite literally king of his family, and only he has political status or rights.[7]

The liberal notion that all citizens have equal rights is grounded in the more basic assumption of rationality. As Jaggar has pointed out,

The fundamental moral values of liberalism are predicated on the assumption that all individuals have an equal potential for reason. This assumption is the basis of liberalism's central moral belief in the intrinsic and ultimate value of the individual.[8]

Thus, for the liberal, the equal rights of citizenship reflect in the political sphere the assumed equality of all with respect to their capacity for reason.

The liberal argument moves from an assumed natural equality to the moral notion of respect for the worth of each individual, and from there to the political notion that each person is due the legal protection of the equal rights of citizenship.[9]

On the face of it, there appears to be no deep problem with this argument. Liberal feminists have assumed it is structurally valid, but can be made sound if only the rationality of women is recognized. From this the fundamental liberal concern for the equal rights of all would no longer apply to men only, but to everyone.

Contemporary feminists object that the underlying conception of rationality cannot and should not be universalized, and hence cannot be used as the basis for extending liberal equality to women. According to Sandra Harding, "Substituting 'A person is a rational animal' for 'Man is a rational animal' systematically and seriously distorts both the intended and achieved reference and meaning of such claims."[10]

An examination of the concept of rationality from the feminist perspective offers some strong reasons for doubting that we can universalize the liberal notion of the rational man. The first involves the idea that liberalism relies on a mistaken metaphysical assumption about mind/body dualism. Since, as Jaggar notes, "contemporary liberalism is not committed to an explicitly dualistic metaphysics,"[11] we need not consider this objection here. What is more important is the assumption of what Jaggar calls normative dualism, "according to which liberals tend to place the highest value on those activities which they perceive as requiring the most use of reason."[12]

This does not in itself constitute a specifically feminist objection; similar points have been made by philosophers who are not especially concerned with gender.[13] The important point for the feminist is that this normative dualism is either based on or promotes judgments about the inferiority or deficiencies of women. Thus, the activities that are most valued because they are most rational tend to be associated more with men than with women.

The liberal tradition has relied on conceptions of morality which value rational behavior above all else. Actions motivated by love, concern, or care for particular others are judged to be morally inferior to those based on rational considerations defined in terms of rights and duties, or by reference to principles of justice. The metaphysical assumption of mind/body dualism is played out, in the moral sphere, in terms of a dichotomy between the morality of justice and that of care.

While past thinkers have simply assumed that women were in fact morally inferior, some recent research might appear to justify the assumption. In his research on moral psychology, Lawrence Kohlberg distinguished six stages of moral development, the highest of which is defined by its rational basis and its focus on a conception of justice as fairness. While Kohlberg claimed that few, if any, people have actually reached stage 6, he found also that men tend to "score higher" than do women.[14] In other words, Kohlberg found that men tend to respond rationally to moral dilemmas more than women do, and that this indicates not just a gender difference but a difference in terms of moral competence. And this is precisely what has been assumed historically by liberal philosophers.

Carol Gilligan, a former colleague of Kohlberg's, also found gender differentiation in moral psychology; like Kohlberg she found that women tend to view moral dilemmas in terms of care and concern for others, while men are more likely to focus on abstract considerations of justice. However, Gilligan argues that the different voice of women is not at all inferior to that of men, but is just a different way of viewing the world and the moral situations in it.[15] Gilligan suggests that the scope of morality should be extended so as to include the very different moral psychology of women, and hence a morality of care should be developed alongside the morality of justice. Thus, if Gilligan is right, to take seriously the psychology of women involves a devaluing of the role that reason has always played in the liberal tradition, and a greater valuing of the moral aspects of care and attachment.[16] However, since liberal theory is determined just by reference to rights, duties, and principles of justice, it is not clear how it could accommodate this broader conception of ethics, which would no longer be marred by an exclusive reliance on a specifically male notion of rationality.

There is a further problem with the normative dualism that Jaggar describes. She points out that the liberal notion of rationality justifies ideals of independence and autonomy, but she claims that these are at odds with the feminist ideals of nurturing, cooperation, and interdependence. These latter values are grounded in the experience of women who live more explicitly within cooperative contexts and who are more frequently motivated by love and commitments to particular people.[17] This view of female experience is supported by research such as Gilligan's, and by studies in gender theory according to which gender emerges from the early, pre-Oedipal relationship between a child and her primary care giver—who is usually a woman. According to this view, gender is determined by social conditions and relations which are, in theory, changeable. Furthermore, the female propensity for nurturing and care is grounded in the specific relationship between mothers and daughters, who in the development of their gender and self-identities do not separate and detach themselves from the mother to the extent that boys do. According to this view, the ideals of autonomy and independence are more fully grounded in the experience of men who developed their identities by just such a detachment and separation.[18] To the extent that liberalism ignores the ideals of nurturance and interdependence, it is therefore irrelevant to the experience of women.

A related objection to the liberal's reliance on rationality is that according to some, women have a distinctive style of thought and of rationality. For example, Sara Ruddick argues that mothers have a distinctive style of thought which is grounded in the particularities and concreteness of their concern for children.[19] Sandra Harding also argues that there are female conceptions of rationality and of the rational person which are incompatible with liberal justice. She takes the point one step further, however, and argues that gender itself is a variable in determining the various conceptions of rationality.[20] Thus, as Genevieve Lloyd argues, ideals of rationality are based on a conception of gender and help structure gender itself. Lloyd writes, "An exclusion or transcending of the feminine is built into past ideals of Reason as the sovereign human character trait . . . [and] the content of femininity has been partly formed by such processes of exclusion."[21]

If this is so, we have strong grounds for questioning why one conception of rationality should be favored over any other, or why any particular conception should be assumed to be the most "natural" or appropriate for everyone. Yet liberalism does seem to make such assumptions, and the liberal feminist is thus confronted with what seems to be a dilemma. To adopt the liberal perspective, she must quite literally "think like a man"—but this involves compromising her specifically female perspective. And apparently, to the extent that she pursues ideals grounded in her experience as a woman, the feminist should leave behind the liberal perspective.

This dilemma may be more apparent than real, however. The liberal and the feminist conceptions of rationality appear to be mutually incompatible; however, if it is the case that each mode of rationality is appropriate for only certain kinds of moral situations, then the dilemma can be resolved. In other words, the dilemma appears only if we assume that the entire moral landscape could be properly determined just by reference to any one of the various conceptions of rationality, for then a conflict arises among competing conceptions. But if the relevant scope of each is limited, no such conflict need arise.

Liberalism takes questions of justice to be most fundamental. Political theory is thus viewed as being primarily concerned with the determination of principles which should guide interaction among rational agents when they would otherwise come into conflict. The mistake of liberalism, clearly pointed to by critics like Jaggar, is to assume that all important interaction would dissolve into conflict without the order provided by principles of justice. This mistake is based on a failure to recognize that many meaningful and important interactions are motivated by particular concerns, commitments, and loyalties and are based on ideals of cooperation, trust, and interdependence. Liberal theorists tend to ignore these ideals, and assume that the model of "rational man" who is bound to conflict with others has universal application. Liberals are correct to recognize that interactions based on personal commitment, loyalty, or love are neither susceptible to assessment by abstract principles of justice nor motivated by universal rules of rationality. They are mistaken in assuming these interactions are therefore outside the scope of moral and political philosophy. The cooperative ideals embraced within the private sphere are central to the living of the "good life" and to the sustenance of the state, and must have a place in any adequate vision of the ideal society.[22] Liberal principles are clearly inadequate for determining every aspect of this ideal.

It does not follow from this that there would be no space for liberal values in an ideal society. Principles of justice may well be an effective means for resolving situations of conflict—and while not every important human interaction would be so marked in the absence of justice, it is naive to think that all interaction can be restructured in terms of cooperation and interdependence. The so-called "circumstances of justice"—that is, circumstances in which questions of justice are relevant—can arise from time to time even for those who are basically cooperative, altruistic, and good-willed. Conflict can arise in a world of altruists just as much as in a world of egoists, and principles for regulating "who gets what" may be needed even there. The important point is that principles of justice can be helpful in those situations where conflict arises. Principles of justice are not needed in all situations, but they may be needed for some. The liberal vision is limited, but it is not therefore without merit. Thus, what theorists like Jaggar view as a conflict between the feminist ideals of nurturing and interdependence on the one hand and the liberal ideals of rational independence and autonomy on the other can be viewed as a challenge for feminist theory: Can we develop a new theory, based on feminist ideals, that can accommodate the insights of liberalism? Can we define the limits of each ideal so as to develop a theoretical whole that encompasses both? Or are they indeed incompatible, as the feminist assumes?

An examination of the ways in which both justice and care are relevant to the development of moral psychology is helpful here. When, for example, we teach a child to share or to wait her turn, we are both teaching the rudiments of justice and encouraging a concern for the needs of others. Annette Baier has argued that we can develop a sense of justice only if we have first developed a sense of trust, which can itself develop only within the context of a caring environment.[23] Baier is thus challenging the liberal assumption that "justice is the first virtue of social institutions."[24] But similarly, to develop a genuine attitude of care and concern for others, one also needs to have a sense that one will be treated fairly by others. A person who feels that her needs and interests are rarely considered to be as important as those of others may have a hard time developing a sense of genuine caring for others. Thus an adequate conception of moral psychology would have to recognize the mutual dependence of both the affective and the rational elements, and of the relationship between the psychology of care and that of justice. A conception of ethics based just on considerations of care would therefore also be marred by a normative dualism that undervalued considerations of justice.

It is easy to slide from the observation of a gender-based "division of labor" in the world of morality and politics to the claim that the masculine ideals are of no relevance to women, or in some way distort the female experience. This conclusion involves an unjustified overgeneralization however. Even those, such as Gilligan, who study gender difference recognize that there is no sharp dichotomy between the moral psychologies of men and women. Their claim is rather that women tend to use considerations of care, nurturance, and interdependence more frequently than do men, but they do not suggest that women never adopt the justice perspective. Furthermore, even Gilligan suggests that certain kinds of situations which highlight conflict, such as that described in the Heinz dilemma, elicit the highest number of justice responses among both men and women.[25] (According to this dilemma, Heinz must decide whether to steal a drug needed to save his wife's life from an avaricious pharmacist who refuses to sell it at a fair price.) This tends to support the suggestion made earlier, that considerations of justice might sometimes be most appropriate. It poses another challenge for both feminism and liberalism, namely, not just to determine how justice and care are interdependent, but also to specify the socially important interactions for which only one or the other perspective is more appropriate. Just as it would be inappropriate for a mother to view all of her interactions with her children as obligations she owes, it is similarly inappropriate for a woman, victimized by unrelenting sexual harassment at work, to be more concerned with the motivations of her tormentor than with her own rights.

The feminist critique of rationality provides strong reasons for rejecting the liberal's assumption regarding the primacy of justice, but it does not provide sufficient grounds for denying that rationality is of value to women, or that justice is of some importance to political theory. Neither does it establish the priority of care and nurturance. In fact, Lloyd has argued that since the moral psychology of women is determined by a social environment which is itself of questionable worth, we should be cautious regarding the validity of the resulting moral ideals. She writes,

The idea that women have their own distinctive kind of intellectual or moral character has itself been partly formed within the philosophical tradition to which it may now appear to be a reaction. . . . The affirmation of the value and importance of "the feminine" cannot of itself be expected to shake the underlying normative structures, for ironically, it will occur in a space already prepared for it by the intellectual tradition it seeks to reject.[26]

The critique of rationality is not itself sufficient to show a fundamental inconsistency between liberalism and feminism. It can be viewed as a challenge to develop a theory which is more closely determined by the moral psychology of men and women. The resulting theory could still have a significant liberal component, but would also be feminist in its fundamental concerns.

PSYCHOLOGICAL EGOISM

Critics of liberalism might still object that the liberal perspective is incompatible with feminism. Jaggar, for example, is concerned about the relationship
between what she describes as neutrality regarding its citizens' various conceptions of the good, and an assumed agnosticism regarding questions of morality. The former is indeed a central feature of liberal theory, and is taken to
reflect the proper role of the state toward issues of morality in a pluralistic and
democratic society. According to Jaggar, this feature of liberal theory depends
on a conception of rationality defined just in terms of the pursuit of already
given ends. The underlying conception of human nature involves an assumption of psychological egoism according to which people will pursue their own
ends and take no special interest in the interests of others. This leads to a conception of rationality according to which it is rational to pursue these ends,
whatever they happen to be, but there is no independent standard by which to
assess the relative merit of various ends. According to Jaggar, the thesis of
psychological egoism and the related conception of rationality are needed to
justify the liberal's commitment to moral agnosticism which itself justifies
state neutrality.

What worries Jaggar here is not so much the validity of the assumption of
psychological egoism or of the conception of rationality but rather the moral
consequences of that assumption.[27] Jaggar argues that feminist theory requires
an ideal or objective conception of the good, according to which we do have
grounds on which to criticize the conceptions of the good that people happen
to have.[28] This ideal conception is needed, for example, to criticize gender-
specific socialization and education, and to object to the practice of pornogra-
phy; it is needed also to understand the "happy housewife" phenomenon, so
puzzling to many feminists and to explain why, if all women are oppressed,
they are not all feminists.[29] Jaggar argues that concepts such as "false consciousness" and "alienation" are required here. One need not adopt specifically Marxist notions to see the importance for feminists of a theory of the
good that does not take given desires as alone constitutive of the human good.
If, as Jaggar suggests, such an ideal theory is incompatible with liberalism,
then we must abandon the project of sustaining liberal and feminist ideals
together.[30]

We should first note that agnosticism regarding the human good need not be
wholeheartedly adopted by liberal theorists. In at least some places, John
Stuart Mill rejects Bentham's earlier assumption that "pushpin is as good as
poetry." Mill suggests instead that certain activities are better than others, that
in the determination of social utility, we must consider the "quality" as well
as the "quantity" of various practices, and that a love of the "higher goods"
should be fostered through education and experience.[31] Although Mill may
have been mistaken in identifying the higher goods with those that are more

intellectually challenging, the point is that he was not totally skeptical in this regard. His theory of the good contains ideal elements even though he advocated extensive state neutrality regarding the individual's pursuit of her or his own conception of the good. Thus a liberal might argue that no one's good is ever realized through subservient, slavish, or demeaning activities even if some people (such as many women) happen to have such desires. If so, the alleged incompatibility between feminism and liberalism in terms of its assumed theory of the good has not been established.

To show this incompatibility, Jaggar suggests that the liberal commitment to state neutrality cannot be maintained unless a skeptical view of the good is assumed. Her argument can be reconstructed as follows. Liberalism assumes that each person is worthy of basic moral respect. This is reflected, in the political world, by the assurance that each person will be able to pursue his or her ends without state interference, so long as this pursuit imposes no harm on others. She argues further that the assumption of moral equality is itself based on the notion of rationality, according to which it is rational to pursue one's given ends, whatever they happen to be. If rationality were defined by reference to an ideal conception of the good, then it would be rational to pursue only those ends one *should* have. But if this idea were adopted, there would be no way to support the liberal assumption of equality, for not all individuals are equally committed to the ideal good, and not all would be equally rational in their pursuit of ends. This notion of rationality and of an ideal conception of the good entails the unequal treatment of people, for some people would then be coerced to behave in ways consistent with the ideal good. The liberal commitment to state neutrality cannot be maintained, therefore, if an ideal theory of the good is assumed.

One way to respond to these objections is to reconsider the connection between this conception of rationality and the liberal assumption of moral equality. Perhaps it is possible to ground this assumption in a way that is compatible with an ideal theory of the good, and that serves nonetheless to support the liberal commitment to state neutrality. Thus rationality would be dissociated from its traditionally assumed connection with the notion of moral equality.

Our rational capacity is morally relevant insofar as we are considered to be moral agents—as persons who, in our activity, have an effect on others and who can act for the sake of morally relevant reasons. Very young children are not yet full moral agents in this sense, and historically the status of moral agent has been denied to women. Jaggar's objections to the notion of rationality focuses on its connection with moral agency. Hence, if her objections hold, the notion of moral equality which is thereby grounded, is also deficient. According to Jaggar, we must all be assumed to be equally rational in our pursuit of our own ends if we are all to be treated as equally worthy of moral respect.[32]

Jaggar has a good point here. I would argue, however, that there is a more

fundamental conception of moral equality often overlooked by liberal theorists. Not only is this alternative account compatible with liberalism, but it is
also consistent with an ideal theory of the good. It might therefore also be
acceptable to the feminist. This alternative notion of moral equality focuses
not on our ability to act as moral agents but rather on our capacity to be the
recipients of moral treatment. We can all—male or female, young or old,
black or white—be benefited or harmed by others, and how we are treated by
others matters a great deal to all of us. It is assumed here that we all have
purposes, goals, or conceptions of the good that we identify as our own, and
that it makes a difference to us whether or not we realize our goals. We can
suffer physical and emotional pain when others prevent us from pursuing our
ends, or when they treat us as if these ends are irrelevant, stupid, or unimpor-
tant. According to this view, we all have the desire and need for others to
respect our basic goals and conception of the good because these are intimately connected with our sense of self. To deny that a person's fundamental
conception of the good is of any value, even to her, is tantamount to denying
that the person who identifies herself with this conception of the good is of
any worth. Thus the moral perspective would require that, as moral agents,
we recognize and respect each person as someone who has a point of view and
a set of goals, ends, etc., that matter fundamentally to her. Accordingly,
moral equality could be derived from our status as the recipients of moral
treatment, rather than as agents.[33] It is thus possible to ground a liberal conception of moral equality without relying on any notion of rationality—and
the feminist objection to moral equality which assumes that it must presuppose that notion is therefore not applicable. Jaggar is correct to the extent that
she is objecting to theories, such as contractarianism, which may well require
an assumption of psychological egoism and instrumental rationality. However
it might be possible to develop a liberal theory which did not contain the of-
fensive assumption.

The question to consider now is how the liberal principle of state neutrality
could be justified by reference to this nonrational conception of moral equality. Jaggar argues that the political principle can be justified only if the liberal
assumes an agnosticism regarding the good. She argues also that it requires
the thesis of abstract individualism—yet this is one further assumption unacceptable to feminists. In the next section, we will examine the notion of abstract individualism, and its relationship to moral goodness, on the one hand,
and state neutrality on the other.

ABSTRACT INDIVIDUALISM

Feminist critics might object to the notion of moral equality developed here on
the grounds that it relies on the plausibility of some form of abstract individu-

alism. Thus it shares with traditional conceptions of liberalism a thesis about human nature which feminists find unacceptable.

Liberalism presupposes that individuals can be meaningfully considered in abstraction from the social, political, and historical networks within which they each in fact exist, and as individuals who are significantly distinct from one another. The state of nature, so familiar within the liberal tradition, is occupied not by real people, but rather by hypothetical individuals who maintain no special connection to or interest in one another, who have no special place in history, and who supposedly have no gender, race, or class membership. The state of nature does not describe any actual state of affairs. It is a hypothetical world occupied by hypothetical individuals who, if left to their own devices, will come into conflict with one another as they pursue their own courses of action. Rules are therefore needed to regulate interaction, and these are the principles of justice.[34]

What constitutes the good for individuals so conceived? Every liberal theory embodies some conception of the good, as determined by reference to an assumed theory of human nature. That which is good must be good for the people involved. Hobbes maintained that the good is simply the satisfaction of a person's desires, wants, or goals, whatever these happen to be. This leads to an agnosticism regarding the good, for there is no external criterion apart from the desires that people have, by which to say that one conception of the good is more worthy than any other. Some form of moral agnosticism is generally shared by liberals, and the political consequence of holding this view is obvious: the state must remain neutral in its treatment of individuals in their pursuit of what they take to be their own good. If any conception of the good is favored, some citizens will sustain an unfair burden while others will receive an undeserved advantage. Where this occurs, the basic moral equality of individuals is not adequately respected by the political structure, and a basic element of the liberal's own case is lost.

However, feminists object that the very notion of abstract individualism, on which the case for state neutrality rests, is untenable. For example, Jaggar argues that "it is a conceptual as well as an empirical truth that human interests are acquired only in a social context and that it is therefore meaningless to talk about individuals in abstraction from the social nexus of which they are necessarily a part."[35] And Naomi Scheman points out that even our basic psychological concepts are interdependent and acquired within the context of socially determined meanings. To think we can conceive of people in the abstract and as distinct from one another is simply false.[36] Although this objection is similar to objections made generally by other communitarian critics of liberalism,[37] feminists focus on the way in which liberalism fails to take into account the central role that families and other social relations based on particular interactions have on the formulation of our motivational structure; and that these kinds of social interactions are determined more by the activities and concerns of women than by those of men.

We can, however, distinguish between the way in which desires, conceptions of the good, etc., are acquired within a social context and the result of that process, namely, an individual who has a distinctive or unique point of view which she calls her own and with which she identifies. Even if we make the radical assumption that all basic desires and preferences are socially determined, it is never the case that two different people have identical experiences and socialization. We are all the product of a multitude of determining experiences, and at some point it is true to say that an individual with a distinct point of view has emerged. Even if individuals are socially determined, each develops a unique point of view, and it is from this perspective that the notion of moral equality, as described above, can be grounded.[38] To treat people as if their emergent identity is without merit is to treat them as if they too are worthless. The assumption of fundamental moral equality remains plausible, despite the feminist objection, and would require that all who have a unique set of preferences be treated with moral respect.

The above argument addresses only one aspect of the feminist critique, however; it addresses only the objection to the assumption of individualism. Feminists also point out that the elements of abstraction, so crucial to liberalism, are at odds with female experience, which is fundamentally determined by concrete relationships and specific interactions. However, the objection loses some force if we accept that liberal standards are relevant only within a limited range of human interactions—only where, for example, the possibility of conflict remains salient. Where differences can be resolved by means of cooperation and mutual concern, the female perspective might well be most effective—for such resolutions often require greater, rather than less sensitivity to the particularities of each person's situation. However, these are not cases in which liberal justice and its assumed values are relevant. Where it makes more sense to resolve differences in terms of fairness and principles of justice, it may well also be appropriate to abstract away the irresolvable differences, and to view the situation in terms of that which is common. And if there are no commonalties at all—neither concrete nor abstract—there would be little chance for any interaction.

We are, however, confronted with an important limitation of liberalism; not everyone has a developed set of preferences and desires, and about these people (young children, especially) liberalism can have little to say. It does not follow from this that the notion of moral equality should be rejected. Indeed, great evils have occurred because people have been treated as if they are worthless. The liberal assumption of equal moral worth is an important one to maintain, but we need to explore the implications of this assumption for the treatment of children who are in the process of acquiring a determinate identity.

It is at this point that we can use an ideal theory of the good to guide us.

Liberals might assume that they should adopt an attitude of neutrality regarding what children learn and how they are socialized. However, if liberalism need not presuppose agnosticism regarding the good, then children—who are in the process of developing a perspective of their own—can be socialized in light of an ideal theory of the good.

This would avoid the element of circularity which Jaggar finds in traditional liberalism. She argues that the worth of particular liberal ideals has been justified by reference to the desires of individuals, yet these desires are inevitably determined by the status quo. Thus she claims that liberalism is constantly self-justifying.[39] If it is permissible to adopt a different perspective for the process of socialization, the circle could be broken. Given the way liberalism has thus far been characterized, there is no obvious objection to this approach to the education and socialization of children. If there is any objection to the social recognition and favoring of a particular conception of the good over other conceptions, the objection can be relevant only with respect to adults. The liberal restrictions on the treatment of adults do not necessarily extend, without modification, to our treatment of children.

The liberal commitment to moral equality is an important value, but its implications have yet to be defined fully. On the one hand, I suggest it is possible to advocate an ideal conception of the good, and that we can and should promote this good in our socialization of children. Indeed this already occurs; we now assume some ideal theory of the good regarding what is permissible or required in the education of children. From the feminist perspective, this would mean that we encourage nonsexist and nonracist attitudes in our children. Yet there are many adults who blatantly assert that women are less than equal to men. The notion of moral equality developed here requires that their views somehow be respected in the political sphere, that they not be prohibited from stating their views publicly. To prohibit public expression of their views is not so much a denial of the stated position, which can be done explicitly in response to their statements, as it is a fundamental denial of *them* as persons with a perspective that matters to them. It is to treat them as if they are children who have not yet developed a distinct perspective. Because they are no longer children and because they already have a unique identity, it would be wrong for the state to ignore them or treat them as if their views did not matter. To try to show others that they are mistaken does not violate their moral equality but in fact shows respect for them. To silence them does not. Thus an argument for state neutrality can be made while adopting an ideal theory of the good and while insisting that these ideals should guide us in our interactions with children. The need for state neutrality can be explained by reference to liberal principles of justice, but the justification of the ideal theory of the good does not fall within the scope of liberalism. Furthermore, it is a mistake to view the socialization of children as a question of justice, and hence this too is an issue which falls outside the scope of liberal political theory.

It is with respect to questions such as these, which clearly fall outside the relevant scope of liberalism, that feminist considerations are of central importance.

Many questions certainly need to be addressed in formulating the relation between liberalism and feminist theory. For example, one might argue that state neutrality is not maintained if it is permissible to adopt an ideal theory of the good in the education of children. This objection fails to take into account the limits of liberal ideals and commitments. State neutrality must be sustained with respect to those who are the subjects of the assumed moral equality. According to the account developed here, it need not extend fully to those who have not yet attained a unique point of view. One might further argue, as does Jaggar, that the liberal ideal of liberty would be compromised if parents were to lose their absolute right to determine fully the nature of their children's education.[40] A full response to this would take us too far afield.[41] We should note, however, that there are important political questions about the relationship between children and adults which need to be considered.

Liberals have assumed that parents virtually "own" their children, but this assumption can be challenged. The exact nature of the relationship between children and adults cannot be answered by liberal theory alone. A feminist theory of mothering, of the relation between parents and children, and between the state and family is more appropriate here. The feminist critique of liberalism from the perspective of human nature provides the basis from which to see some of the previously unrecognized limits of liberalism; it does not, however, establish the incompatibility of liberalism and feminism. I have argued here that the liberal vision includes important insights that might be maintained by feminist political theory, but the result should not be just another version of traditional liberal feminism. In light of the feminist critique, it is clear that the liberal position would be transformed so that its assumed universality and sufficiency as a political theory are called into question; and its compatibility with feminist ideals can be purchased only at the cost of its generally held, but apparently unnecessary, assumption of agnosticism regarding the good. It cannot be assumed that liberal concerns will take priority in the new theory—questions of justice may not be viewed as central in relation to feminist concerns and ideals. In this essay, the possibility of a feminist theory that saves what is of value in the liberal vision is raised, but as yet we have more questions than answers about the details of that theory. These questions pose a new challenge to the development of feminist political theory.

NOTES

1 Mary Wollstonecraft, *A Vindication of the Rights of Women,* 1833, reprint, ed. Charles Hagelman Jr. (New York: W. W. Norton and Co., 1967); Harriet Taylor

and John Stuart Mill, *Enfranchisement of Women and the Subjection of Women,* (London: Virago Press, 1983), with new introduction by Kate Soper.

2 Betty Friedan, *The Feminine Mystique* (New York: Dell Publishing, 1974) and *The Second Stage* (New York: Summit Books, 1981); Janet Radcliffe Richards, *The Skeptical Feminist: A Philosophical Inquiry* (London: Penguin Books, 1982).

3 The differences among some of these categories are discussed at length by Alison M. Jaggar, *Feminist Politics and Human Nature* (Totowa, N.J.: Rowman and Allanheld, 1983); and by Rosemarie Tong, *Introduction to Feminist Thought* (Boulder, Colo.: Westview Press, 1988); some of the historical connections among them are discussed by Hester Eisenstein, *Contemporary Feminist Thought* (Boston: G. K. Hall, 1983).

4 A recognition of the historical and conceptual importance of liberalism is fundamental to the argument developed by Zillah R. Eisenstein, *The Radical Future of Liberal Feminism* (New York: Longman, 1981). See also Jaggar, *Feminist Politics,* p. 28.

5 Jaggar, *Feminist Politics,* p. 28.

6 For a discussion of the historical connections between rationality and the control of nature, see Genevieve Lloyd, *The Man of Reason: "Male" and "Female" in Western Philosophy* (Minneapolis: University of Minnesota Press, 1984).

7 The focus on reason and the assumption that it yields a legitimate dichotomy between the "public" and "private" worlds is not limited to the liberal tradition, but runs throughout the history of Western political thought. For extended discussions, see Susan Moller Okin, *Women in Western Political Thought* (Princeton, N.J.: Princeton University Press, 1979), and Jean Bethke Elshtain, *Public Man, Private Woman: Women in Social and Political Thought* (Princeton, N.J.: Princeton University Press, 1981). See also Lorenne M. G. Clark and Lynda Lange, eds., *The Sexism of Social and Political Theory: Women and Reproduction from Plato to Nietzsche,* (Toronto: University of Toronto Press, 1979).

8 Jaggar, *Feminist Politics,* p. 33.

9 Contemporary liberal theorists do not argue that women are any less rational than men, and they assume therefore that liberal equality applies to everyone regardless of gender. As we shall see below, the feminist critique of rationality applies not just to the exclusion of women, but to the very notion of rationality assumed by liberalism and to any political theory derived thereby.

10 Sandra Harding, Is Gender a Variable in Conceptions of Rationality? A Survey of Issues, in *Beyond Domination: New Perspectives on Women and Philosophy,* ed. Carol C. Gould (Totowa, N.J.: Rowman and Allanheld, 1984), p. 49.

11 Jaggar, *Feminist Politics,* p. 40.

12 Ibid., p. 125.

13 See, for example Alisdair MacIntyre, *Whose Justice? Which Rationality?* (Notre Dame, Ind.: University of Notre Dame Press, 1988); and Bernard Williams, *Moral Luck* (Cambridge: Cambridge University Press, 1981).

14 Lawrence Kohlberg, *The Philosophy of Moral Development,* Essays in Moral Development, vol. 1 (New York: Harper and Row, 1981).

15 Carol Gilligan, *In a Different Voice: Psychological Theory and Women's Development* (Cambridge: Harvard University Press, 1982).

16   Amongst moral philosophers, there is a great deal of interest in the way in which a consideration of the psychology of women entails a new conception of the scope of morality. For some general considerations, see Owen Flanagan and Kathryn Jackson, Justice, Care and Gender: The Kohlberg-Gilligan Debate Revisited, *Ethics* 97 (April 1987): 622–38. An excellent collection of essays on this topic is that of Eva Feder Kittay and Diana T. Meyers, eds., *Woman and Moral Theory* (Totowa, N.J.: Rowman and Allanheld, 1987).

17   Jaggar, *Feminist Politics*, p. 46.

18   For example, see Jane Flax, The Conflict between Nurturance and Autonomy in Mother-Daughter Relationships and within Feminism, *Feminist Studies* 4 (1978): 171–89; Dorothy Dinnerstein, *The Mermaid and the Minotaur: Sexual Arrangements and Human Malaise* (New York: Harper and Row, 1976); and Nancy Chodorow, *The Reproduction of Mothering: Psychoanalysis and the Sociology of Gender* (Berkeley: University of California Press, 1978), and Gender, Relation and Difference in Psychoanalytic Perspective, in *The Future of Difference*, ed. Hester Eisenstein and Alice Jardine (New Brunswick, N.J.: Rutgers University Press, 1985), pp. 3–19.

19   Sara Ruddick, Maternal Thinking, *Feminist Studies* 6, no. 2 (Summer 1980): 342–67. (Reprinted in *Mothering: Essays in Feminist Theory*, ed. Joyce Trebilcot [Totowa, N.J.: Rowman and Allanheld, 1984], pp. 213–30.)

20   Harding, Is Gender a Variable in Conceptions of Rationality?, pp. 52–53.

21   Lloyd, *Man of Reason*, p. 37.

22   Arlene Saxonhouse argues that preliberal political theories did recognize the fundamental importance of the "private" sphere to the life of the polis. See *Women in the History of Political Thought: Ancient Greece to Machiavelli* (New York: Praeger Publishers, 1985).

23   Annette Baier, Trust and Anti-Trust, *Ethics* 96 (1986): 231–60.

24   With this famous (or infamous) claim, John Rawls begins *A Theory of Justice* (Cambridge: Harvard University Press, 1971), p. 3.

25   Carol Gilligan and Grant Wiggans, The Origins of Morality in Early Childhood Relationships, paper presented at philosophy colloquium, University of North Carolina, Chapel Hill, October 1986.

26   Lloyd, *Man of Reason*, p. 105.

27   For further reasons to be skeptical of a wholesale rejection of rationality, on the grounds that it is "male," see Jean Grimshaw, *Philosophy and Feminist Thinking* (Minneapolis: University of Minnesota Press, 1986), pp. 37–74.

28   For a good critique of this conception of rationality, see Mary Gibson, Rationality, *Philosophy and Public Affairs*, 6: 193–225.

29   Jaggar, *Feminist Politics*, pp. 41–46, 194–95.

30   Ibid., pp. 194–95.

31   J. S. Mill, Utilitarianism, in *Utilitarianism and Other Writings*, ed. Mary Warnock (New York: Meridian, 1974), pp. 257–62. See also Susan Wendell, A (Qualified) Defense of Liberalism, *Hypatia* 2 (Summer 1987): 65–94, for a related defense of the view that liberalism need not assume moral skepticism.

32   Jaggar, *Feminist Politics*, p. 33.

33   This account of moral equality is influenced by the discussion of Bernard Williams,

The Idea of Equality, in *Moral Concepts,* ed. Joel Feinberg (London: Oxford University Press, 1969), pp. 153–71. Also, it is consistent with the way in which utilitarianism would ground moral equality; for a utilitarian, any creature capable of experiencing pain or pleasure, happiness or sadness, etc., would be included in the utilitarian calculus.

34 But note that not all liberal theories are state of nature theories. Even in those that are not, such as Rawls's, the assumption of abstract individualism plays an important justificatory role.

35 Jaggar, *Feminist Politics,* pp. 42–44.

36 Naomi Scheman, Individualism and the Objects of Psychology, in *Discovering Reality: Feminist Perspectives on Epistemology, Metaphysics, Methodology and the Philosophy of Science,* ed. Sandra Harding and Merrill Hintikka, (Dordrecht, Netherlands: D. Reidel, 1983), pp. 225–43. For related objections, see Grimshaw, *Philosophy and Feminist Thinking,* pp. 162–86.

37 For example, see Charles Taylor, Atomism, in *Powers, Possessions and Freedom: Essays in Honor of C. B. Macpherson,* ed. Alkis Kontos (Toronto: University of Toronto Press, 1979), pp. 39–61, and Michael J. Sandel, *Liberalism and the Limits of Justice* (New York: Cambridge University Press, 1982).

38 The emergent point of view need not be static; it may well continue to develop over a lifetime, but at any given time, it will be a unique point of view which is distinguishable from all others.

39 Jaggar, *Feminist Politics,* pp. 43–44.

40 Ibid., p. 195.

41 But for an excellent discussion of the place of education in a democratic society, see Amy Guttman, *Democratic Education* (Princeton, N.J.: Princeton University Press, 1987).

CHAPTER 8

Making Connections:
Socialist-Feminist Challenges
to Marxist Scholarship

SANDRA MORGEN

A defining characteristic of the social production of knowledge in the academy in the United States is the fragmentation of knowledge by academic discipline. Within disciplines, competition for legitimacy and hegemony tends to take place between groups who identify with different theoretical or methodological positions. While feminists have been critical of this organization of knowledge,[1] and have advocated interdisciplinary scholarship, most of us continue to work within disciplines, i.e., be employed by, judged within, and identified through traditional disciplines. For example, almost all of the articles in this book consider the impact of feminist scholarship on disciplines or subdisciplines.

In this essay I explore the challenge socialist-feminist scholarship poses for Marxist theory and research. In choosing to consider the impact of one theoretical perspective on another, I undertake a task which is compatible with, though distinct from, the approaches of other articles in the book, which are focused on a discipline. Marxism and feminism are simultaneously concerned with theory and social transformation. Both exist on the periphery of the mainstream curriculum, and both encompass a far-ranging critique of the

The initial version of this paper was presented in a colloquium on Feminist Theory and the Disciplines at Duke University in spring 1985. A revised version was presented in a faculty seminar on Marxism in fall 1985. I would like to thank all of the participants in both seminars for their generous feedback and encouragement. In addition, I am particularly grateful to Carol Smith, Martha Ackelsberg, and Christina Greene for their comments on later drafts of the paper and for their continuing support.

dominant assumptions and theories of mainstream social sciences and humanities. Yet, while "Marxist Studies" exist as a curriculum on some campuses, they are usually taught as political philosophy or as a theoretical framework within a discipline. Socialist-feminism is even less institutionalized; it tends to be taught as a perspective or a theoretical approach within feminist scholarship.

Marxist scholarship enjoyed an intellectual resurgence within the past two decades,[2] gaining legitimacy at roughly the same time as the new feminist scholarship was developing. Both Marxism and socialist-feminism were nurtured by some of the same political and intellectual forces in the larger society and within the academy during this period. Nevertheless, all too often, feminist scholarship and Marxist scholarship, like other critical scholarship including Afro-American studies, developed in parallel rather than convergent ways, remaining theoretically and organizationally separate from each other.

Socialist-feminism is an emerging body of theory and political practice informed by developments in both Marxist and feminist theory. Although nineteenth- and early twentieth-century theorists are the intellectual or political precursors of contemporary socialist-feminists,[3] only since the development of the contemporary feminist movement has socialist-feminism in its present form become a significant force in feminist theory. Socialist-feminism is best understood in its concrete historical context as the major intellectual connection between Marxist and feminist scholarship and between the left and the women's movement.

To understand socialist-feminist theory, we need to situate it in relation to Marxist and feminist, particularly radical feminist, theory. This is commonly accomplished by counterposing the basic propositions of Marxist, socialist-feminist, and radical feminist theories as "ideal types." While this approach is heuristically useful (and I will use it to begin my discussion below), a more productive approach treats these bodies of theory not as ideal types but as evolving intellectual/political traditions. Too often the exploration of the feminist influence on a discipline treats that discipline as more static than it actually is. I hope to suggest, through example, the value of situating the feminist critique of a body of knowledge or a discipline in the historical context of the development of ideas within that body of knowledge.

A note about terminology. The literature I examine below defines itself by using both the term *Marxist-feminism* and the term *socialist-feminism*. One contribution of a socio-intellectual history of this theoretical tradition would be the careful tracing of the differences between the works of Marxist-feminist scholars and those of socialist-feminist scholars. This sort of treatment has yet to be done, and this paper does not aim to do it. My reading of the literature suggests to me a number of tendencies in the usage of the terms.

Marxist-feminism tends to imply a closer relationship to Marxist theory and methodology than does *socialist-feminism*. British and Third World scholars

are more likely than North American scholars to identify themselves as Marxist-feminists. Some might place socialist-feminism within the tradition of
Western social democracy and consider Marxist-feminism more closely
aligned with revolutionary, Third World, or "traditional" Marxism. Finally,
academics may identify themselves as Marxist-feminists more than their
counterparts in the sphere of political practice do. Each of the above distinctions contains some truth and some distortion, and individual theorists probably choose to apply one or the other terms for a variety of political and intellectual reasons which are not consistent throughout the literature. In my own
usage I will consider *socialist-feminism* as the more inclusive of the terms,
and reserve the term *Marxist-feminism* for one tendency within socialist-
feminism. However, in citing or discussing the work of different theorists I
will retain their terminology.

HISTORICAL AND THEORETICAL CONTEXTS
OF SOCIALIST-FEMINIST THEORY

Socialist-feminist theory must be understood as it developed in a particular
historical context over the past two decades.[4] It is a body of scholarship and
political practice that emerged in the early 1970s in the wake of major changes
in the historical situation of women in the West; the flowering of the civil
rights, antiwar, New Left, and women's movements; and the concomitant resurgence of critical theory as a legitimate form of scholarship in universities.
It is first and foremost a branch of feminist theory, developed in the women's
liberation, as opposed to the women's rights, tendency within feminism, and
thus is more akin to radical than liberal feminism. Nevertheless, socialist-
feminism has been deeply influenced by Marxist theory, and, especially in its
early days, by New Left ideas about theory and politics.[5] Socialist-feminism
developed as women, particularly those with experience in left, anti-imperial-
ist, and civil rights organizations sought to develop a "conception of feminism that is socialist"[6] and to "ask the feminist questions, but try to come up
with some Marxist answers."[7]

At its foundation, socialist-feminism is the application of the historical materialist method of Marxism to the question of gender. Socialist-feminists
argue that the "woman question," as the issue is cast in traditional Marxist
theory, or patriarchy, the radical feminist analytic construct, be examined historically. Socialist-feminists conceive of human nature as socially constituted:
that specific historical conditions create the economic, political, social, and
psychological conditions that ultimately shape human action and consciousness. Socialist-feminists have been concerned to analyze the relationship between gender and class oppression, and more recently to understand the intersection of gender, race, ethnicity, and class. They strive to elucidate the

relationship between capitalism and patriarchy, and between political economy and lived reality. Alison Jaggar has described the central project of socialist-feminism as "the development of a political theory and practice that will synthesize the best insights of radical feminism and of the Marxist tradition and that will simultaneously escape the problems associated with each."[8]

Marxist theory takes class to be the most important division in society and emphasizes the ways that members of the same class share a relationship to economic resources and power, and experience similar historical conditions. Traditional Marxism analyzes women's oppression primarily in terms of capitalism. The classic Marxist text on the "woman question" is Engels's *The Origin of the Family, Private Property and the State,* first published in 1884.[9] Engels argued that although the sexual division of labor is universal, the historic defeat of the female sex emerged with the institution of private property (goods or resources with productive potential) as this transformed relations between men and women. With private property, Engels argued, monogamy became institutionalized (to ensure the inheritance of private property to legitimate male heirs) and nuclear families rather than the extended household became the private property-owning bodies.

Marxist theory identifies the material base for women's oppression within the organization of capitalist production.[10] Biological differences between men and women are presumed to explain the original sexual division of labor in society, and to account for many facets of women's subordination in precapitalist formations. Women's liberation is seen in the context of class struggle: women must enter the labor force (social production) and join the revolutionary movement to end capitalism. Once the material base for women's oppression is eroded and a period of socialist reconstruction is under way, Marxists argue, the "ideological manifestations" of women's oppression such as male supremacy and discrimination in superstructural forms (legal, political, family, and social institutions) will end. Since the mode of production is seen as determining the social relations and institutions of the superstructure, these latter aspects of women's oppression are regarded as secondary, derivative, and unresolvable without change in the mode of production. Marxists tend to analyze sexism, like racism, as an ideology used to divide the working class. They have historically downplayed the political issues of the women's movement as largely bourgeois women's concerns that interfere with the unity of the working class in the all-important struggle against capital.[11]

Much radical feminist theory, like Marxist theory, postulates a material base for women's oppression. For some radical feminists, that base is human biology, particularly reproductive biology and the ways societies have organized and controlled women's reproduction and sexuality.[12] Other radical feminists, especially French feminists such as Delphy[13] and Wittig,[14] are developing materialist radical feminist analyses not rooted in biology.

Patriarchy, a core concept in radical feminist theories of women's oppression, was introduced into feminist analysis by Kate Millett.[15] Patriarchy is accorded primacy in radical feminist theory because of its historical precedence (they view it as the first and most long-lasting form of oppression) and because of its presumed universality across time and cultures.[16] Radical feminist theory focuses on the "gender-structuring of human society and human nature,"[17] demonstrating the penetration of "sexual politics"[18] into all aspects of life. The deconstruction and destruction of patriarchy and the development of a woman-centered analysis and social life are radical feminism's central theoretical and political aims.[19]

The feminist movement of the late 1960s and early 1970s was characterized by a radicalism rooted in large part in radical feminist efforts to politicize the "personal," everyday issues facing women. Feminists analyzed sexual politics as the dominant, archetypal form of power. The slogan "the personal is political" in the activist movement and the corresponding analysis of the hidden (i.e., familial, private sphere, "women's culture") lives of women by feminist scholars thematized issues such as sexuality, reproduction, birth control and abortion, daycare, housework, domestic violence, rape, sexual harassment, family and male-female relationships. With the expansion of politics and scholarship to include these issues, radical feminists claimed that women were oppressed *as women,* across race, class, and culture; that women should organize themselves as women, in women's organizations and on the basis of women's culture; that women should place political priority on those issues that confronted them in their daily lives, especially in the areas of family, sexuality, and reproduction. Marxism, like other political philosophies in the Western tradition, was branded as patriarchal in its relegation of women's oppression to a secondary or derivative status. It was therefore regarded as fundamentally flawed for analyzing or guiding women's oppression or liberation.[20]

DEVELOPMENT OF SOCIALIST-FEMINIST THEORY

Socialist-feminist theory is too far-ranging, and the literature too voluminous, to be reviewed here comprehensively.[21] My aims are (1) to examine some developments within socialist-feminist scholarship that suggest both its value and direction and (2) to argue that the convergence of current socialist-feminist thought and a major problematic of Marxist theory make possible a potential for a transformative influence by feminism of Marxist theory. I will organize this selective history of socialist-feminism into three phases,[22] each of which is labeled by a key phrase from the particular body of scholarship being addressed.

"We should ask the feminist questions, but try to come up with some Marxist answers." (Juliet Mitchell, 1966)

In the wake of the feminist movement, many women involved in what is broadly known as "the left" found themselves profoundly affected by the importance of gender, and the issues raised by the women's liberation movement. While they rejected as ahistorical the radical feminist conception of patriarchy, socialist-feminist theorists sought to understand the relationships between patriarchy and capitalism, class and gender, and production and reproduction. Since radical feminist analysis had succeeded in calling into question the validity of Marxist theory as an all-encompassing theory of social life or political action, socialist-feminists carefully reexamined Marxist theory to see what remained of value if the patriarchal aspects of this latter were challenged.[23]

Socialist-feminists produced a series of critiques of the "father" theory. They criticized Marxism for its neglect of gender oppression; challenged Marxist neglect of domains of experience crucial to women (the family, sexuality, housework, procreation), and rejected the uncritical acceptance by Marxists of a natural or biological basis for the sexual division of labor. As socialist-feminists explored women's lives in socialist societies, they concluded that the orthodoxy of liberating women by bringing them into social production and the class struggle was neither a sufficient nor an immediate enough soluation to the "woman question."[24] Moreover, socialist-feminists with previous political experience in the left and/or civil rights movements had experienced the marginalization of women and women's issues; they concluded that theories or movements that refused to make gender a central issue had to be confronted from without.[25] Thus, in the early and middle years of the 1970s, socialist-feminists set a course for developing a body of political theory and practice situated in the interface of radical feminism and Marxism.

During this period much socialist-feminist theory focused on the question of the sexual division of labor. Although this was not the exclusive theoretical concern, the issue embroiled socialist-feminists in debates which characterize this period of scholarship. Traditional Marxist scholarship tends to define the sexual division of labor as a universal and natural division in society; thus, the forces that generate and reinforce it in social life go unexamined. Some early socialist-feminist literature focused on women's unpaid labor in the home to analyze the way this aspect of the sexual division of labor functions within capitalism.

Benston[26] defined housework as a form of production, stimulating a long debate within socialist-feminism and between socialist-feminist and Marxist scholars about the nature of domestic labor.[27] The domestic labor debate raised a series of questions regarding the nature of women's work in the home and its relationship to capital accumulation and the reproduction of labor power and relations of production. Marxist categories and frameworks of analysis were stretched and revised in an effort to understand housework; and the family and the sexual division of labor were problematized. But this debate, especially those aspects of it which concerned highly technical issues such as whether housework was "productive labor" or "unproductive labor" remained rather firmly on traditional Marxist terrain.

"The unhappy marriage of marxism and feminism" (Heidi Hartmann 1979)

A major step forward in socialist-feminist theory was signaled when the terrain shifted, and scholars sought to go beyond questions about the nature of women's labor (domestic or wage) to consider seriously the issues raised by radical feminism (such as the family, sexuality, and reproduction) without assuming the primacy of class relations or the centrality of the "point of production." Thus began a long and tortured literature on reproduction.

One of the first systematic efforts to synthesize traditional Marxist and radical feminist theory was the work of Juliet Mitchell.[28] Mitchell identified four "structures"—production, reproduction, sexuality, and the socialization of children—that are interrelated and that "overdetermine" (following L. Althusser) women's condition in society. Mitchell broke loose of traditional Marxist categories of what constitutes oppression, of aspects of social life that shape human experience, to pose questions that came to be conceptualized in socialist-feminist theory as reproduction.

Trying to be good Marxists and, I would argue, trying to create a theoretical language that paralleled that of Marxists and, thus, was likely to be heard by Marxists, socialist-feminist scholars sought to analyze the issues of family, procreation, and sexuality by conceptualizing a "mode of reproduction" that was to be examined historically in relation to the mode of production.[29] Mary O'Brien's pioneering book *The Politics of Reproduction*, while in this general tradition, sought to understand the particular history and dialectics of the reproductive process, which she portrays as more separable from the social relations of production than do many of the other socialist-feminists of this period.[30]

Socialist-feminist theories of the relationship between the mode of production and the mode of reproduction highlighted a series of relationships that existed between the social organization of fertility and women's reproductive health, the raising of children, women's unpaid work in the home, sex segregation in the labor force, the changing demographics of the labor force, and the organization of production and labor resistance. Yet as several socialist-feminist scholars have noted, the reproduction debate was mired in conceptual confusion.[31] Petchesky's historical exegesis of the concept of reproduction is illuminating. She notes that the concept of reproduction was borrowed from Marxism, which

understood "social reproduction" as simply a dimension of the system of economic production. . . . Recognizing that Marxist theoretical inquiry ignored or distorted whole realms of activity that define human life—such as the bearing and socialization of children, sexual desire and relations, family structure and power, and fertility and its control—feminists tried to reinvent the concept of reproduction in a Marxist-feminist framework. This effort generated two new meanings of "reproduction": (1) the process of intergenerational reproduction and the "reproduction of daily life," which include many of the maintenance and socialization activities of the home and family, and increasingly, institutions—the work of women; and (2) the narrower but also socially mediated process of human biological reproduction and sexuality.[32]

This body of literature aimed in several important directions, each posing significant challenges to traditional Marxist theory. First, women became important as women, not just as part of a genderless class, and the nature of women's oppression expanded to encompass their gender-specific experiences in reproduction. Second, if the mode of reproduction (or relations of reproduction) is granted theoretical autonomy (that is, not subsumed under relations of production), patriarchy is placed in history and given a central theoretical status in the analysis of social formations. Moreover, struggles within social formations over the broadly defined reproductive capacities and activities of women—whether between men and women within families or between men of different classes[33]—are conceptualized as political, and viewed as part of the movement of history. Finally, socialist-feminist theory thematized the relationships between patriarchy and capitalism, gender and class, gender consciousness and class consciousness. If relations of reproduction are not reducible to relations of production, and if they create divisions between and within classes, then gender-specific experiences and consciousness become theoretically and politically important.

For all its important insights and implications, much of the reproduction literature falls prey to a theoretical dualism. This dualism postulates two separate systems of oppression, or the "dualist notion of a social totality as a composite of two discrete systems—patriarchy and mode of production."[34] The theoretical problematic of this dualism is regarded as the failure to encompass and understand fully the relationship between capitalism and patriarchy, class and gender oppression.

"Doubled vision" (Joan Kelly 1979)

Despite the theoretical ground still to be charted by socialist-feminists toward a theory of the relationships among forms of oppression and among gender, class, race, and culture, this body of literature has been invaluable in formulating theories and frameworks that reveal the interconnections among spheres and/or domains of social relations. "Making connections" has constituted the major form and contribution of socialist-feminist theory and political practice. These connections have been revealed on a number of different levels.

The first of these are the connections among different domains or spheres of social life. The public-private theory so crucial to emerging feminist theory in the early and mid-1970s[35] was challenged and ultimately transformed by scholarship such as Rubin's work on the political economy of the sex/gender system[36]; studies of the politics of kinship[37]; research on black women's lives[38]; and other research that demonstrated the interpenetration of public and private, work and family, politics and psyche.[39] This kind of reconceptualization of social life begins to move beyond theoretical dualism to what Joan Kelly called "doubled vision."

"Doubled vision," Kelly argued,

emerged out of changes in women's concrete historical experiences as well as from developments in theory. It allows us increasingly to treat the family in relation to society; treat sexual and reproductive experience in terms of political economy; and treat productive relations of class in connection with class hierarchy. . . . From this perspective, our personal, social, and historical experience is seen to be shaped by the simultaneous operations of work and sex, relations that are systematically bound to each other—and always have been so bound. . . . [We now see] the relation of the sexes as formed by both socioeconomic and sexual-familial structures in their systematic connectedness.[40]

The second kind of connection socialist-feminist theory is now pursuing concerns the intersection of gender, race, culture, and class. From the earliest days of the women's movement, black feminists argued that race was at least as significant as gender and class for understanding the oppression of women of color.[41] Nevertheless, the efforts to understand the relationship between gender and class which consumed socialist-feminist theory in the 1970s generally failed to take race and racism seriously.[42] Black feminists and other feminists of color have argued that unless gender is conceptualized in race- and class-specific terms, feminist theory will fail to include the experiences of women of color and poor women, and will neglect the ways that race mediates patriarchy and class experience and constitutes a crucial dimension of oppression not captured by the analysis of either gender or class.

Among the most influential of black feminist critiques for socialist-feminists were those that shared with socialist-feminism a socialist vision and an analysis of political economy. The Combahee River Collective, for example, defined itself as "actively committed to struggling against racial, sexual, heterosexual, and class oppression and see our particular task as the development of integrated analysis and practice based upon the fact that the major systems of oppression are interlocking."[43]

Angela Davis's work demonstrates how the historical context of black and white women's lives explains differences in ideas and political concerns, for example, concerning reproductive rights.[44] Her analysis of slavery suggests that because of the slave owners' disregard for black families and their use of black women as breeders, black men and women share an interest in reproductive autonomy that has a racial basis that precedes, or at least coexists with, black women's own concern with control of their reproductive lives. Davis's work exemplifies a Marxist-feminist analysis that understands race and racism as central to black women's experience, and argues for the importance of examining the interrelations of gender, race, and class in the capitalist mode of production.

I would argue that the historical shift from dualist thinking to "doubled vision" in socialist-feminist theory is indebted in large measure to the still fledgling incorporation of race, and to some extent ethnicity and culture, in theories of women's oppression and experience. Race upset the applecart, so to speak—those neat models that counterposed gender and class, patriarchy and capitalism. Dualist frameworks such as the public-private and capitalist patriarchy had to be reexamined,[45] and socialist-feminist scholars began to take more seriously not only the gender-specific nature of class experience, but the class- and race-specific experiences of gender.[46] While feminist theory, in general, faced the challenge of understanding differences among women, socialist-feminists confronted that task with a theoretical apparatus at least potentially capable of comprehending both commonalities and differences in women's lives as these are structured by history and political economy.

Socialist-feminist political practice has also been increasingly characterized by the effort to make connections[47] between middle- and working-class women, and among issues that link the concerns of diverse groups of women. For example, reproductive rights organizations such as the Committee for Abortion Rights and against Sterlization Abuse (CARASA) or the Massachusetts Childbearing Rights Alliance[48] linked the issues of abortion and protection from sterilization abuse, working closely with women of color to expand the idea of reproductive rights to include issues besides abortion. Socialist-feminists working in the labor movement moved beyond the traditional issues of trade unions to focus on issues such as sexual harassment, child care, and sexism in unions. In organizing for quality, affordable day care, socialist-feminists raised the needs both of working mothers and of day care workers, linking rather than counterposing issues. While the sophistication of socialist-feminist theory affected the work of socialist-feminist activists, the issues emerging from political practice and the efforts to build and maintain cross-class, multiracial organizations also pushed socialist-feminist theory to make the connections "doubled vision" requires.

What I have tried to indicate here are some of the developments in socialist-feminist theory over the past fifteen years. Despite major advances in this fast-growing body of literature, significant theoretical hurdles still remain to be resolved.[49] Moreover, as numerous commentators have noted, socialist-feminist politics still has a long row to hoe before it achieves its goals of moving women's liberation to the left, becoming meaningful to working-class women in their community and workplace struggles, and influencing the theory and politics of the left.[50]

STRATEGIC OPENINGS AND DIRECTIONS FOR A SOCIALIST-FEMINIST IMPACT ON MARXIST SCHOLARSHIP

Despite the vitality of socialist-feminist scholarship, Marxist scholars have generally failed to appreciate how compelling is its critique of the Marxist paradigm or how promising are some of its theoretical insights. Lise Vogel suggests that much socialist-feminist work is ignored or treated as a "specialist literature" and peripheralized; either way, she concludes "Marxism remains surprisingly untouched by socialist-feminist research."[51] In a similar vein, Stacey and Thorne assess Marxism as "remarkably untransformed," owing to both resistance on the part of Marxist scholars and socialist-feminists' inclinations to develop "autonomous and almost exclusively female institutions, conferences, and publications."[52]

Nevertheless, I believe that socialist-feminism is uniquely situated to offer Marxist scholarship insights which are sorely needed as contemporary Marxism weathers its current theoretical dilemmas.[53] Contemporary Marxist theory, particularly those tendencies which I group here as "critical Marxism,"[54] seeks to move beyond the economic reductionism of orthodox Marxist theory. Critical Marxist theory is embroiled in a debate about the relationship between and primacy of human agency and structure in history. In the process, the issues of ideology and consciousness have come to the forefront of Marxist scholarship to an extent which is unprecedented. I will argue that this constitutes a strategic opening for socialist-feminists, whose work on ideology and consciousness can be a significant force in the current debates and theoretical reformulations.

Both Marxist and feminist theory give a significant role to ideology and consciousness in the process of social transformation, although the theories differ markedly. Traditionally, Marxists have argued that since class is the primary contradication and point of struggle under capitalism, it is class consciousness that has revolutionary importance. On the other hand, feminists have regarded gender consciousness and women's mobilization to be fundamental. Marxists view the formation of class consciousness as a process that takes place primarily at the "point of production" in struggles between labor and capital; feminists argue that gender consciousness emerges as women recognize their shared oppression and organize as women.

Feminist and Marxist scholars do, however, share a number of fundamental assumptions about ideology and consciousness, though these areas of overlap are often overlooked. Both Marxist and feminist theory adopt what John Thompson calls a "critical conception of ideology . . . in which ideology is essentially linked to the process of sustaining asymmetrical relations of power, that is to the process of maintaining domination."[55] For both sets of scholars the study of ideology is inextricably linked to relations of domination. Feminist and Marxist scholarship focuses on the social and historical processes that generate, sustain, and potentially alter ideology and consciousness. And these traditions, while recognizing the pervasiveness of dominant ideology, highlight oppositional ideologies (class or gender based) that exist in given historical circumstances, and assert the power of these oppositional ideologies in political life.

Many feminists (and social scientists) have argued that Marxism is not a useful theoretical framework for understanding ideology or consciousness because, until very recently, Marxism has given short shrift to the realm of ideation. Economic reductionist tendencies in Marxist scholarship have given to the mode of production such a deterministic influence on the superstructure (including ideology) that the analysis of ideology has suffered enormously. When traditional Marxist theory has examined ideology, it has been largely to focus on how relations of production shape institutions and processes that inculcate and reinforce bourgeois ideology,[56] or on how the "vanguard" potential of proletarian ideology, rooted in the material conditions of working-class life, can lead a revolutionary movement for the overthrow of capitalism.

It was not to Marxism, but rather to psychoanalytic and poststructuralist theories[57] that many feminists turned as they sought to conceptualize consciousness, particularly the relationship of the body, sexuality, and consciousness. Much important feminist work owes its theoretical concern and impetus to psychoanalytic theory, albeit heavily revised. Scholars such as Mitchell, Rubin, Dinnerstein, Chodorow, Ruddick, Wittig, and Cixous have highlighted the importance of feelings, the unconscious, language, and women's role as child bearer and child rearer in the development of women's consciousness.[58] I will not elaborate the perspectives of this body of literature further in this paper except to note its centrality in much feminist thinking about consciousness.[59]

Instead I want to argue that the conception of Marxism that led many feminists to reject its value and turn to alternative sources is dated, and in fact, much current Marxist theory takes ideology and consciousness more seriously.[60] Critical Marxist scholarship rejects economic reductionism and stresses the importance of human agency and consciousness in social life and social change. Increased attention to these developments in Marxism will aid the development of socialist-feminist theory and reveal a strategic opening for socialist-feminist scholarship to alter the way women and gender are theorized by Marxists.

I am not the first to note the convergence between socialist-feminism and critical Marxism. Juliet Mitchell's work is indebted to Althusser; Michelle Barrett's work rests on a critical Marxist foundation; and many of the authors in the important collection *Feminism and Materialism*[61] demonstrate a sensitivity to developments in Marxist thinking. On the whole, however, North American feminists, including socialist-feminists, do not evidence a significant engagement with critical Marxist scholarship.

Two major figures in the shift in Marxist theory are Althusser and Gramsci.[62] Both rejected a reductionist concept of ideology as a mechanical reflection of the mode or relations of production. Post-Althusserian Marxism views ideology as "relatively autonomous" from the relations of production; that is, these relations specify "for a particular historical context, the limits to the autonomous operation of ideology."[63] Althusserian theory views ideology as lived experience, exploring how individuals are constructed and reproduced— "interpellated"—in ideology. Chantal Mouffe credits Gramsci with breaking away from the conception of ideology as "false consciousness" and revealing how reductionism wrongly posits a necessary "class-belonging" to all ideological elements.[64]

Michelle Barrett argues that critical Marxist scholarship, with its more sophisticated understanding of ideology, can better "accommodate the oppression of women as a relatively autonomous element of the social formation."[65] She sees feminist theory as part of a general challenge to economic reductionism in Marxist scholarship, and envisions a "fruitful alignment of interests between those who seek to raise the question of gender and its place in Marxist theory, and those who seek to challenge economism in Marxism, insisting on the importance of ideological processes."[66]

While I share this latter vision I would suggest that in fact the debt of socialist-feminist theory to critical Marxism may not be as great as Barrett proposes; that the thinking about ideology by socialist-feminists and Marxists has often been parallel rather than convergent.[67] However, with the continued development of socialist-feminist theory on ideology and consciousness, and greater attention to critical Marxist scholarship, socialist-feminists are in a position to initiate a productive dialogue with Marxist scholars that would open a vein of influence for feminist theory that has gone largely unmined.

SOCIALIST-FEMINIST SCHOLARSHIP ON IDEOLOGY AND CONSCIOUSNESS

In my view, socialist-feminist scholarship offers three main perspectives on ideology and consciousness that have the potential to engage and influence emerging Marxist theories: (1) frameworks for analyzing the relationship of ideology, consciousness, and historical conditions which focus on the process of consciousness formation and change; (2) an analysis of the specificity of class and gender consciousness; and (3) theories of consciousness that take account of the historical/material and the psychological/unconscious forces shaping consciousness and political action.

Sarah Eisenstein's social history *Give Us Bread but Give Us Roses: Working Women's Consciousness in the U.S.—1890 to the First World War*[68] is an important example of this emerging socialist-feminist theory. The book examines changes in working women's social conditions and the available ideologies that shaped women's ideas about themselves and their social roles. Despite the fact that this book represents an unpolished expression of her theory (due to her untimely death), her insights into the processes that underlie collective identity and action are astute. Handicapped by neither an assertion of the necessary class-belongingness of ideas nor an overestimation of ideological hegemony (the dominance of bourgeois ideology), Eisenstein examines the ways that working-class women "selectively filtered through the prism" of their own experiences Victorian ideas about womanhood and the alternative ideas of the socialist and feminist movements.[69]

Like Marxists who argue that as women are drawn into social production their consciousness of social relations of production emerges, Eisenstein explores the ways that entrance into the labor force affected women's consciousness of themselves. She argues that for working-class women, "work in factory or store was their first collective experience in a situation where the social position they share *as women* could emerge" (emphasis mine).[70] In the context of the particular historical conditions of women's overwhelming concentration in "female occupations," their organization into separate (union) locals, and the ideological milieus available to them, women workers' consciousness entailed a collective identity as women as well as members of a class. Beyond her very careful discussion of the ways gender and class consciousness were both fostered by the concrete experiences of women workers, Eisenstein notes, though she does not analyze in depth, the ways that "the awareness of collective identity among women wage-earners was affected in the first instance by variations in their ethnic, regional, and occupational milieux."[71]

Eisenstein does more than reveal the intersection of gender, ethnicity, and class in shaping working-class women's consciousness. She also concerns herself with the process by which ideologies inform action in discrete historical circumstances. Extending Frank Parkin's analysis of the relationship of the working class to the dominant cultural ideology as a process of negotiation—rather than wholesale acceptance or rejection—Eisenstein shows the importance of analyzing both dominant and oppositional ideologies and "the ele-

ments of experience, relationship, and tradition in working-class life which
structure a 'negotiated' response to each."[72] She concludes that

working women in the period under discussion [Victorian] generally accepted the central elements of the prevailing image of womanhood [cult of true womanhood] but they
did so in terms which demonstrate the mediation of their own experiences. Where they
developed ideas which were explicitly critical of prevailing ideology, these did not represent a simple reflection of the arguments of the labor, feminist, or socialist movements with which they were in contact, but a characteristic "negotiation" of them in
light of working women's particular situation.[73]

Eisenstein's work shows how class experience and consciousness are speci-
fied by gender and ethnicity, and it demonstrates an approach for analyzing
the complex process by which ideologies, history, and material circumstances
are interpreted and actively negotiated by women in their efforts to compre-
hend, live with, and change the conditions of their lives.

In addition to other excellent historical scholarship which explores working-
class women's consciousness,[74] socialist-feminist social scientists have studied
political consciousness and activism among contemporary working-class
women in the United States[75] and among peasant and working-class women in
other parts of the world.[76] This growing body of research examines how gender, race, ethnicity, and class shape both the particular experiences of groups
of women and their consciousness and political mobilization.

Women's experience and consciousness of class, for example, is differenti-
ated from men's to the extent that their relation to the mode of production differs
and because women's multiple roles as workers, in families and in communities, gives them a unique structural position within the political economy.[77]
Gender consciousness, on the other hand, is fundamentally shaped by wom-
en's class and race positions, which structure women's work inside and outside
the family, women's reproductive experience, and women's relationship to the
state. Working-class women and women of color often develop an awareness
of gender-based oppression and struggle for their rights and needs as women,
but their gender consciousness is inextricably linked to their race, ethnicity,
and class.[78]

Paying attention to the specificity of class, race, and gender experience and
consciousness will ultimately permit a deeper understanding of what fosters
both accommodation and resistance to oppressive conditions in people's lives.
As I have argued elsewhere, one serious problem with both Marxist and feminist theories of social change is the tendency to associate particular forms of
consciousness with particular forms of political mobilization, e.g., seeing
class consciousness as restricted to or primarily emerging from workplace experience and struggle, or gender consciousness associated with only feminist
issues or "women's issues."[79] Socialist-feminist theory, on the other hand, is

beginning to demonstrate that since social relations of power are constituted by class, gender, and race, the historical analysis of consciousness must encompass the intersection of these social relations among different groups.

Rosalind Petchesky proposes a conceptualization of consciousness that reflects and expresses the multifaceted insights of socialist-feminist theory. She defines consciousness explicitly as a

dynamic process of accommodating the conflicting ideologies and values imposed by the dominant culture and various oppositional cultures on one's own sense of felt need. That sense, in turn, grows out of material and social constraints that may disrupt ideological pre-conceptions rooted in class and life situations and in the unconsciousness and the body. Consciousness is thus a series of negotiations back and forth between ideology, social reality, and desire.[80]

Throughout her definition, the dynamism of consciousness is emphasized. The statement allows for complexity and conflict both within and between dominant and oppositional ideologies while retaining the materialist conception of the importance of historical conditions and class. The feminist recognition of the importance of feeling and of the important contribution of psychology to the understanding of mental and emotional life is, however, incorporated as is the experience of the body, so essential to the theory of radical feminism. The interaction of consciousness and ideology, particularly the way consciousness can break out of the grip of received ideas is underlined and embedded in a framework in which consciousness is socially constituted and constituting.

A focus on process and the emphasis on subjectivity and feeling are themes that have enjoyed a central place in contemporary feminist theory.[81] Socialist-feminist scholars have harnessed these themes to the analysis of political economy.[82] When the analysis of the process of consciousness development is placed in the context of socialist-feminist understandings of the interconnectedness of the domains of "public" and "private" (personal and political, work and family), and of the intersection of gender, race, and class, the ensuing explanatory frameworks can be potent.

CONCLUSION: TOWARD A TRANSFORMATIVE INFLUENCE

It is my contention that the definition of consciousness proposed by Petchesky, and the frameworks socialist-feminists have developed to analyze ideology and consciousness, have the potential to give the Marxist subject (human) an historically and socially constituted consciousness that can ensure a place for agency in theories of social change. Moreover, the work on the gender and race specificity of class experience and consciousness is critical to Marxists as they reassess the concept of class, particularly as a tool for understanding politics.

I chose to focus on the particular potential socialist-feminist perspectives on ideology and consciousness hold for Marxist scholarship, not because these analyses are necessarily the best of socialist-feminist scholarship, nor because they are any more compatible with Marxism than socialist-feminist theories concerning work, family, reproduction, literary criticism, colonialism, or development, for example. Rather, this a strategic decision based on an historical examination of developments within socialist-feminist and Marxist theories.

Socialist-feminism is ultimately concerned with the development of theory to guide and understand change, whether that change be in women's workplaces, in families and communities, or in ideas—including the ideas that are reproduced in the college curricula. I have argued that because of the particular historical situation of Marxist theory today—the themes that are engaging critical Marxist scholars and the weaknesses of existing theories—socialist-feminist perspectives on consciousness and ideology are strategically situated in the field of ideas to offer both the challenges and resolutions. The challenges necessitate fundamental changes in Marxist theory. In this regard, socialist-feminist theory can have a transformative influence on Marxism, an influence that can simultaneously make gender more central in Marxist theory and Marxist theory more powerful as a means of comprehending and informing change.

In addition, I offer this analysis to exemplify a larger point about the strategy of feminists' efforts to reform the curriculum and the research and theoretical agendas of traditional disciplines. A historical analysis of the development of ideas within and between disciplines can indicate particularly productive paths for those concerned with changing the assumptions, theories, and perspectives that engage practitioners in educational institutions. Because the social production of knowledge takes place in particular historical and political contexts, we must recognize that our success in transforming the academy will be linked to both the politics of changing ideas and the strength of organized political movements.

NOTES

1   Ellen DuBois, Gail Kelly, Elizabeth Kennedy, Carolyn Korsmeyer, and Lillian Robinson, *Feminist Scholarship: Kindling in the Groves of Academe* (Champaign: University of Illinois Press, 1985); Sandra Harding and Merrill Hintikka, eds., *Discovering Reality* (Boston: D. Reidel Publishers, 1983); Dale Spender, *Men's Studies Modified: The Impact of Feminism on the Academic Disciplines* (New York: Pergamon Press, 1981).
2   Bertell Ollmann and Edward Vernoff, Introduction to *The Left Academy: Marxist*

Scholarship on American Campuses, vol. 3 (New York: Praeger Publishers, 1986), pp. ix–xxiv.

3   See, for example, Blanche Wiesen Cook, ed., *Crystal Eastman: On Women and Revolution* (New York: Oxford University Press, 1978); Charlotte Perkins Gilman, *Women and Economics* (Boston: Small, Maynard, 1898); Alexandra Kollontai, *Selected Writings* (New York: Norton Books, 1977); Rosa Luxemburg, *The National Question: Selected Writings* (New York: Monthly Review Press, 1976).

4   Barbara Epstein, Thoughts on Socialist Feminism in 1980, *New Political Science* 1, no. 4 (Fall 1980): 25–35; Lise Vogel, *Marxism and the Oppression of Women: Toward an Unitary Theory* (New Brunswick, N.J.: Rutgers University Press, 1983).

5   Lise Vogel, Feminist Scholarship: The Impact of Marxism, in *Left Academy,* ed. Ollman and Vernoff, pp. 1–34.

6   Heather Booth, D. Creamer, S. Davis, D. Dobbin, R. Kaufman, and T. Klauss, *Socialist Feminism: A Strategy for the Women's Movement* (Chicago: Midwest Academy, 1972), p. 3.

7   Juliet Mitchell, *Women's Estate* (New York: Random House, 1971), p. 99.

8   Alison Jaggar, *Feminist Politics and Human Nature* (Totowa, N.J.: Rowman and Allanheld, 1983), p. 123.

9   Frederick Engels, *The Origin of the Family, Private Property and the State* (New York: International Publishers, 1972).

10   Karl Marx, *Capital,* vol. 1 (New York: International Publishers, 1967); Karl Marx, *Grundrisse: Foundations of the Critique of Political Economy* (New York: Vintage Books, 1973); Karl Marx and F. Engels, *Selected Works* (New York: International Publishers, 1968); Karl Marx and F. Engels, *The German Ideology* (New York: International Publishers, 1970).

11   For a feminist overview of traditional Marxist perspectives on women, see Jaggar, *Feminist Politics,* pp. 51–82.

12   See, for example, Susan Brownmiller, *Against Our Will: Men, Women, and Rape* (New York: Simon and Schuster, 1975); Shulamith Firestone, *The Dialectic of Sex: The Case for Feminist Revolution* (New York: Bantam Books, 1970).

13   Christine Delphy, *Close to Home: A Materialist Analysis of Women's Oppression* (Amherst: University of Massachusetts Press, 1984).

14   Monique Wittig, One Is Not Born a Woman, *Feminist Studies* 1, no. 2 (Winter 1981): 47–54.

15   Kate Millett, *Sexual Politics* (New York: Avon Books, 1971).

16   Mary Daly, *Beyond God the Father: Toward a Philosophy of Women's Liberation* (Boston: Beacon Press, 1973); Mary Daly, *Gyn/Ecology: The Metaethics of Radical Feminism* (Boston: Beacon Press, 1978); Susan Griffin, *Women and Nature: The Roaring inside Her* (San Francisco: Harper and Row, 1978); Susan Griffin, *Rape: The Power of Consciousness* (San Francisco: Harper and Row, 1979); Adrienne Rich, *Of Woman Born* (New York: W. W. Norton, 1976).

17   Jaggar, *Feminist Politics,* p. 98. For an overview of radical feminist theory, see Jaggar, *Feminist Politics,* pp. 83–123, 249–302; Hester Eisenstein, *Contemporary Feminist Thought* (Boston: G. K. Hall, 1983); Marilyn Frye, *The Politics of Reality: Essays in Feminist Theory* (Trumansburg, N.Y.: Crossing Press, 1983);

Josephine Donovan, *Feminist Theory: The Intellectual Traditions of American Feminism* (New York: Frederick Unger Publishing, 1985).

18   Millett, *Sexual Politics,* pp. 24–25.

19   Kathleen Barry, *Female Sexual Slavery* (Englewood Cliffs, N.J.: Prentice-Hall, 1979); Marilyn Frye, *The Politics of Reality: Essays in Feminist Theory* (Trumansburg, N.Y.: Crossing Press, 1983); Janice Raymond, *The Transsexual Empire* (Boston: Beacon Press, 1979); Adrienne Rich, *On Lies, Secrets and Silence: Selected Prose, 1966–1978* (New York: W. W. Norton, 1979).

20   Firestone, *Dialectic of Sex.*

21   Zillah Eisenstein, *Capitalist Patriarchy and the Case for Socialist Feminism* (New York: Monthly Review Press, 1979); Lydia Sargent, *Women and Revolution* (Boston: South End Press, 1981); Jaggar, *Feminist Politics;* and Vogel, *Feminist Scholarship.*

22   It is always dangerous to use a term like *phases* when referring to the history of ideas. These phases are only roughly chronological, and individual works may straddle or overlap phases. Mitchell's work, for example, from which I draw the phrase labeling *phase one,* clearly belongs in both phases one and two. I use the term, then, to approximate a sense of development of ideas rather than as labels that can neatly categorize particular ideas or sets of ideas.

23   Some of the early contemporary socialist-feminist writings include Booth et al., *Socialist Feminism;* Charlotte Perkins Gilman Chapter of the New American Movement, *A View of Socialist-Feminism,* 1975, reprinted in *Feminist Frameworks,* ed. Alison Jaggar and Paula Rothenberg (New York: McGraw Hill, 1984), pp. 152–54; Barbara Ehrenreich, Socialist Feminism and Revolution, keynote address, Second Socialist-Feminist Conference, Yellow Springs, Ohio, 1975; Charnie Guettel, *Marxism and Feminism* (Toronto: Women's Press, 1974); Heidi Hartmann and Amy Bridges, The Unhappy Marriage of Marxism and Feminism, working draft, July 1975; Juliet Mitchell, Women: The Longest Revolution, *New Left Review* 40 (1966): 11–37; Sheila Rowbotham, *Woman's Consciousness, Man's World* (Baltimore, Md.: Penguin Books, 1973).

24   Sheila Rowbotham, *Resistance and Revolution: A History of Women and Revolution in the Modern World* (New York: Vintage Books, 1974) (and references in footnotes 21, 23).

25   Sara Evans, *Personal Politics* (New York: Vintage Books, 1980); Lydia Sargent, New Left Women and Men: The Honeymoon is Over, in *Women and Revolution: A Discussion of the Unhappy Marriage of Marxism and Feminism,* ed. Sargent, pp. xiii–xxxii.

26   Margaret Benston, The Political Economy of Women's Liberation, *Monthly Review* 21, no. 4 (1969): 13–27.

27   Pat Armstrong and Hugh Armstrong, Beyond Sexless Class and Classless Sex: Towards Feminist Marxism, *Studies in Political Economy* 10 (Winter 1983): 7–43; M. Coulson, B. Magas, and H. Wainwright, "The Housewife and Her Labor under Capitalism"—A Critique, *New Left Review* 89 (1975): 59–71; M. Dalla Costa and Selma James, *The Power of Women and the Subversion of the Community* (Bristol, England: Fall Wall Press, 1975); Bonnie Fox, ed. *Hidden in the Household: Women's Domestic Labor under Capitalism* (Toronto: Women's

Press, 1980); J. Gardiner, Women's Domestic Labor, *New Left Review* 89 (1975): 47–72; Annette Kuhn and AnnMarie Wolpe, *Feminism and Materialism* (London: Routledge and Kegan Paul, 1978); Pat Mainardi, The Politics of Housework, in *Sisterhood Is Powerful,* ed. Robin Morgan (New York: Random House, 1970), pp. 447–54; Maxine Molyneux, Beyond the Domestic Labor Debate, *New Left Review* 116 (1979): 3–27; Peggy Morton, A Woman's Work Is Never Done, in *From Feminism to Liberation,* ed. E. H. Altbach (Cambridge, Mass.: Schenkman, 1971); Wally Seccombe, The Housewife and Her Labor under Capitalism, *New Left Review* 83 (1974): 3–24.

28   Juliet Mitchell, *Women's Estate* (Baltimore, Md.: Penguin Books, 1971).

29   Lourdes Beneria and Gita Sen, Accumulation, Reproduction, and Women's Roles in Economic Development, *Signs* 7, no. 3 (1981): 279–98; Renate Bridenthal, The Dialectics of Production and Reproduction in History, *Radical America* 10 no. 2 (1976): 3–11; Heidi Hartmann, The Unhappy Marriage of Marxism and Feminism: Towards a More Progressive Union, in *Women and Revolution,* ed. L. Sargent (Boston: South End Press, 1981), pp. 1–41; Heidi Hartmann and Ann Markusen, Contemporary Marxist Theory and Practice: A Feminist Critique, *Review of Radical Political Economics* 12, no. 2 (Summer 1980): 87–94; M. Mackintosh, Reproduction and Patriarchy: A Critique of Meillasoux's *Femmes, Greniers, et Capitaux, Capital and Class* 2 (1977); Roisin McDonough and Rachel Harrison, Patriarchy and Relations of Production, in *Feminism and Materialism,* ed. Annette Kuhn and Annmarie Wolpe (London: Routledge and Kegan Paul, 1978); Bridget O'Laughlin, Production and Reproduction: Meillasoux's *Femmes, Greniers, et Capitaux, Critique of Anthropology* 2 (Spring 1977): 3–32; Women's Work Study Group, Loom, Broom, and Womb: Maintenance and Production, *Radical America* 10, no. 2 (Winter 1981): 29–45.

30   Mary O'Brien, *The Politics of Reproduction* (London: Routledge and Kegan Paul, 1981).

31   Michele Barrett, *Women's Oppression Today* (London: Verso Books, 1980); F. Edholm, O. Harris and K. Young. Conceptualizing Women, *Critique of Anthropology* 3, nos. 9/10 (1977): 101–30.

32   Rosalind Petchesky, *Abortion and Woman's Choice* (Boston: Northeastern University Press, 1985), p. viii.

33   Claude Meillasoux, From Reproduction to Production—A Marxist Approach to Economic Anthropology, *Economy and Society* 1, no. 1 (Feb. 1972): 93–105.

34   Linda Burnham and Miriam Louie, The Impossible Marriage—A Critique of Socialist Feminism, *Line of March* 17 (1985): 39. The Burham and Louie critique is part of a more comprehensive questioning of the assumptions and premises of socialist-feminism. Socialist-feminists have also made the same internal critique of theoretical dualism. See, for example, Barbara Ehrenreich, Life without Father: Reconsidering Socialist-Feminist Theory, *Socialist Review* 14, no. 1 (Jan.–Feb. 1984): 48–58; Zillah Eisenstein, *Capitalist Patriarchy and the Case for Socialist Feminism* (New York: Monthly Review Press, 1979); Iris Young, Socialist Feminism and the Limits of Dual Systems Theory, in *Women and Revolution,* ed. L. Sargent (Boston: South End Press, 1981), pp. 43–69; Judith Van Allen, Capitalism without Patriarchy, *Socialist Review* 14, no. 5 (Sept.–Oct. 1984): 81–91.

35 Michelle Rosaldo, Introduction to *Woman, Culture, and Society*, ed. M. Rosaldo and L. Lamphere (Palo Alto, Calif.: Stanford University Press, 1974), pp. 1–15.

36 Gayle Rubin, The Traffic in Women: Notes on the Political Economy of Sex, in *Towards an Anthropology of Women*, ed. R. Reiter (New York: Monthly Review Press, 1975), pp. 157–210.

37 Rayna Rapp, Ellen Ross, and Renate Bridenthal, Examining Family History, *Feminist Studies* 5, no. 1 (Spring 1979): 174–200; Karen Sacks, *Sisters and Wives* (Westport, Conn.: Greenwood Press, 1979).

38 Bettina Aptheker, *Woman's Legacy: Essays on Race, Sex and Class in American History* (Amherst: University of Massachusetts Press, 1982); Angela Davis, *Women, Race, and Class* (New York: Random House, 1981); Sharon Harley and Rosalyn Terborg-Penn, eds., *The Afro-American Woman: Struggles and Images* (Port Washington, N.Y.: Kennikat Press, 1978).

39 Donna Haraway, A Manifesto for Cyborgs: Science, Technology and Socialist Feminism in the 1980's, *Socialist Review* 15, no. 2 (March–April 1985): 65–107; Emily Martin, *The Woman in the Body* (Boston: Beacon Press, 1986); Michelle Rosaldo, The Use and Abuse of Anthropology: Reflections on Feminist and Cross-cultural Understanding, *Signs* 5, no. 3 (1980): 389–417.

40 Joan Kelly, The Doubled Vision of Feminist Theory, *Feminist Studies* 5, no. 1 (1979): 216–29.

41 Some of the early black feminist writings from the late 1960s and early 1970s include Frances Beale, Double Jeopardy: To Be Black and Female, *New Generation* 51 (1969): 23–28; Toni Cade, ed., *The Black Woman: An Anthology* (New York: Signet, 1970); Pauli Murray, The Liberation of Black Women, in *Voices of the New Feminism*, ed. M. Thompson (Boston: Beacon Press, 1970).

42 See critiques by Davis, *Women, Race, and Class* (New York: Random House, 1981); Bonnie Dill, The Dialectics of Black Womanhood, *Signs* 4, no. 3 (Spring 1979): 543–55, and Race, Class and Gender: Prospects for an All-Inclusive Sisterhood, *Feminist Studies* 9, no. 1 (1983): 131–50; June Jordan, Second Thoughts of a Black Feminist, *Ms.* 5 (1977): 113–15; bell hooks, *Ain't I a Woman: Black Women and Feminism* (Boston: South End Press, 1981), and *Feminist Theory: From Margin to Center* (Boston: South End Press, 1984); Gloria Hull, Patricia Bell Scott, and Barbara Smith, *All the Women Are White, All the Blacks Are Men, But Some of Us Are Brave* (Old Westbury, N.Y.: Feminist Press, 1982); Gloria Joseph, The Incompatible Ménage à Trois: Marxism, Feminism, and Racism, in *Women and Revolution*, ed. L. Sargent, pp. 92–107.

43 Combahee River Collective, A Black Feminist Statement, in *All of the Women Are White, All the Blacks are Men, But Some of Us Are Brave*, ed. Hull, Scott, and Smith, p. 13.

44 Davis, *Women, Race, and Class*.

45 hooks, *Feminist Theory;* Van Allen, Capitalism without Patriarchy.

46 Eleanor Leacock and Helen Safa, *Women's Work: Development and the Division of Labor by Sex* (South Hadley, Mass.: Bergin and Garvey, 1986); June Nash and Maria Patricia Fernandez Kelly, eds., *Women, Men and the International Division of Labor* (Albany, N.Y.: SUNY Press, 1983); Petchesky, Abortion and Woman's Choice; Amy Swerdlow and Hannah Lessinger, eds., *Class, Race, and Sex: The Dynamics of Control* (Boston: C. K. Hall, 1983).

47 I do not mean to imply that other feminist theorists have not "made connections." The seminal concept "the personal is political," for example, comes from radical feminist theory. Black feminists made the connection between racism and sexism more profoundly than others. Lesbian feminists have led the exploration of the relationship between compulsory heterosexuality and traditional sex roles as mechanisms of social and sexual control. However, in this paper the scholars whose work I examine are socialist-feminists who have played a leading role in examining women's lives within the context of political economy, and using the analysis of gender to expand and deepen our understanding of class structure and social relations.

48 CARASA, *Women under Attack: Abortion, Sterilization Abuse, and Reproductive Freedom* (New York, 1979); Adele Clark and Alice Wolfson, Socialist-Feminism and Reproductive Rights; Movement Work and Its Contradictions, *Socialist Review* 14, no. 6 (1984): 110–20; Marian McDonald, *For Ourselves, Our Families and Our Future: The Struggle for Childbearing Rights* (Boston: Red Sun Press, 1981).

49 Jaggar, *Feminist Politics,* pp. 148–63.

50 For example, articles in the series Socialist-Feminism Today, which began in *Socialist Review* 14, no. 1 (Winter 1984), including Wendy Luttrell, Beyond the Politics of Victimization, *Socialist Reveiw* 14, no. 1: 42–47; Meridith Tax, Learning How To Bake, *Socialist Review* 14, no. 1: 36–41; Karen Hansen, The Women's Unions and the Search for a Political Identity, *Socialist Review* 16, no. 2 (March–April 1986): 67–95.

51 Vogel, *Feminist Scholarship,* p. 20.

52 Judith Stacey and Barrie Thorne, The Missing Feminist Revolution in Sociology, *Social Problems* 32, no. 4 (1985): 301–16.

53 For discussions of current theoretical debates within Marxism today, see Stuart Hall, Cultural Studies: Two Paradigms, *Media, Culture and Society* 2 (1980): 57–72; Ernesto LaClau, *Politics and Ideology in Marxist Theory* (London: New Left Books, 1977); E. P. Thompson, Politics of Theory, in *People's History and Socialist Theory,* ed. R. Samuel (London: Routledge and Kegan Paul, 1981); Raymond Williams, Base and Superstructure in Marxist Cultural Theory, *New Left Review* 82 (1973): 973, and *Marxism and Literature* (New York: Oxford University Press, 1977); L. Althusser and E. Balibar, *Reading Capital* (London: New Left Books, 1970).

54 *Critical Marxism* is a term I use to encompass significant twentieth-century Marxist theory which aims to revise Marxism, particularly to counter economic reductionism. Sweeping broadly, I include the Frankfurt school, cultural studies, cultural Marxism, and Marxist "structuralists." There are very significant theoretical and political differences within this large grouping, which are ignored here, as my focus is on the overriding theoretical issues and the potential dialogue socialist-feminists must initiate to participate in and influence these debates.

55 John Thompson, *Studies in the Theory of Ideology* (Berkeley: University of California Press, 1984), p. 4.

56 For example, Samuel Bowles and Herbert Gintis, Schooling in Capitalist America (London: Routledge and Kegan Paul, 1976).

57 See work by M. Bakhtin, J. Derrida, M. Foucault, J. Lacan. For feminist incorporation of these theoretical perspectives, see E. Marks and I. de Courtivron,

New French Feminisms: An Anthology (New York: Schocken, 1981); Gayatri Spivak, Displacement and the Discourse of Woman, in *Displacement: Derrida and After,* ed. M. Krupnick (Bloomington: Indiana University Press, 1983), pp. 169–95; and selected essays by Teresa de Lauretis, *Feminist Studies, Critical Studies* (Bloomington: Indiana University Press, 1986).

58   Juliett Mitchell, *Psychoanalysis and Feminism* (New York: Vintage Books, 1975); Rubin, *Traffic in Women;* Dorothy Dinnerstein, *The Mermaid and the Minotaur: Sexual Arrangements and Human Malaise* (New York: Harper and Row, 1977); Nancy Chodorow, *Mothering: Psychoanalysis and the Sociology of Gender* (Los Angeles: University of California Press, 1978); Sara Ruddick, Maternal Thinking, *Feminist Studies* 6, no. 2 (1980): 342–67; Wittig, One Is Not Born a Woman; Hélène Cixous, The Laughter of the Medusa, *Signs* 1, no. 4 (1976): 875–93.

59   My discussion of critical feminist psychoanalytic theory and feminist encounters with poststructuralist theory does not even pretend to address adequately the complexity of the issues raised in this body of scholarship. I note it merely to acknowledge its compelling influence on some feminist writings about consciousness and ideology.

60   For a summary and overview, see Jorge Larrain, *Marxism and Ideology* (London: Macmillan Press, 1983).

61   Annette Kuhn and Annmarie Wolpe, eds., *Feminism and Materialism* (London: Routledge and Kegan Paul, 1978).

62   Louis Althusser, *Lenin and Philosophy and Other Essays* (London: New Left Books, 1971); Antonio Gramsci, *Selections from the Prison Notebooks* (New York: International Publishers, 1971).

63   Barrett, p. 97.

64   Chantal Mouffe, *Gramsci and Marxist Theory* (Boston: Routledge and Kegan Paul, 1979).

65   Barrett, p. 31.

66   Ibid., p. 85.

67   This is more than an impression, though its demonstration awaits the sociointellectual history of socialist-feminism that I suggest is needed. Checking the bibliographic references cited in articles in two of the important North American collections of socialist-feminist theory, Eisenstein's *Capitalist Patriarchy and the Case for Socialist-Feminism* and L. Sargent's *Women and Revolution,* I found the primary references to Marxist scholarship to be to the works of Marx and Engels. There is little to no reference to critical Marxist scholarship with the exception of articles by N. Hartstock, K. Young, C. Riddiough, and A. Furguson and N. Folbre.

68   Sarah Eisenstein, *Give Us Bread but Give Us Roses: Working Women's Consciousness in the U.S.—1890 to the First World War* (London: Routledge and Kegan Paul, 1983).

69   Ibid., p. 147.

70   Ibid., p. 42.

71   Ibid., p. 147.

72   Ibid., p. 47.

73   Ibid.

74 Ruth Milkman, ed., *Women, Work, and Protest: A Century of U.S. Women's Labor History* (Boston: Routledge and Kegan Paul, 1985); Kathy Peiss, *Cheap Amusements: Working Women and Leisure in Turn of the Century New York* (Philadelphia: Temple University Press, 1986); Deborah Gray White, *Ar'n't I A Woman? Female Slaves in the Plantation South* (New York: W. W. Norton, 1985).

75 Ann Bookman and Sandra Morgen, *Women and the Politics of Empowerment* (Philadelphia: Temple University Press, 1988); Cheryl Gilkes, "Holding the Ocean Back with a Broom": Black Women and Community Work in *The Black Woman,* ed. F. Rodgers-Rose (Beverly Hills, Calif.: Sage, 1980) and Building in Many Places: Multiple Commitments and Ideologies in Black Women's Community Work, in *Women and the Politics of Empowerment,* ed. Bookman and Morgen, pp. 53–76; Karen Sacks and Dorothy Remy, eds., *My Troubles Are Going to Have Trouble With Me: Everyday Trials and Triumphs of Women Workers* (New Brunswick, N.J.: Rutgers University Press, 1982); Kathleen McCourt, *Working Class Women and Grassroots Politics* (Bloomington: Indiana University Press, 1977); Meridith Tax, *The Rising of the Women* (New York: Monthly Review Press, 1980).

76 See various articles by E. Leacock and H. Safa; J. Nash and P. Fernandez Kelly; Claire Robertson and Iris Berger, *Women and Class in Africa* (New York: Africana, 1986); Martha Ackelsberg, Mujeres Libres: Community and Individuality—Organizing Women in the Spanish Civil War, *Radical America* 18, no. 4: 7–19; Carol Andreas, *When Women Rebel: The Rise of Popular Feminism in Peru* (Westport, Conn.: Lawrence Hill, 1985).

77 Sandra Morgen and Ann Bookman, Rethinking Women and Politics: An Introductory Essay, in *Women and the Politics of Empowerment,* ed. Bookman and Morgen.

78 For example, see Andree Nicola-McLaughlin and Zala Chandler, Urban Politics in the Higher Education of Black Women: A Case Study, in *Women and the Politics of Empowerment,* ed. Bookman and Morgen, pp. 3–29.

79 Sandra Morgen, It's The Whole Power of the City against Us!: The Development of Political Consciousness in a Women's Health Care Coalition, in *Women and the Politics of Empowerment,* ed. Bookman and Morgen, pp. 97–115.

80 Petchesky, *Abortion and Woman's Choice,* p. 366.

81 Nancy Hartsock, Feminist Theory and the Development of Revolutionary Strategy, in *Capitalist Patriarchy and the Case for Socialist Feminism,* ed. Z. Eisenstein (New York: Monthly Review Press, 1979), pp. 56–77.

82 Arlie Hochschild, *The Managed Heart: The Commercialization of Feeling* (Berkeley: University of California Press, 1983); Sandra Morgen, Towards a Politics of Feelings; Beyond the Dialectic of Thought and Action, *Women's Studies* 10, no. 2 (1983): 203–23.

Contributors

Elizabeth A. Clark, John Carlisle Kilgo Professor of Religion at Duke University, teaches and writes on early Christian history. Among her publications that pertain to women's issues in that period are *Women and Religion: A Feminist Sourcebook of Christian Thought* (New York: Harper and Row, 1977); *Jerome, Chrysostom, and Friends: Essays and Translations* (New York: Edwin Mellen Press, 1979); *The Golden Bough, the Oaken Cross: The Virgilian Cento of Faltonia Betitia Proba* (Chico, Calif.: Scholars Press, 1981); *Women in the Early Church* (Wilmington, Del.: Michael Grazier, 1983); *The Life of Melania the Younger: Introduction, Translation, and Commentary* (New York: Edwin Mellen Press, 1984); and *Ascetic Piety and Women's Faith: Essays on Late Ancient Christianity* (New York: Edwin Mellen Press, 1986), for which she won the 1986 Adele Mellen Prize for distinguished contributions to scholarship. She has served on the boards of the American Academy of Religion, the American Society of Church History, the Byzantine Studies Conference, and the Duke University Women's Studies Program, and has been President of the American Academy of Religion, Southeastern Region, and currently is President of the North American Patristic Society, President-Elect of the American Academy of Religion, and President of the American Society of Church History.

Kathryn Jackson is Assistant Professor of Philosophy at Montclair State College. She has also taught at Duke University, the University of North Carolina at Chapel Hill, and the University of Toronto. She has published in the areas of ethics, moral psychology, and philosophy of law, and is currently writing a book examining the tensions between liberalism and feminist theory.

Carol Meyers is Associate Professor in Duke University's Religion Department and also serves as Associate Director of the Women's Studies Program. She has had extensive field experience in archaeology and codirects Duke's expedition to Sepphoris in northern Israel. Her research in both biblical studies and archaeology is brought to bear upon her work on women in ancient Israel. Her most recent work on that subject is *Discovering Eve: Ancient Israelite Women in Context* (New York: Oxford University Press, 1988). Currently, she serves as Vice-President of the Albright Institute of Archaeological Research in Jerusalem.

Sandra Morgen, Assistant Professor of Women's Studies, University of Massachusetts, Amherst, was formerly Project Director of the Duke–University of North Carolina (Chapel Hill) Women's Studies Research Center. She is coeditor of *Women and the Politics of Empowerment* (Philadelphia: Temple University Press, 1988), a book which focuses on the political activism of contemporary working-class women in the United States. In addition to articles in journals such as *Social Science and Medicine* and *Women's Studies,* she has contributed work on the women's health movement to a number of collections. Morgen is the Director of the Gender and the Curriculum Project of the American Anthropology Association, a curriculum development project funded by the Fund for the Improvement of Post-Secondary Education, Department of Education.

Kristen B. Neuschel is a specialist in the social history of early modern Europe. She is the author of *Word of Honor: Interpreting Noble Culture in Sixteenth-Century France* (Ithaca, N.Y.: Cornell University Press, 1989). Currently, she is investigating the significance of changed gender roles in the aristocracy for the development of royal absolutism in the seventeenth century. As a member of the Duke University Women's Studies Advisory Board, she has taken an active interest in the intersection of feminist scholarship and the disciplines.

Jean F. O'Barr is the Director of Women's Studies at Duke University. She is also the editor of *Signs: Journal of Women in Culture and Society.* A political scientist with interests in African women and the process of development, she has published a number of articles and edited collections on third world women, including *Passbook Number F 47927: Women and Mau Mau in Kenya* (London: Macmillan, 1985). Her current research interests center on women's education and women's studies. She has edited *Reconstructing the Academy: Women's Education and Women's Studies* with Elizabeth Minnich and Rachel Rosenfeld (Chicago: University of Chicago Press, 1988).

Angela M. O'Rand is Associate Professor of Sociology at Duke University. Her major areas of research interest include gender stratification and the social and cognitive aspects of scientific change. She has published articles in the *American Sociological Review, Social Forces, Sociological Forum, Yearbook of the Sociology of the Sciences,* and *Research on Aging,* and has written a monograph, *Disciples of the Cell: Research Fronts and Traditions in the Biological Sciences* (Dordrecht, Netherlands: D. Reidel, 1989). Currently, she directs the Duke University Round Table on Science and Public Affairs.

Deborah Pope's current research is in women's literature and feminist theory. She has published critical articles on a range of nineteenth- and twentieth-century writers, and the book *A Separate Vision: Isolation in Contemporary Women's Poetry* (Baton Rouge: Louisiana State University Press, 1984). A published poet and Director of the Duke Writers Conference, she is an Associate Editor of *Signs: Journal of Women in Culture and Society.*

Sarah Westphal-Wihl is a Canada Research Fellow in the Comparative Literature Program at McGill University, Montréal, Canada, where she teaches medieval literature and contemporary feminist theory. Her publications include articles on German texts and manuscripts from the later Middle Ages. She is now working on a book about gender, ideology, and courtly love, and is serving as an Associate Editor of *Signs: Journal of Women in Culture and Society.*

Index

Alexandria, Clement of, 90
Althusser, Louis, 152
Ambrose, 93, 97
Anglo-American New Criticism, 25, 30
Apostolic Constitutions, 86
Aquitaine, Eleanor of, 47
Asceticism: and convents, 96–97; history of, 92, 100*n76;* and women's freedom, 101*n77. See also* Patristic writers
Augustine, 91, 97

Baier, Annette, 128
Barnes, Annette, 33
Barrett, Michelle, 152
Benbow, C., 112–13
Benston, Margaret, 145–46
Benton, John, 46, 58*n8*
Bible: Eve in, 62, 67, 68, 76; female subordination in, 70–71; New Testament of, 64, 83, 85, 86, 87, 88–89, 91, 95, 96; Old Testament of, 56, 62, 66–67, 68, 76*n1,* 85, 90, 94, 95; Revised Standard Version of, 68; women in, 69, 85. *See also* Gender issues; *Women's Bible, The*
Biblical scholarship: and ancient Israel, 68; and androcentric translation, 67; and archaeology, 66, 72–75; doctrine, 67; feminist, 65–70, 81–82; methodological advances in, 66, 69; on position of women, 82; and scholars outside seminaries, 66; and twentieth-century religion, 68. *See also* Canon; Gender issues; Women's movement
Bingen, Hildegard of, 49, 58*n7*
Bleier, R., 110–12, 114
Bumke, Joachim, 48–49

Canon: biblical, 62, 76*n1,* 85; literary, 28–29, 31, 38, 44. *See also* Feminist theory

Champagne, Marie de, 47, 58*n6*
Chodorow, Nancy, 151
Christianity: and asceticism, 91–97; and convents, 96–97; deaconesses and, 96; early development of, 86–87, 89, 92; Gnosticism and, 87–89; heretical sects and, 86–87; and martyrdom, 93; and women leaders, 88–89; and women's freedom, 92, 94–97
Chrysostom, John, 83, 85, 91–92, 94, 97
Cixous, Hélène, 38, 151
Class interests: and biblical texts, 71; and courtly love literature, 13; and founding convents, 97; and Gnostics, 88; intersect with race, 148–49; and notion of talent, 107; and patristic Christianity, 81; and socialist-feminist practice, 149; and women's consciousness, 154; and women's liberation, 143
Clement of Alexandria, 90
Courtly love, 13, 44, 50–51, 57*n2*

Darwin, Charles, 25, 64
Davis, Natalie, 18
Dinnerstein, Dorothy, 151

Eagleton, Terry, 25
Eisenstein, Sarah, 153–54
Eleanor of Aquitaine, 47
Eliot, T. S., 30
Ellmann, Mary, 40–41
Engels, Frederick, 143
Epistemology, 23–24, 28, 29, 107

Family: analysis by archaeology, 73–76; in ancient Israel, 69–70; and capitalism, 143; and liberalism, 133–34; men as sovereign within, 124; and women's personal lives, 15; women's power within, 12; women's

171